Where to
SELL
Anything &
Everything

Where to
SELL
Anything &
Everything

Henry A. Hyman

World Almanac Publications
New York, New York

Cover design: Nancy Bumpus
Interior design: Abigail Sturges
First published in 1985.
Distributed in the United States by Ballantine Books, a division of Random
House, Inc., and in Canada by Random House of Canada, Ltd.

10   9   8   7   6   5   4   3   2   1

Newspaper Enterprise Association ISBN No. 0-911818-21-9
Ballantine Books ISBN: 0-29777-6
Printed in the United States of America.
World Almanac Publications
Newspaper Enterprise Association, Inc.
A Division of United Media Enterprises
A Scripps-Howard Company
200 Park Avenue
New York, New York 10166

Contents

Introduction

Garage sales are an American tradition. Homeowners continually make disastrous mistakes when pricing common-appearing items. A Maryland man sold a tin can at a rummage sale for $12; let's hope he never finds out that the collector who bought it would gladly have paid $2,000. The Long Island family that sold a $2 sweetmeats dish couldn't help but be dismayed when the same dish appeared on the cover of a half-dozen antiques publications after reselling for $66,000. Recently, nearly a dozen $20 duck decoys purchased at a New England sale were resold for more than $300 each, far less than the record $38,000 for a single decoy. Horror stories like these can be told endlessly.

If you think it doesn't matter how, where, and to whom you sell a cigar box, a corkscrew, or a cast iron bank, you'd better think again. The record price for a cigar box at this writing is $975, for a corkscrew over $1,100, and for a cast iron bank a whopping $18,500. And each of these three examples was originally sold for next to nothing at a house sale. There are duck decoys, dolls, carnival glass bowls, and comic books worth $1,000 or more; but you probably don't know which are the ones worth big money.

How Where to Sell Anything and Everything Helps You

Where to Sell Anything and Everything introduces you to hundreds of collectors and dealers ready to buy everything from electric trains to old dishes. These are specialists committed to helping you get the best price for the least amount of effort. If you already sell things, Where to Sell Anything and Everything will give you hundreds of new customers, eager to send you their "wants lists" and to pay top price.

The experts have derived a steady income from selling to these buyers for many years. Now it's your turn to convert everyday items into cash the easy way. Sell by mail through Where to Sell Anything and Everything.

Finding Your Buyer

The buyers listed in Where to Sell Anything and Everything have been divided into broad categories based on their principal interests. Most of these buyers are fascinating people, interested in many different things. That means the reader can't determine everything a buyer wants from the section of the book in which his or her entry appears. If you are looking for a buyer for a specific item, it is essential that you use the index. Thousands of items have been carefully referenced for your convenience.

The item you are looking for might be one of those listed under a number of different headings in the index. A collector of Coca-Cola wallsigns might be found under such diverse headings as "advertising," "signs," "Coca-Cola," or "paper." If you understand a little bit about the different types of collections, it will prove helpful when you are trying to use the index.

Some collections are item-specific. In other words, the person collects a single type of thing, such as stamps, figural bottles, barbed wire, valentines, or art glass. In other cases, your potential buyer might collect according to theme, such as "anything about Great Danes" or "anything from Nevada." This latter type of collector usually wants cards, photographs, catalogs, and a wide range of other items.

It is to your advantage to think about what you have and to take the time to find your best market. To whom, for example, would you sell a hand-drawn postcard sent by Teddy Roosevelt depicting a Great Dane in downtown Hoboken? A postcard collector? A presidential memorabilia collector? A Great Dane collector? A Hoboken collector? Any one of them is a good prospect, and all should be considered.

In general, any item you own might be wanted by a variety of persons. To get the best price, you should consider collectors of items that are:

1. Made from that material (glass, macerated money)
2. Made in that shape (cats, dogs, fire trucks)
3. Made for that purpose (cigar boxes, figural whiskey bottles)

4. Associated with that event (Jamestown Exposition or Mardi Gras)

5. In that size (miniature beer bottles, books less than three inches high)

6. Made by that factory (Avon, Colt, Hummel)

7. Illustrated by that artist (Schreyvogle, Rockwell, Mucha)

8. Created during a particular time in history (pre-1800 newspapers)

9. From a particular place (Nevada or Salem, New Jersey)

10. Made for use in a particular place (railroad china)

11. Sold in a particular place (souvenirs of anywhere)

Virtually anything can be collectible for any reason. So when examining your goods, you must consider that someone might want it, not only because of what it is, but also because of what it is made of, when it was made, where it was made, how it was made, why it was made, and sometimes even for whom it was made. A colorfully labeled Civil War bottle containing a patent medicine made from opium and sold by C.D. Kenney Company in western mining towns would be easy to sell to many different types of collectors.

You should be careful not to overlook the sales potential of small paper items. A high percentage of the people listed in Where to Sell Anything and Everything are serious researchers, authors of one or more books and articles on their hobbies. These part-time historians play a major role in preserving our American heritage. They are the ones who write about political buttons, jukeboxes, radio premiums, farm machinery, prisons, cigar labels, inkwells, and the other everyday minutiae that made 19th- and 20th-century daily life what it was. For little more reward than personal satisfaction, they do the difficult, time-consuming job of collecting, organizing, and interpreting data, and then writing about it. Because their topics are so specialized, they often assume the expense of publishing their research themselves, as well.

Independent researchers need all the help they can get in their historical data gathering. Items as seemingly insignificant as a $1 postcard can thrill a researcher if the information or picture is new. Pamphlets, instruction manuals, catalogs, photographs, letterheads, and magazine illustrations are all potentially useful. Keep in mind that "useful" doesn't necessarily mean extremely valuable, but it can. Some collectors search for years seeking a single photograph, engraving, or advertising card and will pay you well to obtain it. Ellen Dubrow, for example, offers to pay $5,000 for a single catalog of the Belter Company.

To Whom To Sell

There has been much debate over the years whether it is better to sell to a collector or a dealer. That isn't an easy question to answer, if for no other reason than the fact that many collectors are also dealers, and vice versa.

Traditionally, it is thought that one advantage to selling to collectors is that they are accustomed to paying end-of-the-line prices for things, so they may offer you more than anyone else for something good. As one collector put it, "If I don't have a doll that I want, I'll pay more than any dealer in the country for it. If I do have it, I'll still pay a fair price, but there are others who might pay more."

Many collectors will buy duplicates of items they already have. When they do this, they can rarely afford to pay you top dollar, since the item is being purchased for trade or resale to another collector. When any collector or dealer buys your item for resale or trade, he's finding your market for you. That's a service for which an auction house will charge as much as 20 percent, if not more. You pay an auction house gladly, recognizing that it deserves a fee for what it does. So, too, a collector or dealer who assists you by tying up his own money buying a duplicate item deserves some consideration in the form of a slightly lower price for that effort. Selling to full- or part-time dealers has an advantage: Even if they don't pay more, they are likely to buy a wider range of items because they're buying for resale as well as for their private collections.

The only answer to the "to whom to sell it" dilemma is that there is no answer. Every transaction depends on the particular item being sold and the needs of the particular buyer.

Describing What You Have to Sell

Each listing in Where to Sell Anything and Everything identifies not only what that person wants to buy but also how he would like you to describe what you have.

There's a great deal of difference in the amount and nature of information requested by collectors. Some buyers need to know little more than a brand name and model number, while others require many specific details, including dimensions, colors, and the like. If you want the best offer, give each buyer the specific data requested.

Most collectors don't want pen pals, although you will find a few that specifically request them. When writing to someone found in

Where to Sell Anything and Everything, you should clearly state your business. Don't be vague. Always describe your items completely. Price your items when you are confident about their relative value.

Almost everyone wants to know an item's dimensions. Normally, you give dimensions across (length), front to back (width or depth), then up and down (height). It has been customary in this country to measure in inches, although more and more collectors find it easier to work in centimeters, as the art world has done for centuries.

An item's color is often requested. Color is particularly important when the item is made of glass. Advertising and paper items are usually described as "black and white," "monochrome" (a single color and black), or "multicolored." If the item consists of two or three solid colors only, identify them. If many subtle hues are present, say so, describing the predominant colors. Some things are common in one color but extremely valuable in another. It would be a shame to miss a big sale because you failed to accurately describe an item's color.

Condition

Condition is probably the single most important factor in most people's decision to buy. Some collectors report that they send back about 15 percent of what they buy through the mail and that the reason is almost always condition.

All collectors want everything they have to be as perfect as the day it left the factory, but realistically will settle for something less. They will not settle for junk, ever. A scratch or two, a spot of rust, or other minor damage, though it depreciates an item, usually does not make it worthless, but it does sharply reduce an item's value in most cases. For example, a $10 gold certificate worth $125 if perfectly crisp is worth $15 in used condition. A cigar box worth $40 if perfect might be worth $10 if not, and have no value at all if badly soiled. A toy worth $250 might be worth only $45 if the paint isn't complete, and so on. Much as an automobile depreciates most in its first year, a collectible depreciates most with its first substantial damage. Most collectors have little or no interest in anything with more than minor damage.

Jukebox collectors, radio collectors, and a few others who can salvage parts from damaged mechanisms are in the unusual position of being able to buy damaged goods, but even then at greatly reduced prices. There are few takers for torn, faded, beat-up, rusty goods, even if you price them very cheaply.

Glass and china should be as nearly perfect in both manufacture and condition as possible. Chips, nicks, rough spots, or imperfections in the painting or design should all be noted. Even hairline cracks are your responsibility to describe to the potential buyer, since they reduce the value of a piece. If you have something perfect, you may be able to get top dollar for it. But if your item is flawed, please don't offer it for sale expecting enormous profits or a line of waiting buyers.

Collectors don't want you to use words like "good condition" or "fair condition" when you describe something. Probably the scariest phrase of all to a collector as "good for its age." Your idea of good condition is unlikely to be theirs. Even members of collector's clubs find it very difficult to agree on objective standards that permit something to be described in a word or two to everyone's satisfaction. One man's "fine" is still another man's "good." You must always be specific about condition. Indicate whether your item has any damage, dents, chips, flakes, scratches, water stains, foxing (brown spots on paper), names written in the flyleaf, tears, creases, cracks, broken parts, missing parts, or whatever. Describe what the damage is, where it is, how extensive it is, and what is affected.

Photographs

If a collector asks for a photograph or a photocopy, or describes one as "advisable," it is to your advantage to send one with your first letter of inquiry. Even if you are an expert in antiques and collectibles, it is hard to know exactly what a given collector wants to know about a given piece. Sometimes minor variations, some small detail you might not even notice, could make the item worth two or three times as much money. One active mail buyer stated, "On the average, I pay 50 percent to 100 percent more when someone includes a photocopy, because then I can be sure of what I'm getting."

A blurry photo isn't worth much, though. Buyers often complain that dealers send fuzzy blobs taken from eight feet away, along with a note saying, "They didn't turn out too well, but it gives you a rough idea." All too often the "idea" is too rough to have much meaning. Only if you take the time to do it right will a photograph pay off for you. Use 35mm whenever possible, as a good slide is hard to beat. A Polaroid is your next best choice. Most snapshot cameras do not allow you to get close enough to your subject. But no matter what you use, it is important to steady your camera. Use a tripod or set your camera on a table or other solid surface while you are shooting. A hand-held snapshot is usually a waste of time. Use a close-up lens whenever possible and appropriate.

Photocopies are useful when selling paper goods, especially song sheets, pamphlets, brochures, advertising, catalogs, old photographs, and the like. Many people have access to photocopy machines where they work. Most employers will permit machines to be used at lunchtime or after work for personal business if you pay a small charge. Copy machines can also be found in post offices, schools, libraries, courthouses, and government offices. Many of these can be used for fees ranging from a dime to a quarter. In large cities, or near colleges and universities, small businesses called "copy centers" exist to help students copy papers and dissertations. They will copy what you have for a nominal charge.

Sending a photograph or a photocopy does not relieve you of the responsibility for accurately describing what you have and pointing out all its defects. A picture is helpful, but is no replacement for honesty and careful observation.

Rubbings

Rubbings are sometimes requested. This is usually the best technique for showing the fine details of engraving, stamping, or casting on swords, silver, medallions, and the like.

Rubbings are simple to make. Take a thin piece of paper; plain white typing paper will usually do. Find a soft pencil; one marked "B" would be best, but "F" or "No. 2" will also do. If you are handy with a knife, it is best to sharpen the pencil so that more lead than usual shows. Flatten this lead slightly on a piece of fine sandpaper or just by rubbing it on a piece of paper. You want a flat area about the size of two or three pinheads. If you're not handy with a knife, sharpen your pencil in a pencil sharpener and use the side of the lead.

Place your paper on top of the item to be rubbed, and gently rub the pencil back and forth, gradually making your impression darker. You can go in more than one direction; it's not as if you're sanding wood. Practice a few times until you get a good, clear rubbing. It is not necessary that you make a perfect representation of the design, but try to make it show sufficient detail. Remember, the more the buyer knows, the more likely he is to be able to fairly assess what you have. The hardest part is keeping your coin or medal from moving. A tape loop on the bottom will hold it steady to the table while you make the rubbing.

Pricing

Most collectors want your item priced, although most everyone included in Where to Sell Anything and Everything has pledged to assist amateur sellers who might have no idea of an item's worth by making an appraisal or purchase offer.

Asking your potential buyer to "make an offer" is a technique commonly used by uncertain sellers who want to be sure that they don't sell something valuable well below its market price. Considering the skyrocketing value of many collectibles, and the difficulty for anyone to be knowledgeable about the many fields of collecting, it would seem a good practice to let the expert set the price. It could prove to be especially important on expensive items, where the difference between what you might ask and the item's true worth could be enormous. This may also hold true for less expensive items. Unless you're an expert in the field, it is easy to underestimate values. Some fad items have surprisingly high values. Some unusual collectibles have only a few dozen important collectors competing for the rarities, but those few will pay very well if you offer them something good.

Asking the buyer to set the price avoids another common problem. Amateurs have a tendency to grossly overestimate the worth of many items, and by overpricing, to lose the sale entirely.

If you ask a reputable dealer or collector to quote a price, it is unlikely that he will offer you only $5 for an item that retails at $50. He would be likely to offer you $35, though. Mail buyers will usually pay more than your local antique shop, but they can't be expected to pay full retail price for all items. Some collectors claim that the better the item, the more likely they are to pay close to top dollar, because of not wanting to risk losing the item. One collector said, "If I figure an item should retail at about $8, I'll offer $5. But if an item is currently worth $100, I'm likely to offer $125. If it's something good, I want to make certain that I get it."

So what do you do? If a collector prefers you to set a price, it is best to do so if you have some reasonable estimate of the item's value. If not, you are well advised to take advantage of an expert's willingness to share expertise. Don't be reluctant to ask someone to make an offer. You should be prepared to accept the offer if it is reasonable, however.

It is not fair to waste an appraiser's time. One disgruntled soul writes, "I received a letter requesting an appraisal of six items. I took the time to do so in detail, and made an offer for them. I never got a response. A few weeks later, while visiting a flea market almost two hundred miles from home, I came across the exact items I had appraised, priced at exactly the same amount I had offered a few weeks before. I bought them, but couldn't help feeling cheated that a seller had taken advantage of my knowledge and then not acted fairly by selling to me." Certainly, if someone offers you twice as much money, you should feel no obligation to sell for the lesser amount, but when dollar values are close, you owe courtesy to those who assist you in your efforts to sell.

This does not mean that you must accept the first offer you get. There is nothing wrong with soliciting second opinions about an item's value. However, as a general rule it is not a good idea to offer to sell your goods to "the highest bidder." You will cut down your response greatly by so doing. Unless the item is extremely rare, many collectors will simply throw your letter away rather than enter into a bidding war with their colleagues over unseen merchandise. Sending photocopies of lists of stuff, along with a request for someone's "best offer," will generally bring very poor results.

Answering mail is a time-consuming business. It takes a good correspondent a great deal of time to set up, think about, and answer your letter. All the people in Where to Sell Anything and Everything have pledged their willingness to do so, however. But if you are asking for "bids" from many different people, be fair and say so. Give buyers the option to choose not to participate.

Appraisals

One Where to Sell Anything and Everything listee notes, "Regarding 'mail appraisals' and offers for unpriced items: I would be happy to provide these to amateur collectors and have gladly done so many times in the past. But in more cases than I like to remember, after researching the item and going to the expense of writing or telephoning for an additional description, I have gotten no response to an answer I sent containing a self-addressed stamped envelope. This is maddening. But I approve of the goal of Where to Sell Anything and Everything of helping the seller who honestly has no idea of the value. I just want sellers to be fair and honest with us buyers."

Remember, you are asking for a courtesy and the collector involved owes you nothing if you are requesting information but not offering something that he is interested in buying. Don't always expect a prompt, or for that matter any, response. Many of these people lead extremely active lives professionally or with their hobbies and really don't have the time or the set-up to answer large volumes of irrelevant requests.

Phone Calls

Don't call people collect. It is extremely presumptuous to do so
without permission. If you write them first, and your item is a good
one, they'll call you. Collectors often like you to phone them, as
evidenced by the large number of listees in Where to Sell Anything
and Everything who include their telephone numbers. It is handy
when someone telephones because it gives the buyer the opportunity to ask questions about what you have for sale. Just don't make
that call collect unless the buyer has requested that you do so.

Sending Unrequested Items Through the Mail

Don't send unrequested items through the mail unless you intend to
give them away. A collector is under no obligation to pay for,
return, or even acknowledge anything sent without permission.
Note that a small minority of collectors included in Where to Sell
Anything and Everything do encourage you to send items directly
for an offer without first contacting them. This is always noted in
the entry. But unless someone's listing specifically grants you that
right, don't send anything without invitation and expect to be paid.

Self-addressed Stamped Envelope

Next to condition, the most important consideration in writing to
collectors is the self-addressed stamped envelope, usually referred
to as an SASE. If you expect your letter to be answered, almost
every collector insists that an SASE be included when you write.

What is an SASE? It is a long (no. 10) envelope, with your own
name and address on it in the place for addresses, and a first-class
postage stamp in the corner. Fold the envelope and include it with
your letter. If you are sending pictures that you wish to have
returned, increase the postage on your SASE so it is sufficient to
cover the extra weight.

The purpose of an SASE is to make it both easy and inexpensive
for a collector to respond to your letter. Many of the people listed
in Where to Sell Anything and Everything answer a few dozen
letters every week. When asking an expert to draw upon his or her
years of experience and expertise to give you a free opinion about
an item, you owe the courtesy of providing the stamp and envelope.

One collector explained, "I spend an average of twenty minutes each responding to letters with requests for appraisals, offers, or both. That's about six to eight hours a week, every week of the year. I rarely answer letters that don't include an SASE. I take that as a sign that the seller doesn't care whether they are answered or not. I'll answer if it's something valuable which is priced right, but otherwise the letter gets discarded."

If you are asking for information, for an appraisal, or for someone to make an offer, then make cartain to always include an SASE. If you are simply offering a priced item for sale, and don't care whether you receive a response, tell the buyer to "answer only if interested" and then you may omit the SASE. As a general rule, it is best to always include an SASE, since the collector will often send "wants lists" or other interesting material in response to your inquiry.

Residents of the United States should not include an SASE when writing to Canadians, or vice-versa, because they will not be able to use an envelope with foreign postage. What you should do is to include a loose stamp, which your foreign correspondent can then use on an SASE sent to your country.

Wants Lists

A fairly high percentage of collectors offer what are called "wants lists." As the name suggests, these are lists of things the collector wants to buy. Collectors see them as a convenient way of informing dealers and other collectors about those things they are most likely to purchase.

"Wants lists" are generally a single page, perhaps on both sides, but a few collectors will provide you with four or more pages of great detail explaining what they would like to find. Some "wants lists" are simply long, dull lists, but there are those that are written with wit and style. Some are illustrated with photographs, and a few contain drawings and artwork of obvious skill. Many are informative and enable you to develop insight into the nuances and pleasures of a particular collecting hobby.

Some "wants lists" are "priced," meaning a price or a range of prices to be paid for various items is quoted. These priced lists can be a great help when you are trying to decide on a value for what you have.

It is not possible to price all things exactly in a "wants list." In those hobbies wherein all the collectible items are clearly defined, such as figural bottles or coins, it is easy for a potential buyer to understand what you have and to evaluate it. He is then safe writing in his "wants list" that a particular figurine, for example, is worth $35 to him, for essentially all those items are the same.

On the other hand, someone who collects salt-and-pepper shakers is faced with the fact that there are tens of thousands of different salt-and-pepper shakers. It might be possible to say "glass shakers, $1-$5 pair" but not possible to list every glass shaker known.

Instructions on "wants lists" should be taken seriously. If one reads, "We buy U.S. stamps only," don't offer your collection of African colonies just because you think they're pretty.

The Buyer Contacts You

Mail transactions between buyer and seller can take a number of patterns. In most instances, the seller writes, quoting a price. The buyer accepts, rejects, or makes a counteroffer, and sends a check. Once the offer is accepted, the seller ships his goods, although with large items purchasers will often come and pick them up. If the buyer likes the merchandise received, and does not notify the seller within five days of receipt that a problem exists, the deal is completed. It is assumed that everyone is happy.

Occasionally, when a potential buyer receives your description and a request to make an offer, it is impossible for him to determine an exact value based on the information given. In that situation, some buyers will make an offer in the form of a price range, saying something like, "I'll pay between $15 and $30." In these cases, the buyer feels that he must actually see what you have before a final determination of value can be made. Sometimes there are subtleties that an amateur could not be expected to know, and that a buyer cannot anticipate, that could greatly affect value, often in your favor. In these cases a check will not always be sent with the buyer's response, or if one is sent, it will be for the minimum of the two quoted values. If the item proves to be worth more upon receipt, most collectors are very good about adjusting their payments according to their original offer.

It is important for you, the seller, to understand that when engaged in mail buying and selling, the buyer always has the right of ultimate acceptance based on any criteria he wishes, although more often than not it is unsatisfactory condition that is the cause of rejection. If a buyer does not like what he receives, he is obligated to notify you and return it promptly, usually within five days of receiving it. The seller must return the purchase price upon the return of his goods in safe condition. The cost of postage may or may not be returnable. If the item was misrepresented, deliberately or accidentally, it is customary for the cost of postage both ways to be borne by the seller. If returned for reasons other than unsatisfactory condition or misrepresentation, the buyer usually pays the cost of postage in exchange for the privilege of examining the item.

Shipping

Once a deal is completed, it is the seller's responsibility to ship the item, packaged properly so that it does not get damaged in transit. Remember, the practice in mail buying is that it belongs to you, the seller, until the buyer accepts it. If it arrives broken or damaged, he is not going to accept it. Insurance is optional. Some folks use it regularly, others never do. Shipping is at your risk. When shipping one-of-a-kind items, many people believe it is foolish not to have some protection.

Ship via either the U.S. Postal Service or United Parcel Service. Mail can go parcel post, but first class or priority rate (as it is called over twelve ounces) is often suggested for anything that weighs only a few pounds and has a retail value of $25 or more.

Some large items, like cash registers or jukeboxes, can be extremely difficult to crate and ship. It is best to get specific instructions from the buyer on how he wants you to proceed. Many buyers of large, heavy items will make all arrangements to have private truckers pick up the item at your home or shop.

This cannot be emphasized too much: When shipping through the mail or United Parcel Service, it is essential to pack your goods carefully. Start your packaging with a sturdy cardboard box. Boxes that held liquor, paper, books, or other heavy items are best. Book boxes are particularly good, since they are not only strong but usually clean of outside advertising. Do not use shoe boxes or other packages of lightweight cardboard. Also, never ship antique photographs or paper goods without heavy cardboard stiffener in the envelope to protect them. Shirt cardboard, unless three or four thicknesses are used, is not strong enough, except for very small items. Remember, if it is damaged, you're the loser because it will be returned.

Use a box big enough to provide plenty of space for protective packing. Four to six inches of space around your item should be enough. Plastic peanuts make the best packaging for most items.

Other Styrofoam is also very useful. Styrofoam protects the contents, and its light weight does not add much to shipping costs. If you do not have any of these, upholstery foam may work well. It can be purchased in larger dime and department stores, or obtained very reasonably in scrap form from upholstering shops. When all else fails, use crumpled newspaper, a resource readily available to all. Crumpled paper should be bunched fairly tightly, so it has the disadvantage of adding weight, especially on larger packages. Many collectors prefer to pack their items in a second cardboard box, floating in a sea of crumpled paper. This is undoubtedly the best way to package breakables.

Boxes should be sealed well. Strapping tape or duct tape are best suited for sealing the package. The latter, manufactured for sealing air-conditioning ducts, is particularly effective because its two-inch width permits a good solid seam along the edges of a box. Label all packages clearly, including zip codes and return address.

Satisfactory Transactions

If you have read the entries in Where to Sell Anything and Everything carefully, described your items fully to the appropriate buyer, arrived at a fair price, and packed well, chances are you will find mail selling to be an enjoyable and profitable venture. However, any transaction between human beings runs a certain risk of misunderstanding and dissatisfaction.

Some of that can be avoided by knowing who you are dealing with. The people selected for listing in Where to Sell Anything and Everything are, in many cases, the most important people in their fields, and you should have no problems. Many others were selected because they are very active buyers through the mail, something not all collectors are willing to be. Still others were included to provide a variety of subject matter in the listings.

If you have any doubts about the person with whom you are dealing, contact the reference, if one was provided as part of the listing. The Better Business Bureau, too, can be a valuable source of information about those collectors who are also full- or part-time dealers. If you have an item worth hundreds or thousands of dollars, no legitimate collector or dealer will object to your request for additional references. In most instances this should not be a problem, since valuable items are seldom shipped without prepayment; but it is sometimes necessary to do so. Do not hesitate to investigate if you are unsure.

If you believe that you have been treated unfairly by someone listed in Where to Sell Anything and Everything, please contact us. Although no one involved in the production of Where to Sell Anything and Everything can act in a legal capacity on your behalf, we can take appropriate steps to look into the matter and determine whether the listing should be withdrawn in future editions.

Henry A. Hyman

1
Animals

CATS

Marilyn Dipboye
Cat Collectors
31311 Blair Drive
Warren, Michigan 48092

This fifteen-year veteran collector-dealer wants to buy any representation of a domestic cat including figurines, books, paintings, graphics, posters, netsukes, incense burners, matchsafer, baby spoons, hooked rugs, postcards, china, jewelry, toys, games, puzzles, playing and greeting cards, quilts, advertising, and folk art.

Cats may be made of metal, glass, pottery, porcelain, chalkware, paper, ivory, or wood. Some of the most sought-after cats are made by Royal Doulton, Herend (Hungary), Meissen, Cybis, Boehm, Galle, Lalique, and the like.

As long as your cat is in good condition ("I buy no damaged figurines") you are likely to find a buyer here. Marilyn Dipboye wants to know what it is, any markings on the piece, and the condition. If you want her to make an offer, Marilyn says, "I usually ask the piece be sent to me for a five-day inspection. At that time, the piece will either be returned or paid for."

Marilyn publishes Cat Talk, a bimonthly newsletter. She has written widely about cat collecting and is always glad to hear from other cat fanciers.

CATS ON ADVERTISING

Ellen Yanow
457 Fullerton Parkway
Chicago, Illinois 60614

Ellen Yanow is a collector of antique advertising for products that used a cat as a trademark or a central part of the design. "The cat must be important in the advertising illustration, not just a tiny detail."

She buys signs, tins, product packages, cigar boxes and labels, large advertising die-cuts, tip trays, thermometers, match holders, and Victorian games on which the cat and the name of the product are shown on the box. "Please note," she writes, "that I am not interested in art, calendars, postcards, or trade cards."

A complete description of the item is requested, including age, condition, size, and color. Any historical information is helpful. A photograph would be appreciated and returned if you include an SASE. She requests that you price your item, but will make offers.

SCOTTIE DOG ITEMS

Donna Newton
Country Scottie
P.O. Box 1512
Columbus, Indiana 47202

Donna Newton wants "anything pertaining to the Scottie dog, including bronzes, figurines, prints, posters, books, advertising, magazine ads, postcards, glass, wood, or textiles. I buy both old and new items, including contemporary handcrafted Scotties. Depression glass Scotties are especially desired."

This collector-dealer publishes a quarterly newsletter and always seeks reference material about Scotties or products featuring Scotties. She also expresses interest in "new artwork that can be used for note cards or stationery for resale."

Please describe your item fully, including its size, the material it is made of, and its condition. A photograph or photocopy is very helpful. She would also like to receive historical background on the items. She does not make offers and requests that you state the price you want in your initial correspondence. "I appreciate consideration given to the fact that I will resell many of the items," she notes.

DOGS

John D. Fornaszewski
3007 Nameoki Road
Granite City, Illinois 62040
(618) 877-5510 or (618) 877-3475

John Fornaszewski is an active collector of dog figurines made of porcelain, bronze, iron, wood, or other material. Any breed can be represented (although fox terriers are his favorite), but he wants figures that are good specimens of the breed.

In addition to figurines, John buys books and magazines concerned with dog breeding (especially early issues), paintings and prints of dogs, and other representations of thoroughbred dogs, from jewelry to canes to doorstops.

He would like to know the breed (if possible), the material from which it is made, the dimensions, the coloring, and any maker's marks that can be discovered. Make certain to indicate damage, repairs, or defects. You may price your item or request an offer.

GREAT DANE ITEMS

Leon Reimert
9 Highland Drive
Coatesville, Pennsylvania 19320
(215) 383-6969

Leon Reimert wants old items pertaining to Great Danes, especially prints, lithographs, magazine covers, bronzes, postcards, porcelain, and calendars. If you have anything old featuring a Great Dane, it's worth a try.

He wants to know what it is, what is is made of, its size and color, approximate age, and condition. He prefers you to set an asking price, but will make offers on unpriced items.

Leon has been a Great Dane breeder for more than twenty years and a collector for fifteen.

DOG AND HUNTING LICENSE TAGS

James C. Case
P.O. Box 1076
Corning, New York 14830
(607) 962-2504

Jim Case specializes in dog license tags issued before 1920 by all states, especially those by towns and cities in New York State.

He also buys (1) dog tags issued before 1946 by the ASPCA, the New York Conservation Department, or the city of Buffalo; (2) dog tags issued before 1920, especially before 1900, by any other state or country; (3) any dog tag shaped like the written year of its issue.

Among other licenses of interest are (1) New York State hunting, fishing, or trapping licenses and license buttons before 1942, especially those for nonresidents and aliens; (2) New York State game warden, fire warden, or guide badges and buttons; (3) New York State sidewalk or sidepath license tags issued by towns or counties before 1920; (4) all dates of New York State set line tags, fyke net or trap net tags, minnow net tags, eel pot tags, and sturgeon line tags; (5) pre-1940 New York State game law booklets and conservation commission reports; (6) Pennsylvania resident and nonresident fishing license buttons before 1955; (7) Pennsylvania hunting license back plates before 1942.

Jim wants to know the date of issue and the condition. "In the case of dog tags, a pencil rubbing is helpful."

He will do free appraisals *when only* a few items are involved, and will make offers on items for sale. Upon request, he will send you a brief, priced wants list.

ANIMAL LICENSE TAGS

Karen Lea Rose
4420 Wisconsin Avenue
Tampa, Florida 33616
(813) 839-6245

Karen Rose collects animal license tags, ASPCA tags, and Humane Society tags. "While I collect license tags from any animal, anywhere, I am particularly interested in pre-1900 tags and tags from Chicago, Wahington, D.C., Baltimore, Indianapolis, Savannah, and anywhere in Florida.

"A rubbing or tracing of your tag would help me to set a value," Karen says. "Be certain to describe the origin and date as well as the condition of the tags. I will answer all letters. Please enclose a self-addressed stamped envelope."

Karen has written articles on the subject of animal license tags and is president of the International Society of Animal License Collectors.

ARABIAN HORSE ITEMS

John R. Graney
44 Main Street
Le Roy, New York 14482
(716) 768-8420

John Graney has been collecting paintings, prints, bronzes, tapestries, books, magazines, and catalogs pertaining to the Arabian horse for more than three decades.

This veteran collector-dealer would like to know what you have. Your detailed description should include the size of the item, its color(s), the publisher (of books and prints), and its condition. Include a photograph if possible.

A wants list may be requested. John is available for appraisals and to make offers on unpriced items.

OWL-RELATED ITEMS

Donna L. Howard
The Owl's Nest
P.O. Box 5491
Fresno, California 93755

For eleven years, Donna Howard has been a collector-dealer of owl-related items, especially old children's books containing owls, postcards, prints, carvings, netsukes, and advertising, including items from Owl Drug Store. "I want any unique owl item," she notes.

Among the things Donna would like to know about your owl are: what is is made of, its size, color(s), age (if known), country of origin, and previous ownership. She buys only mint-condition items, and will make purchase offers on desirable items she is offered.

Donna is publisher of a bimonthly newsletter, The Owl's Nest.

—— 2 ——

Around the Home:
American and Foreign

MISSION OAK FURNITURE

William Porter
908 Pierce
Birmingham, Michigan 48009
(313) 647-3876

Bill Porter wants to find marked or unmarked Arts and Crafts (mission oak) furniture made by Gustav Stickley's Craftsman factory in Eastwood (Syracuse), N.Y.; Charles Rohlfs in Buffalo, N.Y.; Charles P. Limbert Co. in Holland and Grand Rapids, Mich.; Stickley Bros. Co. of Grand Rapids, Mich. (inlaid pieces only); Tobey Furniture Co. of Chicago; and various unknown makers who worked in similar heavy oak construction and (usually) dark finishes.

Mission oak furniture was made early this century and can be recognized by its square lines and simple, often pegged, construction. It is seldom decorated or turned. Most of these pieces are marked with the name of the manufacturer, but it can sometimes take a little looking to find.

When describing furniture, provide details including dimensions, condition, and an indication of whether it still has its original finish. If you find its maker's mark or label, tell where on the piece it was discovered. Bill prefers you to send a photograph or detailed sketch with all queries.

The value of these items has risen sharply recently, so you would be wise to take advantage of Bill's willingness to make an offer. Please do not abuse this generosity, however, by contacting him about furniture that is not genuinely for sale. He does not make appraisals and does not wish to become part of a bidding war with other collectors.

He lectures widely on the furniture of this period and is responsible for at least one museum show on all facets of the Arts and Crafts movement. Fidelity Bank of Michigan, at 101 South Woodward in Birmingham, can provide references.

MIRRORED ART DECO FURNITURE
Barbara "The Bizarre Lady"

Notrog's
P. O. Box 1252
Dayton, Ohio 45401
(513) 253-5073

Barbara, often called "The Bizarre Lady," is a longtime dealer in many different collectibles, particularly of the Art Deco period. But her specialty and favorite items to buy are mirrored glass furniture and decorative items.

Vanities, dressing tables, liquor cabinets, clocks, end tables, coffee tables, plant stands, radios, picture frames, and a number of other pieces can be found. She will be happy to arrange for shipping on larger pieces.

The glass can need resilvering, but no broken glass, please. Be certain to describe all defects. Give the measurements and include a photograph whenever practical. She prefers you to set the price you want, but will make offers on unpriced items.

TWIG FURNITURE

Mary K. Darrah
33 Ferry Street
New York, Pennsylvania 18938
(215) 862-5927

There are four different styles of twig and rustic furniture, and Mary Darrah buys them all. The Gothic style in the years 1870 through 1880 was usually made of roots and pieces of burl and constructed with cut nails. It is generally very naturalistic in form. Later twig furniture often contains designs bent into the wood, especially hearts. Some furniture was machine made with woven seats and backs; this style is usually labeled or stamped with the name of the maker. Perhaps the fanciest is the Chinese style intended as a country-house version of Chinese Chippendale. She wants chairs, tables, stands, etc., in any of these styles for her own collection or to supply to museums and other collectors.

A good clear photograph is almost essential, but if you draw well, a sketch will do. If you know the age, origin, or type of wood, tell her. Condition is critical, so make certain to mention broken, loose, or missing parts.

For a nominal fee she will do appraisals of items not for sale. If your photos are good, and the item is desirable, she will make offers.

'HIGH STYLE" AMERICAN
19TH-CENTURY FURNITURE

Joan Bogart
P.O. Box 265
Rockville Centre, New York 11571
(516) 764-0529

Joan Bogart is one of the nation's most important dealers in high-quality mid-19th-Century ornate American Rennaissance and American Empire furniture.

She buys and sells the work of Belter, Roux, Meeks, Herter, Phyfe, Allison, Hunzinger, and Lannuier. Unfortunately, most of these pieces are unmarked: some are highly ornate, while others are more simple.

It is almost essential to send a photograph when offering large items such as these, which can have values well in excess of $1,000. Send a statement of condition, noting any defects or repairs, no matter how minor they might appear to you.

She offers an illustrated wants list that you can request in exchange for an SASE. Joan prefers you to indicate the price you would like, but is willing to make appraisals and offers as well as to verify makers through the mail at no charge if descriptions and photos are accurate. Folks at Citibank, 297 Merrick Road, Rockville Centre, New York 11570 can provide references for this well-known expert.

In addition to the furniture described above, Joan also buys Astral and Argand lamps, ornate gas chandeliers, and catalogs from these furniture or lamp companies.

PAIRPOINT LAMPS

Edward Malakoff
276 Princeton Drive
River Edge, New Jersey 07661
(201) 487-1989

Ed Malakoff has specialized in lamps made by the Pairpoint Mfg. Company of New Bedford, Massachusetts, for two decades.

He buys all Pairpoints, whether scenics, fruit, or florals, plain or puffy. In addition, he buys bases or shades from Pairpoint lamps.

When describing lamps, pay close attention to condition. Note if there are any hairline cracks or tiny chips around the rim. Also check the condition of the paint and let him know about defects, including sloppy application, wear, and the like. If there are cracks or wear in the base, point that out. Ed will do appraisals for a fee and will make offers on your lamps, some of which can be worth many hundreds of dollars.

GRAY GRANITEWARE

Reginald P. Corrigeux
2503 North Julia
Spokane, Washington 99207
(509) 487-9797

Reginald Corrigeux describes himself as "an advanced collector" who is looking only for "rare and unusual pieces" of American-made gray graniteware.

Pieces he seeks include ABC plates, gravy boats, dust pans, pancake turners with nineteen holes, mold pans with a strawberry or a rabbit pattern, salt boxes, and female urinals.

He also wants paper items related to gray graniteware, including trade cards, cookbooks, catalogs, and other descriptive ephemera.

He wants to know what it is, and its exact size and shape. Describe its condition, noting all chips, no matter how minor. He prefers to have you set the price, but he will make offers on unpriced items.

FIGURAL COOKIE JARS

Judy Posner
P.O. Box 1124
Teaneck, New Jersey 07666
(201) 836-1754

Judy Posner wants to buy ceramic figural cookie jars that were factory-produced in the United States between 1930 and the present. The most collectible cookie jars are based on well-known fantasy characters such as Popeye, Casper the Ghost, Peter Pan, Dennis the Menace, Snow White, black mammies, and others. She likes the black mammy jars so well that she will buy them even if they are made in Japan.

She also buys other ceramic kitchen accessories such as salt-and-pepper shakers, teapots, canisters, sugars, creamers, and spice jars, especially figurals of Little Red Riding Hood.

A description should include the type of figure, all colors, and any marks on the bottom. Condition should be accurately described. "I want to know about any crazing, chips, cracks, and factory flaws. Minor defects are acceptable, but I must be told about them." She requests that you price your jar, but she will make offers for desirable items.

RACIST KITCHENWARE

Jacquie Greenwood
156 Schmitz Terrace
Mt. Arlington, New Jersey 07856
(201) 398-7113

Jacquie Greenwood is a collector of general black Americana, with a special interest in kitchen items such as cookie jars, egg timers, clocks, lamps, string holders, salt-and-pepper sets, and wall plaques. "Of these, my favorites are mammy and Negro chef cookie jars, although I'm still looking for my first mammy wall clock." A detailed list of twenty-seven distinctly different cookie jars that she will purchase can be yours for an SASE. She urges you to phone collect if you have one to sell.

Like many serious collectors, Jacquie also wants research material such as manufacturers' records, patent illustrations, and other historical documents about any figural item depicting a mammy or Negro chef.

An accurate description should include details on condition, markings, color, and design. A photo is not necessary but is helpful in identifying a piece. When the seller sets the price it greatly speeds the transaction. "I am also interested in trading with other collectors or dealers." The Black Memorabilia Collectors' Monthly Newsletter was founded by Jacquie in 1982. Send her an SASE for more information.

THERMOMETERS

Warren D. Harris
6130 Rampart Drive
Carmichael, California 95608
(906) 966-3490

"I wish to buy interesting, unusual, decorative thermometers manufactured before 1940. I am not interested in heavy industrial models, clinical (fever) thermometers, or those with advertising. I will buy them in any reasonable condition, and generally the older they are the better."

Warren Harris wants to know about:

1. The original purpose of the thermometer (household, chicken hatching, automobile, or whatever)

2. Its approximate age and any history that accompanies it, no matter how minor

3. Its physical condition, including all blemishes

4. The materials used in its construction, including the color of the liquid

5. Any writing or symbols on the instruments, including the name of the manufacturer and any dates

He will make offers for those he can use for his collection.

CHILDREN'S LUNCH BOXES

Robert J. Carr
7325 Cornell Avenue
St. Louis, Missouri 63130
(314) 721-8232

"I buy and sell children's lunch boxes and Thermos bottles."

"My main interest," Bob Carr goes on to say, "is in cartooned or children's character lunch boxes which date from about 1920 to the present. These lunch boxes depict everything from Mother Goose to Howdy Doody to the Beatles. In addition, I also collect the kind of children's school lunch boxes and Thermos bottles that are still manufactured today. The first of this style was made in 1950 by Aladdin Industries and pictured Hopalong Cassidy. Since then, new school lunch kits have been issued each year by a number of other companies. They can be made of metal, vinyl, or plastic.

"I want the name of the item for sale along with a detailed description of the condition. I only buy lunch boxes and Thermos bottles that are in excellent condition: paint intact, colors bright, no rust, no major dents, etc. I cannot stress too strongly that I only buy items in excellent condition. I would appreciate a picture of the item for sale if possible and will return your photo if you include a self-addressed stamped envelope. You may set your price or ask me to make an offer."

PERFUME ATOMIZERS

Norma Sanders
2195 South John Hix Road
Westland, Michigan 48185
(313) 721-1323

Norma Sanders is an advanced collector of De Vilbiss perfume atomizers, preferably those on pedestals from the 1920s. She also buys perfume lamps by De Vilbiss and any catalogs or advertising for the lamps and atomizers.

She wants lamps and atomizers that are complete and in good condition, but it is not essential that they be in working order. She will also purchase damaged ones with good bulbs and hardware.

Your description should include a clear photograph or accurate sketch, an indication of the color of the glass, and a statement of condition. If it is marked, tell her where. If you know the age, make certain to say so. You may request an offer if your description is complete and includes mention of all damage.

ORIENTAL RUGS

Arthur B. Halpern
Renate Halpern Galeries, Inc.
325 East 79th Street
New York, New York 10021
(212) 988-9316

This veteran husband and wife team has been in the business of buying and selling Oriental rugs for more than two decades.

They are always seeking to buy fine Oriental rugs, tapestries, and textiles from Russia, China, Persia, Turkey, Central Asia, and the Greek islands. Rugs, textiles, and shawls made by North or South American Indians are also often of interest, as are fine European tapestries. Some American hooked rugs and samplers are purchased.

They also buy books and catalogs related to Oriental rugs, textiles, and weaving. Please send a photocopy of the title page or complete standard bibliographic information.

Because of their complexity, rugs are difficult for the amateur to describe. A clear, sharp photograph is almost essential. Although Mr. Halpern normally does appraisals only for a fee, he has promised to assist amateurs to sell their Oriental rugs because of the complexity and variety of these items, as well as their potential value. He will make offers on items definitely intended for sale.

BOOKMARKS

Margaret Wattman
7 Raintree Road
Chadds Ford, Pennsylvania 19317
(215) 388-7091

Margaret Wattman is a fairly new collector of bookmarks.

She wants bookmarks made of woven silk, or advertising bookmarks made of paper or celluloid. "No handmades, please," she asks.

Describe your bookmark, including the name and address of the advertiser. Note any tears, creases, chips, or other damage, no matter how small. Give its approximate age if you can. Margaret does not make offers on these inexpensive collectibles, and she requires you to set the price you would like.

CHRISTMAS DECORATIONS

Robert M. Merck
7585 SW Westgate Way
Portland, Oregon 97225

Bob Merck has been collecting antique Christmas decorations for seven years and wants:

1. Pre-1940 figural Christmas ornaments made of glass, cardboard, or cotton in the shape of animals, people, vehicles, etc.

2. Figural glass Christmas lightbulbs in milk glass or clear glass that has been painted (lightbulbs need not work)

3. Pre-1940 Santa Claus figures made of papier-mache, bisque, cotton, cloth, cardboard, etc.

He wants a complete description and asks that you set your own price, although he will make offers and claims "top-dollar paid." A wants list may be requested for an SASE.

AVON and C.P.C. PRODUCTS

Dick Pardini
3107 North El Dorado Street
Stockton, California 95204
(209) 466-5550

Dick Pardini is a nationally known expert on products made by Avon and its predecessor, the California Perfume Company (C.P.C.).

He wants early toiletries and other products made by California Perfume Company (C.P.C.); Perfection (household items made by C.P.C.); Goetting and Company; Savoi; Hinze Ambrosia Company; Gertrude Recordon; Marvel Electric Silver Cleaner; Easy Day Automatic Clothes Washer; or other names used by Avon and C.P.C.

Among specific wants are the 1909 and 1910 C.P.C. calendars; C.P.C. catalogs; pre-1950 Avon catalogs; the 1915 Baby Mine book; and pre-1958 Avon gift of soap sets.

"I don't want Avon figural bottles or single-item toiletries. The only Avons wanted are those sets and items specifically mentioned."

Dick runs a public museum of Avon collectibles, and he urges readers to use one of the many fine books on Avon to determine values of items they have. If you want to sell something you believe of interest to him, please indicate whether it has the original box and contents. State the price wanted, though he will consider making appraisals and purchase offers for beginners and nondealers.

If you want an answer, you must include a self-addressed stamped envelope.

ROUND OAK STOVE MEMORABILIA

William Krohne
Doe-Wah-Jack Antique Woodstoves
92224 County Road 687
Hartford, Michigan 49057
(616) 424-3450

William Krohne wants to buy Round Oak brand stoves and ranges.

He also wants to buy calendars, tin signs, paper signs, hot pads, match-safes, catalogs, and other advertising ephemera from the woodstove industry. He is particularly interested in items marked "Round Oak Stove Co.," "Doe-Wah-Jack" or "Dowagiac."

If you are offering him a stove, he wants you to copy all letters and numbers. Describe the condition carefully, especially noting any cracks. If possible, send a photocopy of advertising items, although a good description is adequate.

Krohne has more than ten years' experience buying and selling antique woodstoves.

BRASS FIREPLACE FIXTURES

Frank P. Jank
The Hearthstone
2711 East Coast Highway
Corona Del Mar, California 92625
(714) 673-7065

Frank Jank has been collecting and dealing in antique brass items, especially fireplace fixtures, for almost twenty years.

His interests include andirons, fenders or screens, tool sets, wood boxes, and the like in both brass and unusual wrought iron. Although the Hearthstone specializes in fireplace fixtures, Jank's customers have more varied tastes, so you should inquire if you have unusual antique brass items, such as umbrella stands, candlesticks, planters, and picture frames for sale.

He would like you to photograph what you have and include a ruler or yardstick in the picture so he can get an idea of size. Items he buys are generally intended for resale, so they must be in prime condition. You are asked to set the price wanted.

DOORKNOBS AND HARDWARE

Charles W. Wardell
P. O. Box 195
Trinity, North Carolina 27370
(919) 434-1145

Charles Wardell will buy heavily decorated doorknobs, escutcheons, plates, door hinges, knockers, doorbells, mail slots, store door handles, push plates, and anything else that could be considered builder's hardware. He'll take one "orphan" piece or a hundred, and also wants any catalogs and other printed matter picturing these items (1840 - 1940).

All hardware offered must be decorated in some fashion. Human faces, animals, scenics, lodge emblems, and names of public buildings on the hardware are particularly desirable. His beautifully illustrated wants list indicates that he will pay as high as $200 for an 1870 doorknob featuring a hound dog surrounded by a leaf border. Other decorated knobs bring $3 and up. No plain hardware is wanted.

A photograph, photocopy, rubbing, tracing, or drawing is almost essential to help describe what you have. He will make offers in cash or in trade, and notes, "After twenty years of collecting, I have many resources from which to draw and can offer a wide range of items in trade."

Tell him the type(s) of item(s) you have and the material from which it is made (brass, iron, glass, or wood). He also wants the size, condition, and any facts you know about where the hardware was originally used (hotel, courthouse, home, school, etc.). When describing printed matter, provide the size, date, number of pages, name of manufacturer, number of items illustrated, and overall condition of the catalog or pamphlet.

DECORATIVE CERAMIC TILES

Lewis Jaffe
1919 Chestnut Street
Philadelphia, Pennsylvania 19103

For nearly ten years, Lewis Jaffe has been collecting the decorative tiles that have graced fireplaces, bathrooms, and kitchens since the days of the Babylonians.

He is particularly interested in pre-1930 American and European tiles that are hand-painted or silk-screened with decoration, figures, or scenes. The older tiles can be recognized because they are usually about a half-inch thick instead of a quarter-inch like newer tiles. Often when a home is remodeled the older tiles are used as trivets, so check carefully.

Make a good clear photograph or drawing of what you have, noting its dimensions. Make certain to indicate any chips or damage. He makes appraisals for a fee and prefers not to make offers on unpriced items, so you set the asking figure.

DOORSTOPS

Martin Kelly
Doorstops
P.O. Box 421 D
Waterville, New York 13480

The Kellys are dealers who have specialized in cast iron, glass, and marble doorstops for the past five years.

If you have doorstops you wish to sell, include a complete description. If the doorstop is cast iron, please indicate whether it is solid, hollow, or fully three-dimensional, and whether it has a flat or concave back. Provide details of its height, width, and depth, as well as the condition of the finish, including mention of any cracks, chips, or other imperfections. "Drawings or photographs are most helpful."

Martin notes: "The margin of profit in this specialized field is small, and we do not wish to become involved in extensive correspondence. Please provide the description and the price wanted (including postage) in your first letter. If we are interested, you will have our acceptance within a few days."

FIRE GRENADE BOTTLES

Larry Meyer
4001 Elmwood
Stickney, Illinois 60402
(312) 749-1564 eves.

For more than eleven years, Larry Meyer has been collecting glass fire grenade bottles.

Fire grenade bottles are usually embossed with the company name and the words "fire grenade" or "hand fire grenade." They can be found in a variety of shapes and colors and contained a fire-snuffing liquid. Many had imaginative and colorful names extolling their virtues, but the truth is that they often bounced when thrown at a fire. They disappeared at the turn of the century, after discovery of the fire-fighting properties of carbon tetrachloride.

Send him a detailed description, including color, shape, measurements, embossing, and labels. Note any damage such as cracks, chips, holes, stains, or discoloring. He does not perform appraisals but will be pleased to make an offer for your grenades.

In addition to grenades, Larry would like to purchase examples of unusual, early hand-held fire extinguishers. Other early fire department relics may also find a home with Larry, a veteran of sixteen years as a fireman. Tell him what you have.

OLD TELEPHONES AND PHONE PARTS

Ron Knappen
Phoneco
RD 2, Box 590
Galesville, Wisconsin 54630
(603) 582-4124

For more than eleven years, Ron Knappen has been buying large numbers of old telephones and telephone parts "in any condition and any pre-1937 style."

He suggests that you order Phoneco's detailed and heavily illustrated catalog so that you can familiarize yourself with the retail value of old phones and phone parts. It's free for the asking and, although in very small print, is certainly worth obtaining.

Rom encourages you to contact him if you are unsure about what you have. He will ask specific questions about your old phones, so as a courtesy make certain that the items are available at the telephone number you give.

Ron has published three editions of The History And I.D. Of Old Telephones, the latest one a mammoth 824 pages. He also has a price guide to phones, which may be ordered for $4. Phoneco charges a fee for large, formal appraisals but will quote a price for phones you would like to sell.

UNUSUAL OLD TELEPHONES

Gerry Billard
Billard's Old Telephones
21710 Regnart Road
Cupertino, California 95014
(408) 252-2104

Since 1966, Garry Billard has been supplying old telephones and telephone parts to collectors all over the world.

Unusual styles of antique phones, primitive dial phones, phones with front-mounted cranks, pay phones with dollar slots, extra-long wooden phones, and phones with wooden receivers are among those that Gerry seeks for his collection or for resale.

He also wants assortments of phone parts, early phone directories, phone catalogs, and other early books and signs related to phones.

For $1 you can order a fine illustrated catalog from Gerry that pictures approximately one hundred varieties of phones. If you have phones to sell, the catalog is extremely useful since each of the basic styles is pictured and numbered, making it much easier for you to describe what you have.

Gerry will do appraisals and make purchase offers on unpriced items that he can use. You may correspond in French or Spanish if either of these languages is more convenient.

PENS

Mrs. Ky
P.O. Box J
Port Jefferson Station, New York 11776

Good quality pre-1940 pens and related items are sought by this veteran collector.

She wants glass pens, old stylus pens, fountain pens, fountain pen tools and repair kits, and fountain pen nibs. She also buys catalogs, counter displays, advertising, trade cards, repair manuals, and other paper ephemera related to writing instruments. Brands of fountain pens she seeks include Waterman, Parker, Shaeffer, Wahl, Le Boeuf, Chilton, Moore, and Montblanc.

She is interested in single items or large collections. Give the name of the maker (and model when you can), the dimensions, and the color(s). Sketch any unusual decorations. She wants to know how the pen is filled. Absolutely every defect must be noted: scratches, wear, chips, stains, cracks, or anything else. She offers an illustrated wants list and will make purchase offers, although she prefers you to tell her how much you would like.

NOVELTY PENDULUM CLOCKS

John and Lynnette McCormack
3816 North Massachusetts
Portland, Oregon 97227
(503) 287-7594

The McCormacks want to buy American-made animated alarm clocks and novelty wall clocks made by Keebler, Lux, Columbia, Westclox, and others. They will send you a priced wants list upon receipt of your SASE.

These wall clocks are generally made with a pendulum, usually incorporated into the design. John and Lynnette want to know what that design is, what color the clock is, and who the maker was. Whether it runs is not important in their decision to buy.

The McCormacks have bought and sold novelty clocks for twenty years and are in contact with clock collectors all over the country.

CAST IRON KITCHEN TOOLS

George R. Fougere
67 East Street
North Grafton, Massachusetts 01536
(617) 839-2701

George Fougere is a relatively new buyer and seller of a variety of kitchen items, including:

1. Small cast iron kitchen tools, such as nutmeg graters, nut crackers, bottle openers, ice shavers, apple corers

2. Flatirons or sadirons and trivets that are four inches or less in length. They can be made of cast iron, tin, pot metal, wood, or glass. "Nonelectric irons only, please."

3. Stoneware crocks and jugs that are marked "F. B. Norton, Worcester, Mass." He is not interested in Norton jugs made in Vermont.

He would like you to describe what you have as fully as possible. The condition is critical and must be described carefully, including all chips, cracks, repairs, or broken parts. He asks that you make a tracing of the bottom of any irons or trivets; mention any names, numbers, or dates found on the items for sale.

COOKBOOKS

Roberta Deal
C109 University Park
Ithaca, New York 14850

Roberta Deal has an extensive collection of old cookbooks and specializes in those put out by various companies to encourage use of their products. Among items she seeks are pre-1930 advertising cookbooks, especially hardcover; fund-raising cookbooks; pre-1910 cooking magazines; Jell-O insert recipe booklets; turn-of-the century grocer's catalogs; pre-1950 cookbooks with unusual subject matter; illustrated cookbooks by famous people; bibliographies and reference books about cookbooks; histories of food companies.

Condition must be at least "good," since no books with severe damage are wanted. She would like to know the title, author or company, publisher or corporate sponsor, date of publication, number of pages, number and type of illustrations and whether they are in color or black and white. If you cannot find a date, describe the cover carefully, as it may provide clues.

Roberta is willing to make offers for cookbooks she can use.

ANTIQUE LAMPS

Dan W. Besant
Besantiques
60 Meaford Road
Buffalo, New York 14215
(716) 833-8138

Dan Besant is a longtime buyer of lamps of all sorts:
 1. All models of student lamps, including table, wall, hanging, single, double, full-sized, miniature, complete or not
 2. Astrals, sinumbras, and mantel lamps
 3. Lamps with reverse painted shades
 4. Desk and table lamps with colored glass shades
 5. Desk and hanging leaded glass lamps
 6. Hanging cranberry prism lamps
 7. Pairpoint puffy shade lamps
 8. Art glass lamps and shades
 9. Signed lamps by Tiffany, Handel, Pairpoint, Jefferson, Classique, Moe Bridges, and others
 10. Unusual or rare antique lamps of all types.

After nearly three decades in the lamp business, Dan knows what to ask: Is it an original antique? Is it complete? Is it in good shape? What is wrong with it? What parts have been replaced or repaired? Is there a return guarantee? Is the item pictured in a particular reference book? Do you have other, similar items for sale? Is the price negotiable? Can you send a photograph? Dan will make offers on well-described lamps, some of which can be worth more than $1,000.

NUTCRACKERS

Hal A. Davis
1815 West 18th Street
Santa Ana, California 92706
(714) 558-7800

After thirty years, Hal Davis is a most experienced collector of nutcrackers. "I have one of every one I've ever seen," he says, but points out that "new ones keep turning up."

He seeks all types of nutcrackers, big or small, made of almost any substance you can name: wood, brass, bronze, ivory, porcelain, or glass. Include a description, sketch, or photograph of the nutcracker. Give the dimensions, age (if known), color, and material from which it is made. Copy any marks or writing.

Hal is also interested in articles about nutcrackers.

JUICERS AND REAMERS

Edith Esposito
735 Bryant Avenue
Roslyn Harbor, New York 11576

Edith Esposito wants to buy orange, lemon, and grapefruit extractors made of fine china, silver, or glass in black, cobalt, red, teal green or colored slag. She also wants figural ceramic juicers shaped like clowns, elephants, dogs, pigs, Donald Duck, Mickey Mouse, and other characters. "No mechanicals, please."

In addition to juicers, Edith wants to buy both pie birds and cast iron figural bottle openers.

"Describe and price," she requests, but indicates that she will make offers on unpriced items, as long as you don't forget to include an SASE.

CANNING JARS

Tom and Deena Caniff
1223 Oak Grove Avenue
Steubenville, Ohio 43952
(614) 282-8918

The Caniffs are collector-dealers of antique fruit-canning jars, specializing mainly in pre-1925 items. They buy:

1. Canning jars in unusual colors, such as amber, emerald green, cobalt blue, milk glass
2. Canning jars with unusual closures
3. Recently made canning jars that were produced in limited quantities either as samples or as mistakes
4. Limited-production presentation jars or bottles made by Kerr, Ball, and others to honor retiring employees, company anniversaries, and the like
5. Advertising items (tin signs, displays, posters, letter openers, etc.) from manufacturers of canning jars

When writing them about an item for sale, please include the maker of the jar, color of the glass, type of closure, and size, dimensions, or capacity. Note any cracks, chips, stains, missing lids, scratches, and other defects.

The Caniffs are members of numerous bottle clubs and authors of a variety of articles in antiques publications. "We will attempt to answer all questions to the best of our ability, and if we are unable to help, will attempt to forward questions to someone in the bottle or jar hobby who can help. Requests regarding the antique bottle or jar collection hobby itself will be happily answered." The Caniffs are available for appraisals and will make offers on unpriced items you wish to sell.

EYE CUPS

W.T. Atkinson, Jr.
P.O. Box 4112
Hampstead, North Carolina 28443
(919) 686-0921

This longtime collector-dealer wants to purchase antique eye cups, but only those made of fine china or colored glass, "not common clear glass."

Please send a complete description, including any markings on the bottom of china cups. A good close-up photo would be helpful for determining the exact color.

Atkinson will evaluate your cup in light of his own collection as well as its resale potential. He will make offers if you ask him to, and don't forget to include an SASE.

RAZOR BLADE BANKS

Herb Shearer
904 La Puente Drive
Bakersfield, California 93309

After thirty years of collecting, Herb Shearer probably has the largest collection of razor blade banks in the world, but he says that there are thousands of them he still seeks.

Razor blade banks are small containers, made between 1925 and 1960, designed to hold used double-edge razor blades. They are made of ceramic, tin, metal, paper, wood, glass, and plastic. Some are simple jars, but they also come in a variety of figural shapes. The figurals are, of course, the ones Herb most wants, especially those shaped like a barber's chair.

Banks are generally worth between $1 and $10 each. If you have one for sale, describe it well and price it. He will make offers on unpriced items he would like to buy.

FANCY STRAIGHT RAZORS

K. John Ruckh
P.O. Box 26525
St. Louis Park, Minnesota 55426
(612) 545-9439

John Ruckh wants to purchase fancy old straight razors in good condition.

He indicates a preference for those with handles of stag horn, bone, tortoise shell, genuine ivory, worked bone, mother of pearl, silver, or intricately designed celluloid. He also will purchase boxed sets, seven-day sets, or razors with plain handles but heavy engraving on the blade.

Please provide a description of both the blade and the handle. When describing the blade, indicate whether it is new, sharpened, ground, discolored, rusty, etc. Provide a photograph, good drawing, or photocopy of artwork on the handles or blades. An SASE is a must if you want an answer.

You may ask John to make an offer for what you have if you provide a good enough description.

UNUSED RAZOR BLADES

Gerald Hanes
Contract Station 18
Windsor Park Mall
San Antonio, Texas 78218
(512) 655-3562

For fifty years, Gerald Hanes has been building the largest razor blade collection in the United States, more than four thousand of them.

"There are still many I don't have," he points out. "Some European collections go over ten thousand blades." He wants unused blades that are individually double-wrapped, with colored wrappers, in boxes, cartons, or on display cards. He is primarily seeking unusual private brands for his collection but will purchase duplicates for trade.

Gerald will make an offer in cash for your blades, but because individual blades are not particularly valuable you may find it profitable to work out trades. He is a multi-faceted collector with a wide variety of other items to trade.

When describing, indicate the brand and variety (single-edge, double-edge, blue steel, white steel, gold, stainless, autostrop, etc.). Tell how they are packaged, the condition, and how many you have for sale or trade.

BAROMETERS

John N. Lewis
156 Scarboro Drive
York, Pennsylvania 17403

John Lewis buys, sells, and restores old barometers.

If you have one for sale (or would like yours restored), he wants to know the name of the maker, the type of barometer, and the condition. Note whether it is still working. If there are any paper labels, make certain to provide as much information as practical.

John will generally request that the instrument be shipped to him for inspection before he sets a value or a price for restoration. He will discuss with you the problems of shipping a restored instrument (you may have to pick it up) and will send a shipping crate for your use, when appropriate. If the instrument is for sale, he would prefer the seller to set the price, but is willing to negotiate after making a free and honest appraisal.

The Hamilton Bank of York, Pennsylvania, can provide references for this long-established craftsman.

FOUNTAIN PENS AND FLASHLIGHTS

Stuart Schneider
P.O. Box 64
Teaneck, New Jersey 07666
(201) 261-1983

Stu Schneider wants rare fountain pens, pens with comic characters or personalities on them, and pens made with a mechanical pencil at the other end. He also wants signs, banners, clocks, tokens, catalogs, pamphlets, and brochures related to old fountain pens.

In addition, Stu seeks old unusual flashlights. "I do not want ordinary two-cell flashlights. When flashlights were first made, they came in many unusual shapes or heavily decorated. These are the ones I want." He has a page of illustrated examples that you may request if you include your SASE.

If you have pens to sell, he suggests that you place them on a photocopier covered with a piece of plain white paper. Indicate the color and manufacturer's name. "An adequate description" of your flashlight, preferably accompanied by a life-size drawing, is all that's needed.

Stu is author of Collecting and Valuing Early Fountain Pens and publisher of a monthly newsletter for pen fanciers.

TEXAS INSTRUMENTS' WRISTWATCHES

Matthew Murphy
9 Beacon Place,
Melrose, Massachusetts 02176

Bob Murphy specializes in wristwatches, but only those made by Texas Instruments. It doesn't matter whether they are new or used, LED or LCD types, Bob wants to hear from you if you have one to sell.

He wants to know whether it is new or used and whether it is working. He also wants to know what the case is made of, the model number, and the color.

He does not perform appraisals but will make purchase offers on unpriced items.

WRIST AND POCKET WATCHES

Miles F. Sandler
Maundy International Watches
9071 Metcalf, Suite 108
Overland Park, Kansas 66212
(913) 383-2880 or (800) 235-2866

Miles Sandler advertises himself as the country's largest mail-order dealer in watches of all types. He buys "anything from the dollar watch to the museum timepiece, one watch or ten thousand." He also buys watch dials, movements, and cases.

You may write to him about your watch, giving the name of the watch company, the number of jewels, the type of case and the metal from which it is made, but he must see the watch before giving estimates or making purchases. Make sure to include your telephone number, as he is likely to phone you upon receipt of your watch.

Miles is an attorney and former city prosecutor. He offers a catalog with good descriptions of antique watches priced from $100 to more than $1,000. The president of the Peoples Mercantile Bank in Kansas City, Missouri 64114, can provide reference.

POCKET AND WRISTWATCHES

Roy Ehrhardt
10101 Blue Ridge
Kansas City, Missouri 64134
(816) 761-0080

Better-quality men's and women's wrist and pocket watches are purchased by Roy Ehrhardt.

He also buys trade catalogs for clocks, watches, cut glass, pocketknives, and stringed musical instruments, especially violins. Auction catalogs of clocks and watches from "any auction house, anywhere, any date" are also purchased.

Provide him with complete information, maker, model (if known), gold content, number of jewels, serial number, and type of band. A photocopy is suggested for catalogs, although a good description including the publisher, number of pages, and date will suffice.

When necessary, he will make offers on items he needs.

CARTOON AND ADVERTISING WATCHES

Maggie Kenyon
One Christopher Street, #14G
New York, New York 10014

Maggie Kenyon collects watches with promotions, advertising, cartoons, or caricatures on the face.

Tell Maggie the brand name of the watch and what is on the face. Note the condition of the case, crystal, and band. If you know how old it is, make certain to tell her that, too.

All watches should be priced. Requests for offers are considered requests for an appraisal and should be accompanied by your check for $3 to cover the appraisal fee.

MOUSETRAPS

Tom Edmonds
6161 Birkewood Road
Huntington, West Virginia 25705

For fifteen years, Tom Edmonds has been a collector of antique moustraps.

He is particularly interested in obtaining pre-1920 traps that catch the mouse alive.

Send him as complete a description as possible, including a photograph or simple drawing. He will make offers on unpriced items.

FLOWER FROGS

Bonnie K. Bull
P.O. Box 106
Trumbull, Connecticut 06611
(203) 261-2398

For nearly ten years, Bonnie Bull has been a collector of flower frogs.

She wants glass, porcelain, and pottery figures that contain holes for arranging cut flowers. "I do not want metal and wire flower frogs or plain round frogs which do not depict a person or object."

Provide her with a description, size, condition, manufacturer (if known), and your asking price. She expresses a willingness to make offers on unpriced items, however.

She is interested in hearing from other frog collectors, as she would like to start a national club.

FLYTRAPS

Maris Zuika
1717 Shaffer Road, 208
Kalamazoo, Michigan 49001
(616) 344-7473

Maris Zuika is a fairly new collector of flytraps, especially those made of glass.

She buys flytraps made of other materials as well, if they are unusual. She also buys literature and advertising about flytraps.

She would like you to provide a photograph or sketch of the item, including its dimensions and the color of the glass. If there are any defects, especially chips or cracks in the glass, please note them in your first letter. You are asked to set the price wanted, but an offer may be requested.

KNIVES

J. Bruce Voyles
Bruce Voyles Company
P.O. Box 22171
Chattanooga, Tennessee 37422
(615) 894-0339

For more than a decade, Bruce Voyles has bought and sold a wide variety of knives and knife-related items, including:

1. Antique bowie knives, especially those with English or American markings
2. Pocketknives with bone handles and fine-condition etched blades "made by anyone," including specific companies
3. Any knives made in Massachusetts or Connecticut
4. Knives made by Remington, Winchester, Marbles, Keen Kutter, Schatt & Morgan, New York Knife Company, Walden Knife Co., Diamond Edge, Western States Cutlery, Cattaraugas Cutlery, Sequine, Hardenbrook, Watson, Little, Case Bros., M. Price, Will & Finick, Kesmodel, Schivley, Searles, and Samuel Bell
5. Advertising for cutlery, including store signs and displays, window banners, catalogs, single-sheet flyers, giveaways, boxes, magazine advertising
6. Magazines (such as American Cutler, The Cutlery Journal, and Paine's Cutlery Journal) and ads for knives from sporting and other magazines
7. Large display knives

He recommends that you lay your knife or other item(s) on a photocopier and include all information about the manufacturer and any other markings that can be found. He will not give free appraisals or make offers on unpriced knives. Since a few knives can have values in excess of $50, some research on your part is necessary. Bruce is the author of the Official Price Guide to Knives; perhaps you can obtain his book through your local library.

CLOTHESPINS

Linda Campbell Franklin
P.O. Box 383 Murray Hill
New York, New York 10016
(212) 679-6038

Linda Franklin wants to buy hand-carved wooden clothespins.

She is not interested in mechanical pins with springs or in common wooden round knob-topped clothespins. If the clothespins you have are wooden, hand-carved, doll-like, and between five and seven inches long, drop her a line, describing them well. She requests that you tell her the approximate price you'd like, but she is willing to make offers.

POCKETKNIVES

Frances Bacharach
6232 North 13th Street
Philadelphia, Pennsylvania 19141

If you have a knife or letter-opener that has a blade which folds into the handle, there is a good chance that Frances Bacharach may buy it.

In addition to penknives, jackknives, and pocketknives, she also buys old advertising, catalogs, literature, or European books that feature folding knives.

When describing knives, indicate the maker (usually stamped into the tang of the blade), all other markings, the length, the number of blades, and the material from which the handle is made. A statement of condition should include all wear, stains, rust, breaks, or other imperfections. A sketch or photocopy is helpful.

Please indicate the approximate price you would like, and don't forget your SASE if you want an answer.

SEWING NEEDLE BOOKLETS

Nita Markham
P.O. Box 221
Pacific Grove, California 93950
(408) 373-6018

Nita Markham collects sewing needle booklets given away by merchants during the 1920s, 1930s, and 1940s. She also collects sewing kits designed for travelers or for carrying in a purse.

Make a photocopy of what you have or describe it thoroughly. Include all the items found in the kit. Count the number of needles, if any, still remaining in the sewing needle booklet. If the items aren't in perfect condition, tell her what is wrong.

If you have a price in mind, ask for it. She will also make you an offer for these relatively inexpensive items.

INDUSTRIAL SEWING MACHINES

Victor L. Kin
Insewmac
P.O. Box 713
New York, New York 10116
(212) 594-3552

Insewmac wants to purchase used home, industrial, and shoe sewing machines, especially those made by Willcox & Gibbs.

Victor Kin is an internationally known specialist in establishing clothing manufacturing plants, and he uses these machines, once reconditioned, in Third World countries. He will buy either the treadle, hand-crank, or electric models, since basically they are all the same machine. His company is not interested in stands or tables but will buy attachments or assortments of parts. He also purchases older, pre-1870, sewing machines for his personal collection.

Willcox & Gibbs machines were manufactured, virtually unchanged, between 1900 and 1940. They are usually black and resemble the letter "G" from the rear. You may find (and Insewmac will buy) machines made by Willcox & Gibbs but marked with the name of a different company, such as Western Electric, New Home, or National. "Don't get excited about early patent dates," he warns, "as most of the machines carry dates in the 1880s and 1890s."

Send an SASE for drawings of the machines Insewmac wants. Values range from $5 to $35 apiece for more common machines.

ANTIQUE THIMBLES

Marie R. Siwiec
Marie's Antiques
152 Mt. Bethel Road
Warren, New Jersey 07060
(201) 647-1492

Marie Siwiec is a longtime collector who buys and sells thimbles of all sorts.

She is interested in thimbles with unusual designs, styles, colors, or materials, and is particularly fond of antique thimbles of precious metals that are hallmarked and have some history with them. She buys and sells thimbles of gold, silver, bronze, brass, aluminum, ivory, white metal, plastic, tin, iron, wood, stone, marble, glass, porcelain, enamel, bisque, fabric, and leather. She is also interested in obtaining any books about thimbles you might find.

If you wish to sell one thimble or one hundred, "give a brief description as to kind, quantity and asking price in your first letter. All inquiries will be answered if they include an SASE."

SEWING THIMBLES OF PRECIOUS METAL

Roz Belford
The Collector's Choice
1313 South Killian Drive
P.O. Box 12600
Lake Park, Florida 33403
(305) 845-6075

Perhaps this nation's most important thimble collector-dealer, Roz Belford is seeking only unusual thimbles made of gold or silver.

As part of the description, include a drawing of any hallmarks. Also indicate the age and country of origin if you know them. A statement of condition is mandatory.

Her wants list may be requested, but you will still be required to set your own price. If you wish, she will appraise your thimble; there is a $5 fee.

SEWING MACHINES

Carter Bays
The Sewing Machine Museum
3214 Foxhall
Columbia, South Carolina 29204
(803) 787-3167

Carter Bays has been collecting for a little more than five years, but he has been doing it very seriously and now owns the largest private collection of antique sewing machines in the country.

He pays from $30 to $300 for pre-1870 machines he can use in his collection or can resell. "Of greatest value," according to Carter, "are treadle machines with serial numbers of four digits or less and small, hand-operated machines in the form of animals."

He points out that there are many sewing machines that may be sentimental family favorites but lack value to collectors. Machines with a nickel- or chrome-plated flywheel are common, as are those with high serial numbers, no matter how old or unusual they might look.

When contacting Carter, include the maker, the serial number, and a photograph whenever possible. He promises that all mail will be answered if an SASE is included. For $20 he will sell you reprints of a long series of articles he did for The Antique Trader Weekly that contain more than one hundred photographs of common and desirable machines. Carter is a professor of computer science and is available to do appraisals on sewing machines that are not for sale; he charges a nominal fee for this service, but there is no charge for offers on items for sale.

QUILTS

Herbert L. Wallerstein, Jr.
Calico Antiques
2163 San Ysidro Drive
Beverly Hills, California 90210
(213) 273-4192

Herb Wallerstein advertises widely in the antiques press for pre-1940 quilts for resale in his Beverly Hills shop.

Calico Antiques buys only quilts that are in near-perfect condition, with no rips, tears, holes, or stains, since all quilts are for resale. Navy blue and white are his favorites.

To offer a quilt for sale, send a description of the materials used, the colors, the size, the approximate age, and a brief history if available. Include a statement of condition and a photograph whenever possible. If you know the name of the pattern, identify it.

Herb prefers you to price the item you wish to sell, but he will make purchase offers. All quilts are subject to final approval after inspection.

ANTIQUE QUILTS

Margaret Cavigga
The Margaret Cavigga Quilt Collection
8648 Melrose Avenue
Los Angeles, California 90069
(213) 659-3020

Owner of one of the world's largest private collection of quilts, and operator of a kaleidoscopic quilt shop and museum, Margaret Cavigga is always looking for more quality pieces.

Besides rare and unusual pre-1940 American quilts, she also purchases antique woven American coverlets, sewing birds and other interesting sewing memorabilia, pre-1940 books about quilts, photographs depicting early quilts in use, and cigar felts and silks.

Margaret wants only items in fine condition, "no holes, stains, or tears." Good quilts generally bring $100 and up, so it is advisable to send a photograph of any quilt or coverlet you have for sale. Margaret expects you to set the price, so research is in order, as most quilts are moderately priced but a few are quite valuable. She wants the seller to specifically state that she has the right of seven-day approval or return.

AMERICAN QUILTS

Michael Council
Quilts
842 Mohawk Street
Columbus, Ohio 43206
(614) 443-0696

This beginning collector-dealer wants to purchase hand-sewn American quilts dating before 1940.

Although Michael Council collects silk quilts and deals in all 19th- and 20th-century pieced and appliqued quilts, he considers his specialty to be quilts of the Depression era.

He does have a wants list and indicates a willingness to make purchase offers if items are photographed and well described. He wants to know the pattern, color, size, age, and origin of quilts and coverlets you offer. He specifically states that he is not interested in items with holes or stains unless they are very old or rare.

PATCHWORK QUILTS

Eli Leon
5663 Dover Street
Oakland, California 94609
(415) 652-9486

Eli Leon is a ten-year veteran collector-dealer of patchwork quilts.

"I am chiefly interested in pre-1950s handmade quilts in good condition but will consider any quilt with redeeming characteristics, especially in one of my specialties: quilts by black women; friendship quilts signed by a number of people; quilts that are signed, dated, and have a known history."

You must describe the condition of the quilt in detail, including all wear, loose stitches, tears, and stains. Give its dimensions, its age, and the name of the pattern if you can. A photo is strongly suggested if you are not familiar with traditional quilting patterns. He will make offers on well-described items.

VINTAGE CLOTHING

Mrs. Bess Hill
Hill House Costume Shop
1914 Newport Boulevard
Costa Mesa, California 92627

Bess Hill has been a well-known buyer of vintage clothing for twenty years. She is interested in:

1. 1950s clothing, such as beaded and sequined sweaters, poodle skirts, crepe and other thin blouses, men's gabardine jackets, Ivy League shirts, Hawaiian shirts, and leather jackets
2. White Victorian dresses, especially wedding gowns
3. 1920s beaded dresses, as well as nightware and underwear
4. Men's morning coats and hats from all periods
5. Velvet and satin dresses of the 1930s and 1940s (the long slinky ones) and the lingerie to wear with them
6. Designer clothes of all periods
7. Fine hats, shoes and gloves of all periods
8. Lace, linens, and tapestries of good quality

"I hate to make an offer for something I haven't seen," Bess says. If you want an offer, you must write her first, listing what you have, the dates, the materials, the styles, and the colors. Indicate the label, and of course, any damage, no matter how small. She will tell you which items should be sent on approval. "If you price your stuff and it's reasonable, I usually will take a chance and buy outright, but I seldom answer a letter that doesn't include an SASE," she notes.

VINTAGE WOMEN'S CLOTHING

Janet Cormier
Cormier's Vintage Interiors
14 Harvard Street
Brookline, Massachusetts

Janet Cormier wants to buy women's dresses, blouses, and fashion accessories dating between 1890 and 1950. She especially wants hats sold between 1920 and the late 1940s. Women's shoes from the same period are also of interest if size 8 or larger.

Art Deco accessories, costume jewelry, perfume bottles, and decorator items are also wanted.

Describe yout item fully, making certain to note all damage, tears, stains, wear, fading, scuffs, etc. Janet does not do appraisals and prefers the seller to set the price wanted.

Fashion magazines, especially Vogue and Harper's Bazaar from the 1920s thorugh the 1950s, are also of interest.

WOMEN'S CLOTHING AND SHOES IN LARGE SIZES

Ralph S. Sullivan
346 Ivy Avenue
Westbury, New York 11590
(516) 334-5188

In thirty-five years of collecting, Ralph Sullivan has amassed an assortment of more than five hundred pairs of women's shoes plus hundreds of clothing items. He is, therefore, very specific in his needs.

Ralph wants large women's clothing (size 40 and up) and shoes (size 10 and up) that show evidence of being used. "I want worn clothing and shoes only. I do not want unworn or so-called mint-condition clothes or shoes. I want to look at the clothing and see wear and know that it comes from the period it represents. I want items to have the look, the feeling, and the smell of age and wear."

He writes: "If there are mature women in their seventies or eighties with collections of Lane Bryant clothing (underwear, suits, shoes, etc.) dating from 1920 to 1945, I would like to hear from them. The clothing must be size 40 or larger and conservative in nature. I especially want underwear and dressy business suits, dresses, skirts, and blouses in black, brown, dark blue, or gray, in striped or plain material. Silk and rayon is preferred, but cotton and wool will be considered. Please, nothing frilly or in loud colors."

Other high-quality or custom-made clothing that fits the general description will also be considered, Ralph indicates, but notes, "The only formal wear that I am interested in is flapper dresses from the 1920s. No other formal wear is of value to me."

Shoes, too, should show evidence of wear. "I want black kidskin, brown kidskin, black calf, brown calf, black patent leather, brown-and-white spectator pumps, oxfords, and sandals with high heels. I want shoes specifically of the period 1920-45 in large sizes (10M, or 9-12 E, EE, or EEE). People who will be wearing these shoes are large in stature and must have the large sizes to feel comfortable."

He warns: "Please do not send me new shoes, cloth shoes, suede shoes, vinyl or plastic shoes. I know the difference between plastic and skin shoes. I also know the difference between a 1931 kidskin pump, a 1957 stiletto high heel, and a 1970 vinyl pump, and have no interest whatever in the latter two."

If you are the original owner of the shoes or clothing for sale, Ralph would like to know the year you purchased them, as closely as you can remember. He will make generous offers for items he finds suitable.

FUR COATS

Linda Green
P.O. Box 311
Utica, Michigan 48087
(313) 739-4053

Linda Green wants men's or women's fur coats made between 1920 and 1950 of raccoon, muskrat, mink, monkey, black seal, and other good-quality furs. She does not want Persian lamb, mouton, or any other curly fur.

Although she wants coats in all sizes and lengths, she does not buy capes, stoles, neck pieces, collars, muffs, or other fur pieces.

Tell her the size and approximate age of your coat and describe the style in detail, including the type of collar, cuffs, buttons, etc. A drawing would be most helpful. As for condition, she also wants to know: Are there any skin splits or tears in either the fur or the lining? Is there noticeable wear in the fur or the lining? Is the coat in clean and shiny condition?

"I do not buy coats that need cleaning or smell of cigarette smoke or other odors except mothballs." But she does make offers, to be confirmed after inspection.

COSTUME JEWELRY

Elenore Ernst
Ronelle Sales
P.O. Box 517
Merrick, New York 11566

Elenore Ernst, a mail-order dealer known to her customers as Ronelle Sales, buys and sells quality costume jewelry dating between the turn-of-the century and 1930. "I'm primarily interested in unique necklaces, mosaic jewelry of all types, cameos, jewelry with Art Deco design, marcasite jewelry, and gold-filled bangle bracelets. But I will buy other jewelry as well," she writes.

Jewelry can best be described with a close-up photograph, a sketch, or a photocopy. Indicate all colors, the type(s) of metal and stones, and any markings. If you know when and where the piece was originally purchased, tell her.

Elenore is confident in her knowledge of costume jewelry and is willing to make appraisals, but only when actually examining your item. Describe what you have well, and she will make offers, subject to inspection.

VINTAGE RAYON LINGERIE

Irene Turner
Irene Turner Antiques
P.O. Box 14
Quincy, Massachusetts 02269

Irene Turner seeks rayon lingerie and accessories from 1920 to the present. "Rayon items should be made by the spun or multifilament process," she writes. "This material is very soft, similar to silk but heavier and very durable.

"I am seeking the following lingerie undergarments that were manufactured of 100 percent rayon, silk rayon, or rayon acetate: chemises, teddies, slips (full or half), bloomers, knickers, step-ins, briefs, and all styles of panties." Please identify your underclothing by the style, size, color, and (most important to her) the brand name on the sewn-in tag. Although she has a list of specific brand names that are popular sellers, she is prepared to negotiate if the style, size and color you have are of a different brand but something she can use. "Everything has some value," she points out.

Books, magazines, and sewing literature that in whole or part deal with the past, present, or future of undergarments are also purchased.

Irene promises to answer all inquiries promptly but will perform appraisals only after actually seeing the item(s). "We will reimburse all your shipping costs, but we insist that shipments be insured, securely boxed, and a return receipt requested to insure the safety of your items."

HATPINS AND HATPIN HOLDERS

Lillian Baker
Hatpins & Hatpin Holders Club
15237 Chanera Avenue
Gardena, California 90249
(213) 329-2619

Lillian Baker is a freelance writer and founder of an international club for collectors of hatpins and hatpin holders, her specialty for thirty years.

She will buy "authentic period hatpins, hatpin holders, and dresser sets which have hatpin holders as part of the set. I will buy one piece or an entire collection."

Lillian also wants to buy Art Deco jewelry and miniatures on a scale of one inch to one foot. When offering any of these items for sale, provide a full description and a photograph if possible. She prefers you set your own price, but will make offers on items she finds desirable. You may request an illustrated and priced wants list, valuable information for the beginner.

She is the author of two books on jewelry and one on hatpins.

ANTIQUE OR BROKEN DIAMONDS

Kal Newfield
Newfield Trading Corp.
98 Meridian Street
Greenfield, Massachusetts 01301
(413) 774-4106

Kal Newfield buys broken and chipped diamonds in all sizes, shapes, colors, and grades. He also buys some good-quality antique jewelry and mountings, "with artistic merit" and with or without stones, for his personal collection.

Kal suggests he is willing to pay "realistic" prices. "I can offer bank references and the names of satisfied jewelers and other customers with whom I do business regularly."

The procedure requires that you ship your stones to him for inspection and an offer. He will submit an individual bid for each stone. "Once my bid is accepted, a check is sent immediately. If they reject my bid, their parcel is returned promptly. If substantial value is involved, I will travel to inspect the stones at the seller's convenience."

MECHANICAL AND BATTERY-OPERATED BANKS

H.E. Mihlheim
Mechanical Bank Collectors Association
P.O. Box 128
Allegan, Michigan 49010
(616) 673-4509

Mr. Mihlheim, Secretary of the Mechanical Bank Collectors Association, especially wants to buy old and unusual cast iron mechanical banks dating between 1870 and 1920, but also will buy battery-driven mechanical banks made in Japan during the 1940s and 1950s.

If you have a cast iron mechanical bank for sale, your first step is to stand the bank upright on a piece of paper and trace closely around the bottom of the bank with a sharp pencil. Accuracy is important when tracing since the size will affect the amount he will offer for the bank. He also wants a statement of condition that includes your estimate of percentage of the original paint that still remains.

If your bank is battery-operated, be certain to mention whether it is still in working condition and whether it has its original box. Battery-operated banks should be in mint to near-mint condition to be of interest. No plastic banks, please.

Mr. Mihlheim has been collecting for more than a dozen years. You may write for an unpriced wants list and also request appraisals or purchase offers.

STILL BANKS

Ralph Berman
3524 Largo Lane
Annandale, Virginia 22003

Ralph Berman writes: "I am interested in buying still banks that are old, original, and have no broken parts or need of repairs. They can be of cast iron, pot metal, or tin, but I am seeking only fine-condition, unusual or interesting still banks. I do not buy mechanical banks."

The seller should list the size (height, width, and depth) and the type of metal from which the bank is made. The condition of the paint is very important, as are any names or numbers you might find. If you are familiar with banks, he wants you to refer to standard bank reference books and give the assigned number. He would like all historical information that is available.

Ralph requests that the seller set the price, but amateur sellers may look to him for assistance.

CIGARETTES, SMOKING TOBACCO, AND SNUFF

"Tobacco Bill" Hatcher
713 Parott Avenue
Kinston, North Carolina 28501

Bill Hatcher wants "memorabilia, paraphernalia, and ephemera" from the cigarette, pipe tobacco, chewing tobacco, and snuff industries. He'll buy tins, tags, packages, signs, advertising, premium books, and catalogs. Particular interest is expressed in:

1. Tin tags from obsolete chewing tobacco plugs
2. Premium catalogs from manufacturers showing merchandise that could be obtained by sending in tin tags or coupons
3. Tobacco company histories, house organs, or advertising booklets such as "Lorillard Magazine" or "Durham Whiffs"
4. Advertising labels from the ends of tobacco crates
5. Other interesting pre-1930 items

Bill has been involved with the tobacco industry for more than twenty-five years and a collector of tobacco memorabilia for almost that long. He asks that you provide him with a complete description, including the size, color, brand name, manufacturer, and date when possible. He prefers you to set the price wanted, and requests that you send a photocopy whenever possible. If your photocopy and description are clear and complete and you include a self-addressed stamped envelope, Bill will make offers on items from amateur sellers.

Bill is a tobacco auctioneer, a well-known figure in the collecting world, and active with a large number of clubs, museums, and historical associations.

RARE PIPES AND TOBACCO LITERATURE

Ben Rapaport
Antiquarian Tobacciana
5101 Willowmeade Drive
Fairfax, Virginia 22030
(703) 830-8584 eves.

Ben Rapaport wants to buy antique meerschaum, porcelain, or wooden European or Oriental pipes. He is seeking old, rare, decorative, or unusual items only, please.

Ben is also the world's largest dealer of tobacco books and literature and author of an international bibliography of materials available on smoking and tobacco. A linguist and retired army colonel, Ben buys books, catalogs, prints, posters, and other ephemera related to tobacco, tobacco manufacture, smoking, pipes, cigarettes, and cigars. His twenty years' experience make him the international authority on tobacco literature in at least five languages.

When describing a pipe, tell Ben its condition, its overall length and height, the materials from which it is made, and indicate any damage or missing parts. When describing books, provide standard bibliographic information. Please make photocopies of any unusual items, prints, advertising, and the like. Ben will make an offer based on its potential resale value.

TOBACCO LUNCH BOX TINS

Robert J. Carr
7325 Cornell Avenue
St. Louis, Missouri 63130
(314) 721-8232

Bob Carr is a longtime member of a tin container collectors organization and well known for his collection of children's lunch boxes.

Bob also buys early tobacco tins shaped like lunch boxes. These were manufactured between 1900 and about 1930, were approximately six by nine inches and about five inches high. They are characterized by wire bail handles on top and colorful lithography all around.

Some of these can be worth over $1,000., so you are urged to contact Bob if you think you have what he is looking for. But be cautioned--tin collectors are among the fussiest of people when it comes to condition, so write him only if your tobacco lunch box is in excellent condition.

Ask Bob to set the price, as he keeps current with the market in tins. A picture of what you have is appreciated, although most brands are well known to collectors.

PIPES, SMOKING TOBACCO, AND SNUFF

L. Page Maccubbin
1724 20th Street, NW
Washington, D.C. 20009
(202) 387-6688

Page Maccubbin wants pre-1920 items associated with pipe smoking or snuff taking, including snuff boxs and tools, snuff advertising, and books.

He also wants unusual early pipes, especially those with small bowls, water pipes, carved meerschaums, and the like. He will purchase antique cigarette rolling papers or advertising for them. "No cigar items, please," he says emphatically.

All items, no matter how old, must be in fine condition, as Maccubbin buys for resale in his shop. Include a complete description, noting all defects, dings, or damage. Photographs or sketches, depending on the item, are helpful. He will make offers for items he can use.

CIGARETTE PACKS

Richard Elliott

61 Searle Street
Georgetown, Massachusetts 01833

Dick Elliott collects rare and obsolete packages, tins, and boxes of U.S.-made cigarette brands, either singly or in albums.

He does not buy common brands, foreign items, or anything still manufactured. "No Lucky Strike green or Chesterfield fifties needed, thanks." Send him a self-addressed stamped envelope and he will send you a page of brands and the prices he pays (generally from $3 to $10).

"Write first, before sending anything," he urges, "giving the brand name, describing its condition, and identifying the series number on the tax stamp." He prefers you to set the price, but will make offers on unpriced items.

CIGAR BOXES AND MEMORABILIA

H.A. "Tony" Hyman
5816 N. Rowland Avenue
Temple City, California 91780
(818) 285-5905

Tony Hyman wants to obtain cigar boxes that are unusual in shape or size, especially very large or very small boxes, or boxes shaped like books, mailboxes, trunks, bottles, and the like. He also buys wooden cigar boxes with colorful or unusual labels, particularly those featuring nudes, gambling, sports, bathing beauties, animals doing human things, women in traditionally "male" roles, women's liberation or suffrage, humor, cartoons, patriotic themes, Uncle Sam, war, Indians, blacks, any ethnic practices or characteristics, religion, medicine or health claims, U.S. presidents, entertainers, Christmas or other holidays, special events, local scenes or personalities, elections, clubs or organizations, and the like.

Tony also buys "virtually everything" having to do with growing cigar tobacco, making cigars, selling cigars, making cigar boxes, manufacturing cigar tools, printing cigar labels, making cigar or other tin cans, printing tax stamps, taxation, the Cigar Makers International Union, Samuel Gompers, etc.

He wants catalogs, photographs, brochures, label catalogs, tax booklets, company records, salesmen's sample kits, postcards, trade cards, signs, posters, cigar lighters, premiums and giveaways, tip trays, cigar store Indians and other figures less than three feet tall, mechanical tools, and "anything else you can think of" if it has to do with the cigar industry.

Make a photocopy of the inside lid of your cigar box or other item for sale. Tony buys mint or near-mint-condition boxes only, but historical ephemera is considered in less than perfect condition. You may price what you have or request an offer.

CIGARETTE SILKS

Kenneth Silverman
Thieves Market
P.O. Box 654
Tiburon, California 94920

Ken Silverman wants cigarette silks, those small decorated silks included with cigarette packs around the world at the turn of the century.

He will buy any amount, from any country, "even duplicates." He also buys quilts or other items that have been manufactured of cigarette silks.

Ken wants to know how many you have, the subject matter, and their condition. If you want him to make an offer, it is advisable to first ship them to him for inspection.

CIGAR BANDS

Myron H. Freedman
International Seal, Label & Cigar Band Society
8915 E. Bellevue Street
Tucson, Arizona 85715

Myron Freedman is a thirty-year veteran collector of cigar bands and is the founder and publisher of the newsletter of the International Seal, Label & Cigar Band Society.

He is primarily interested in cigar bands, but also buys labels and trade cards from the tobacco industry and sample books of cigar bands and labels.

Tell him the number and type of bands and their condition. A photocopy of some of the pages would be most helpful. There is a fee for appraisals, so ask for offers only if you seriously intend to sell. You may request his illustrated wants list.

CIGAR BANDS

Jack Shapiro
3201 South Monroe Street
Denver, Colorado 80210
(303) 756-8235

Jack Shapiro buys Cuban, American, and European Cigar bands, but the latter only in complete sets.

If you have bands for sales, a good description should include information about the person who collected the bands and where he lived. He would also like to know the type of book the bands are mounted in, the percentage of bands that are duplicates, and the condition, noting how many are wrinkled, torn, or soiled. Any unusual or particularly colorful bands should be pointed out.

Appraisals may be requested, but Jack will make them only after actually examining what you have, and a fee is charged. He will make an offer for your bands based on your description, but it will probably be substantially lower than if he actually sees the collection before making the offer.

CIGARETTE SILKS AND CARDS

Charles Reuter
6 Joy Avenue
Mount Joy, Pennsylvania 17552

Charles Reuter wants to purchase premiums issued by the cigarette industry between 1880 and 1920, including trade cards, silks, albums, and posters. "U.S. companies only," he clarifies.

He buys cigarette premiums, no matter what the topic (flags, rugs, ball players, butterflies, etc.,) but note that he specifically wants cigarette premiums, not those of the cigar or tobacco industry. They are not the same.

Make a photocopy of what you have or describe it well, especially the condition. He will make offers for what he can use, or you may set the price you would like.

BOTTLE OPENERS

Tom Morrison
2930 Squaw Valley Drive
Colorado Springs, Colorado 80918
(303) 598-1754

Tom Morrison collects figural, unusual, or intricately carved bottle openers, whether made from wood, ivory, pot metal, or silverplate. If the handle of your opener is made of sterling silver, Tom wants it even in common dinnerware patterns.

He also buys combination corkscrew/bottle openers that are made with sterling handles or in unusual designs. "If in doubt, write me about any odd or unusual bottle openers. So far, I've bought every sterling silver opener I've ever found."

Tom has been collecting for five years and promises to answer all mail that includes an SASE. He suggests a photocopy or a clear life-size sketch as the best technique for describing what you have. If you know the name of the pattern or the manufacturer, mention it. Describe the condition and give Tom an idea of the price you're seeking.

CORKSCREWS

Aaron Corenman
Brookside Antiques
P.O. Box 747
Los Altos, Califonia 94022
(415) 948-6174

Corkscrews made between 1700 and 1930 are Aaron Corenman's pleasure, especially miniature, pocket, table, and large mechanical bar-mounted types. He prefers those with wood, silver, horn, ivory, iron, mother-of-pearl, or brass handles. You are well advised to send for his beautifully illustrated wants list.

If you have something to sell, a photo with measurements or a full-size tracing is preferred, along with an accurate description of condition. Make certain to tell him about any markings or hallmarks. "I don't like to make offers without actually seeing the item," he notes, so he prefers sellers to set the price. He has said, however, that if the seller badly underprices a corkscrew, he will pay more than the asking price.

He will not answer if you fail to include an SASE or if you offer items "to the highest bidder."

BEER CANS AND OTHER BREWERIANA

Jeffrey C. Cameron
P.O. Box 43
Colmar, Pennsylvania 18915
(215) 699-3014

Jeff Cameron writes, "I am seeking quality brewery advertising items, particularly pre-WW II beer cans, trays, lithographs, reverse on glass signs, and tin pieces of all types. I will consider all brewery items, but my main interest is in older, rarer advertising pieces."

He goes on, "When you inquire, details are important. Make certain you identify the type of piece (tray, can, mug, stein, lithograph, photograph, sign), and describe it as best you can. Identify what brand is advertised, its brewery, and any cities that are mentioned. Note any flaws such as scratches, dings, dents, tears, fading, rust, and the like. Identify any colors."

Jeff prefers items to be priced, but indicates that he will make offer based on rarity and condition. On more valuable items, it may be necessary for him to see the piece before making a firm offer.

A full-time collector-dealer since 1973, Jeff is promoter of a national convention of beer collectors, author of The Class Book of U.S. Beer Cans, and publisher and editor of Brewery Collectibles Magazine.

CAST IRON FIGURAL BOTTLE OPENERS

Bonnie K. Bull
P.O. Box 106
Trumbull, Connecticut 06611
(203) 261-2398

For nearly ten years, Bonnie Bull has collected cast iron figural bottle openers.

She describes them as "three-dimensional cast iron figures of people, animals, fish, etc., which open bottles. The opener is incorporated into the design of the figure. The were manufactured predominantly by two Pennsylvania companies, Wilton and Wright."

Note the condition, including how much of the original paint is left. "A drawing or picture would be very helpful," she says. You should set the price you'd like, but Bonnie is available to do appraisals and will make offers on unpriced cast iron openers you have for sale.

BEER BOTTLE OPENERS AND CORKSCREWS

Donald A. Bull
P.O. Box 106
Trumbull, Connecticut 06611
(203) 261-2398

Don Bull is an advanced collector of beer bottle openers and corkscrews. He is primarily interested in finding unusually shaped openers or corkscrews that contain advertising for a beer or brewery, especially for breweries which predate Prohibition.

When you write him, it is important to include a clear tracing of your opener. Tell him about any writing or labels. You may request his handsome illustrated wants list, which pictures examples of openers and corkscrews he seeks.

If you accurately describe what you have, Don will make an offer.

Don is an extremely active collector and researcher, author of four books on breweries and beer openers, and editor and publisher of Just for Openers, a quarterly newsletter for collectors of openers.

STEINS

Lottie Lopez
P.O. Box 885
Santa Paula, California 93060
(805) 525-8833

Lottie Lopez is an advanced collector of steins, seeking fine, rare, and unusual pieces.

She lists Mettlachs, the early bluegray steins by Westerwald, and all good character steins as being of interest. So, too, are those of glass, faience, or pewter. Mettlach wall plaques are also sought.

"A photo and detailed description are most necessary. List size, condition, and decorations. Include the number and marks on the bottom of the stein. Please describe all defects, missing parts, and repairs. State the price range you hope to get."

Lotti can provide a priced wants list and is willing to make offers on items she can use.

BEER TRAYS, BOTTLES, AND OLDER CANS

Steve Daniels
P.O. Box 1362
Dedham, Massachusetts 02026

Steve Daniels wants to buy beer trays, beer bottles, and older beer cans.

When describing what you have, begin by indentifying the beer and the brewery. Describe items thoroughly, making certain to indicate the colors. A statement of condition should be included. He will provide you with a priced wants list if you send him a self-addressed stamped envelope.

This seven-year veteran collector-dealer will make offers on unpriced items that he can use for his collection or his shop.

SWIZZLE STICKS

Edy J. Chandler
P.O. Box 20664 S
Houston, Texas 77225
(713) 668-7864 or (713) 527-8402

Edy Chandler will buy swizzle sticks made of glass, plastic, or wood, but only fancy or figural ones with people, animals, airplanes, designs, corporate logos, etc. No plain, straight sticks or spoons.

The best way to describe swizzle sticks is to lay them on a photocopy machine. You may request Edy's permission to ship items on approval. Edy will make an offer on sticks she wants, but you are reminded that these are not items of great value.

METTLACH STEINS AND PLAQUES

Gary Kirsner
Glentiques, Ltd.
P.O. Box 337
Glenford, New York 12433
(914) 657-6261

Gary Kirsner is a ten-year veteran collector and dealer in steins, plaques, and other wares made by Mettlach.

He also purchases other fine-quality regimental or character steins made of glass, pewter, faience, or stoneware. Any high-quality steins in silver, gold, or ivory are wanted. No modern or souvenir pieces, please.

An accurate description is requested, including the stein's capacity (often marked on the bottom), height, maker's marks, etc. Send a photograph whenever possible.

Gary is the author of The Mettlach Book and a member of Stein Collectors International. He is available to perform estate appraisals of steins for a fee, but is willing to make offers on fine items offered by amateur sellers.

HAMM'S BEER

Peter J. Nowicki
2239 24th Avenue
San Francisco, California 94116
(415) 566-8445

If it has to do with Hamm's Beer or the Hamm's Brewery, Peter Nowicki will probably buy it.

He asks for all displays, advertising, packaging, souvenirs and "related items" including: cans, bottles, bottle caps, signs, openers, kegs, tappers, glasses, steins, trays, shirts, photographs, lithographs, postcards, and so on, from Hamm's Beer or any other brand made by Hamm's. These are Buckhorn, Velvet Glove, Matterhorn, Burgie, Right Time, Old Bru, and Waldech, according to Nowicki.

If you have anything relating to Hamm's, describe its size, the material from which it is made, all writing on it, and its condition. It is particularly important to copy writing exactly when describing cans and glasses. "Photos are appreciated," he says, but not necessary.

He has a wants list, makes appraisals for a fee, and will quote you an offer for items he can use in his collection.

MINIATURE BEER BOTTLES

Alexander C. Mullin
1029 Windsor Road
Collingdale, Pennsylvania 19023
(215) 532-7185

Alex Mullin wants to buy foreign and American miniature beer bottles.

He points out that there are five different types of miniatures:

1. Pre-Prohibition bottles are about five to six inches tall and were generally filled with real beer and had cork stoppers and wire closures. "I am interested in bottles which are embossed or have a label in reasonably good condition."

2. Post-Prohibition bottles are from three to a little over four inches tall and were usually produced as salt-and-pepper shakers or as company give-aways. Some were filled with water and labeled "Does not contain beer." Most will be marked "Muth" or "Bill's" on the bottom. Labels are decals, foil, or paper, and most will have neck labels. "These bottles are of interest only if they have labels in very good condition."

3. Foreign bottles are generally from the 1950s or 1960s. They usually have shaker or solid caps and are similar to American bottles. "For me to purchase them, they must be in excellent condition."

4. Bottle-opener bottles are miniature wooden or metal operners with handles shaped like beer bottles. They have labels similar to the glass miniatures and must be in excellent condition, with all labels intact, for him to buy.

5. Miniature cans, barrels, and mugs are also collected, but only exellent-condition items from American breweries are wanted.

When writing, tell him about the size, the brand name, the brewery, any embossing, and the condition of the item. Make special mention of the label, since all nicks, tears, scratches, fading, or cracking greatly affect the value.

BREWERIANA FROM LEHIGH COUNTY BREWERIES

Herb Brown
P.O. Box 306
East Texas, Pennsylvania 18046
(215) 398-2176

Herb Brown buys beer cans, trays, tap knobs, foam scrapers, coasters, labels, steins, signs, openers, glasses, and other advertising, but only from breweries located in Lehigh County, Pennsylvania.

Lehigh County breweries include Neuweiler, Horlacher, and Daeufer (Allentown); Bushkill, Kuebler and Seitz (Easton); Widman's, Beth Uhl and South Bethlehem (Bethlehem); Eagle, Viking & Kostenbader (Catasauqua); and Northampton (Northampton).

Tell him clearly and exactly what you have for sale. A photograph or drawing would be appreciated. State the condition accurately. You may set your price or ask him to make an offer.

BEER CANS AND OTHER BREWERIANA

Jim "Jeemy" Hunter
P.O. Box 608
Mountain Home, Arizona 72653
(501) 449-5447 after 6 p.m.

Jeemy Hunter described his wants: "Any older cone-topped beer cans that required a bottle opener. I also buy older flat-topped cans that you used a beer can opener to open." Jeemy also purchases other selected breweriana, including beer signs and trays.

Jeemy is a serious collector, as well as editor and publisher of the monthly American Can Collector for the past six years. He is also a member of nearly a dozen clubs and organizations connected with can collecting and beer industry research.

He wants a photograph when possible, but a complete description of the item, including an exact description of condition, will suffice. If you have quantities of the item, let him know. He asks that you set the price, but will make offers on unpriced things he can use.

BEER TRAYS AND OTHER BREWERIANA

Lynn Geyer
The Brewery
1605 North 7th Avenue
Phoenix, Arizona 85007
(602) 252-1415

Lynn Geyer says that he wants (1) older beer trays with pictures of factories, animals, women, children, scenes, food, bottles, and the like; (2) framed and unframed calendars with beer names; (3) old advertising signs that have the name of a beer or brewery on them; and (4) miscellaneous minor breweriana including mugs, glasses, knives, matchsafes, pocket mirrors, miniature bottles, booklets, statues, tap knobs, blotters, postcards...anything with a brewery name on it.

"If describing a tray, note its size and shape, the scene pictured, the brand name of the beer, and the colors of the tray. On most items," he goes on, "the size, scenes, colors, and condition are important."

Lynn will do appraisals, but only on items he sees personally, not through the mail. He will, however, make conditional offers.

He is a member of numerous beer collectors clubs and has been featured in articles and on television. He operates The Brewery Auctions, which accepts items on consignment.

CALIFORNIA WINERY MEMORABILIA

David F. Schmidt
1901 Court Street
Redding, California 96001
(916) 223-0555 eves.

Dave Schmidt wants to buy a wide range of items from pre-Prohibition California wineries, vineyards, and wine companies. "To be of interest," he writes, "an item must date before 1920 and must list the name of a California winery, vineyard, or wine company."

Interests include signs, calendars, trade cards, business cards, letterheads, envelopes, labels, labeled bottles, wine lists, booklets, photographs, stereoview cards, stock certificates, and advertising glasses. In exchange for a self-addressed stamped envelope, Dave will send you an illustrated and priced wants list. He offers to pay a finder's fee to anyone who helps him locate good items from California wineries.

When you write to him, your description should include all information printed on the item in question. Data such as the lithographer's name, alcoholic strength, contents, tax stamps, district and compliance with the Pure Food & Drugs Act often provide clues to an item's age.

CERAMIC FIGURAL WHISKEY BOTTLES

Fred Runkewich
Fred's Bottles
P.O. Box 1423
Cheyenne, Wyoming 82003
(307) 632-1462

Fred Runkewich buys miniature and large sizes of Jim Beam and other modern ceramic whiskey bottles shaped like men, animals, buildings, and the like. Although he will buy them full or empty, bottles must be complete with all labels and stoppers and have no chips or cracks.

Tell Fred the brand name of the whiskey and the year it was issued, often marked on the bottom of the bottle. He prefers you to set the price wanted. but since he publishes the quarterly Price Guide to Modern Bottles, you can call upon him for assistance if you don't know anything about bottles.

Fred is a retired military officer who has been collecting and dealing through the mail in ceramic figural whiskey bottles for fifteen years.

COCA-COLA

Randy Schaeffer and William Bateman
C.C Tray-ders
Route 3, Box 3
Kutztown, Pennsylvania 19530
(215) 683-3333

Bill and Randy are serious advanced collectors of Coca-Cola memorabilia who want to buy advertising and promotional items issued by that company prior to 1940.

Their interests include, but are not limited to, trays, signs, calendars, cardboard cutouts, magazine ads (pre-1932), clocks, glasses, novelties, games, toys, stationery, historical records, trade cards, lights, convention items, jewelry, and bottles. "All items must carry the trade mark 'Coca-Cola' or other identifying features. No reproductions or recent items are wanted."

A description should include what it is, the material from which it is made, its size, and its colors. Any fine print in the lower right or left corner is particularly important. If you are offering magazine ads, you must include the exact page and date of the magazines as well as a brief description of the artwork. Include an SASE and, if you have one, your asking price. Randy and Bill will make offers, however.

SODA BOTTLES

Victoria Herberta
P.O. Box 8154
Houston, Texas 77004
(713) 523-4346 days/eves.

This avid and wonderfully eccentric collector wants to buy soda pop bottles from all over the world, as long as they have the names painted on and are new to her collection.

Victoria Herberta is trying to accumulate as many different brands of soft drinks as possible, so she is particularly eager to obtain products from small local bottlers, short-lived brands, and early bottles issued in commemoration of events. There are many hundreds she is aware of not having.

Every nick, scratch, chip, worn spot, or area with faded paint must be noted. The condition of the painted label is the most important consideration. She asks, "Include your price per bottle, or entire group of bottles." She is willing to perform appraisals and will make offers on bottles she can use or trade.

SLEEPY EYE MEMORABILIA

E.W. Kolbe
Sleepy Eye, Minnesota 56085
(507) 794-6464

Sleepy Eye was a droopy-lidded Sioux Indian for whom a Minnesota town, a creek, and a lake were named. E.W. Kolbe says he wants to buy "most anything associated with Sleepy Eye, the town of Sleepy Eye, or the Sleepy Eye Flour Mill," especially the thousands of premiums and giveaways distributed by the flour mill, which operated between 1883 and 1921.

Kolbe buys stoneware, bronzes, thermometers, paperweights, cloth pillow tops, aprons, postcards, trade cards, and anything else you can find that was associated with Sleepy Eye. He also wants postcard views of small Minnesota towns, and Minnesota souvenir spoons.

For Kolbe, a complete description includes size, color, and age. State whether it is all original, and give its condition, noting all damage. He does not want to make offers, and will do so only for something exceptional. He asks you to set your own "low dollar."

3
Toys, Dolls
and Playthings

CHILDREN'S TOY TRAINS

Dr. H.D. Lazarus, Research Editor
Toy Train Operating Society
14547 Titus Street, Suite 207
Panorama City, California 91402
(213) 762-3652 eves.

Dr. Lazarus wants "the larger, very 'toy-like' trains played with by children as opposed to scale-model trains, which were usually intended as an adult hobby."

Trains can be foreign or domestic, as long as they are in "reasonable" condition. Some of the more popular brands of trains he seeks are Lionel, American Flyer, Hafner Overland Flyer, Ives, Dorfan, Bing, Marklin, Hornby, Bassett-Lowke, Boucher, Voltamp, Carlisle & Finch, Karl Bub, Fander, and Carette.

Literature related to toy trains is also wanted, including mail-order and department store catalogs from companies such as Sears & Roebuck, Montgomery Ward, Butler Brothers, Charles Williams, Blackwell-Wielandy, and others that include pages of ads for children's toy trains.

Willy, as he is known to his friends, is a serious researcher with thirty-five years of experience and dozens of articles to his credit. He would like "a very complete description of the item(s) or good close-up slides or photos." Any serial numbers and names should be given. Don't forget to mention the color(s) of cars, etc. Make certain to accurately describe what you have, noting all rust, scratches, dents, chips, and the like. If there are parts or pieces missing, note them. If you know whether it works, tell him.

Dr. Lazarus will give written appraisals for a fee of 5 percent of the item's value. When he buys, he pays 75 percent of current retail. Contact him for details. The Panorama City branch of the Bank of America can provide references, as can the Toy Train Operating Society, 3770 Canfield Road, Pasadena, California 91107; (213) 351-0022.

MODEL TRAINS

Thomas J. Ryan
234-04 Bay Street
Douglaston, New York 11363
(212) 423-3732

Electric trains of all sorts interest Tom Ryan, but especially pre-World War II trains made by Lionel, American Flyer, Ives, and Voltamp, among other U.S. and European manufacturers.

Trains do not have to be in operating condition, as this ten-year veteran collector rebuilds and overhauls all trains he buys.

He wants to know how many cars the train contains and the color of each. Indicate the type of car (passenger, oil tanker, flatcar, etc.). If you can find any numbers on the engine, make certain to provide them.

Tom will make offers on any train he can use.

SMALL TOY CARS AND TRUCKS

Alan F. Sabol
220 Outlook Drive
Mt. Lebanon, Pennsylvania 15228
(412) 343-1643

Alan Sabol wants to buy small automobiles, trucks, buses, and other vehicles that fit certain conditions. Toys may be made of cast iron, pot metal, sheet metal, or rubber, and they may be from Tootsietoy or other manufacturers.

But they must have wheels that are either metal or white rubber.

Let him know the type of vehicle, its length, and the condition of the original paint. If wheels or other parts are missing, note that fact. If you can give the manufacturer's name, you can usually add to the value of your vehicle. Alan will make offers.

MINIATURE TOY PISTOLS

G. Frazier
P.O. Box 16352
San Francisco, California 94116

Mr. Frazier buys toy pistols less than five inches in length, working or not.

If you have any for sale, he would like to know the size, the manufacturer, the type of gun, and what it is made of. If you know the year in which it was made, tell him.

Make certain to describe the condition as well as you can. He claims to be interested in "almost any miniature pistols you might have," but asks that you set the price you want. He does not make offers.

VOLTAMP TOYS AND TRAINS

H. Bart Cox
11305 Riverview Road
Ft. Washington, Maryland 20744
(301) 292-1333

Bart Box wants to buy items manufactured between 1904 and 1925 by the Voltamp Electrical Manufacturing Co. of Baltimore, Maryland.

Products include, but are not limited to, electric toy trains, toy motors, train accessories, train tracks, radio components, and radio testing equipment. In addition to the products themselves, Bart wants catalogs, letterheads, and other paper ephemera from this company, and is willing to travel to inspect large collections.

All toys should be complete, or in at least restorable condition. If you want him to set the price, you must include a clear photograph, an SASE, and a $10 money order for each item you want evaluated. "If I can use the item, I will offer to buy it, and any fee charged will be returned if my offer is accepted," Bart explains.

TIN CARS AND TRUCKS MADE IN JAPAN

Rex Barrett
P.O. Box 254
Medinah, Illinois 60157
(312) 893-8312

Rex Barrett wants post-World War I tin lithographed toy cars, trucks, boats, airplanes, and the like, especially windup, friction, or clockwork toys made in Japan.

Many popular American cars and other vehicles were scaled from six to fifteen inches long by Japanese makers. "In all cases, I prefer those which most accurately reflect their real counterparts, the more detailed the better."

To describe one of these toys, you must include the type of vehicle it is, who the manufacturer is, the dimensions, what type of mechanism it has, whether the mechanism works, and what condition it is in. Appraisals and offers are free if the item is for sale to him. Otherwise there is a fee.

TOY FARM TRACTORS

Mark L. Egli
Egli Farm Toys
RD 3
Jolley, Iowa 50551
(712) 297-8728

Mark Egli says, "I want to buy toy farm tractors, construction vehicles, and industrial equipment in any condition from mint in the box to junk. I buy any make or model made by any company, and will buy one piece or a truckload."

He would like to know the manufacturer of the tractor or other vehicle you have for sale, as well as the name and model. Tell him if any parts are missing, whether it has been repainted or otherwise repaired, and describe the condition of the wheels and tires. "It is best to include a picture and an SASE to get a prompt reply," advises Mark.

He prefers the seller to establish the price, but he will make offers if necessary to help amateur sellers.

FARM AND CONSTRUCTION MODELS

Raymond E. Crilley
Farm Model Exchange
1881 Eagley Road
East Springfield, Pennsylvania 16411-9739
(814) 922-3460

Ray Crilley is a collector-dealer in business for nearly thirty years; he specializes in miniature farm models, including toy farm sets, small-scale animals, farm machinery models, and tractors. He also collects and deals in truck and construction models.

Ray asks simply for a description of the item, a statement of condition, and your asking price. A description should include dimensions, colors, maker's identifications, etc. He will make offers on items he can use.

The well-known monthly Miniature Tractor and Implement is his publication, and he coauthored Collecting Model Farm Toys of the World with Charles Burkholder.

AMERICAN FLYER TRAINS

R.E. Zeigler
P.O. Box 286
Alief, Texas 77411
(713) 879-1753

American Flyer trains of all types are wanted by Mr. Zeigler. The trains he seeks run on a two-rail track and are marked "American Flyer," "American Flyer Lines," or "A.C. Gilbert." They come in a variety of colors, metals, and plastics.

"I buy trains in almost any condition, but the better the condition, the better I pay." He wants to know the color of each item and any numbers printed thereon. Tell whether there are plastic parts. Always note if the individual cars or the set itself is in its original box and give any model numbers from the lid or end of the box.

Offers will be forthcoming, but "it becomes almost imperative for a collector to actually view the merchandise first. People who are not collectors generally overestimate condition."

LARGE TOY TRUCKS AND CARS

William E. Hall
15 Conrad Drive
West Hartford, Connecticut 06107
(203) 521-8169

If you have very large toy trucks and cars made of aluminum and tin, Bill Hall is an eager buyer.

Smith-Miller, Miller-Ironson, and Doepke were the three most important manufacturers of these rubber-tired fire trucks, cement mixers, moving vans, cab-overs, road graders, and other specialized vehicles. Most of their toys are marked or have decals with various corporate names and logos on the doors.

Bill is most concerned with the general overall appearance. Pay particular attention to the condition of the wheels and whether the vehicle has been repainted. Identify all damage, noting everything that is in need of attention. If possible, please send a picture of each side of the vehicle. He will gladly make purchase offers if your description is complete.

TOY GUNS

Charles W. Best
Charles Best Antiques
6288 South Pontiac
Englewood, Colorado 80111
(303) 771-5870

Toy guns and cap shooters of all types are Charles Best's interest.

Although he mostly seeks unusually shaped pre-1900 pistols and guns, especially those made from material other than iron, Best is interested in learning about almost any other fine-condition pre-1945 toy pistol, rifle, or BB gun. He has a lengthy wants list, but it is not illustrated.

If you have a gun for sale, send him a sketch, including dimensions, markings, names, or numbers. When you describe condition, make certain to indicate every chip, nick, scratch, or other damage. It is not necessary to set a price, as Best will make an offer on any gun that he would like for his own collection or for resale.

SAND PAILS AND OTHER TOYS

Kendra Krienke
Whistler's Daughter Gallery
88 South Finley Avenue
Basking Ridge, New Jersey 07920
(201) 766-6222

Kendra Krienke is a relatively new dealer of toys who wants to purchase a number of pre-1920 items: embossed tin sand pails; any pail or bucket that reads "good boy" or "good girl;" candy or Christmas pails; children's watering cans; tin animals; baby cups, rattles, and whistles; drums or tin horns (but only those twenty-two inches long); dachshund toys, especially on wheels by Steiff, but including "folksy" ones as well.

If you have any of these for sale, indicate the materials from which it is made, the dimensions, the colors, its approximate age, and any of the history that you know. She will make offers for toys she can use.

TIN, IRON, AND STEEL TOY VEHICLES

Greg Wolfe
P.O. Box 333
Conyngham, Pennsylvania 18219
(717) 788-2007

Greg Wolfe is a dealer in old toys with nearly twenty years' experience. He needs "just about any type of cast iron, tin, die cast, or steel automotive, boat, aviation, horse-drawn, or comic character toy," including the following:

1. Tootsie toys with steel or white rubber tires
2. Pre-1964 Dinkys, English or French
3. Steel vehicles, airplanes, and trains of the 1920s made by Buddy L, Keystone, Turner, Metalcraft, Kingsbury, Kel-Met, or Sturditoy
4. Schoenhut animals, dolls, dollhouses, and circus sets
5. American, German, or French tin clockwork autos, ships, aircraft, or carousels by Bing, Carette, Marklin, Fischer, Lehman, Marx, Strauss, Unique Art, or Mueller and Kadeder
6. Smith-Miller, Miller-Ironson, or Doepke toys, 1945-55
7. Cast iron automotive, aircraft, horse-drawn, construction, and farm toys by Arcade, Hubley, Kenton, Ives, Kilgore, Dent, Unidex, or Williams
8. Pre-1950 children's pedal cars and planes
9. Metal and plastic dealer promotional cars, trucks, and farm machinery dating between 1948 and 1965
10. Robots and space toys

He requests a "full description," which should include what it is, who made it, how big it is, and what condition it is in. Note any missing or damaged parts and whether it works. Its "general overall appearance" should be described as well.

Greg prefers you to set the price you would like, but he is willing to assist by making offers. He is available for consultations and appraisals on estates or large collections.

TIN TOY BOATS

Joe Sanko
4750 Kildare Road
Mound, Minnesota 55364
(612) 472-1282

Joe Sanko is a relatively new collector of tin toy boats, so he wants a wide range of them, all ages and sizes.

"My collection consists mainly of pleasure boats, cabin cruisers, and runabouts, although I have recently begun collecting ocean liners, warships, and submarines. If your boat is made of metal, no matter how simple or intricate it is, I would like to hear from you."

A description should include the type of boat, the type of propulsion (windup, battery, etc.), the manufacturer, and the condition. "In most cases, a photograph combined with the measurements tells it all. They may set the price or I will make offers. All items returnable, of course."

OLD TOYS

Larry Bruch
P.O. Box 25
Mountaintop, Pennsylvania 18707
(717) 678-7395 after 5 p.m. EST

Larry Bruch is a relatively new dealer who buys and sells a wide range of toys. He claims, "I will pay top dollar for quality antique toys" such as:

1. German and American tin windup toys
2. Large trucks and construction models (Buddy L, etc.)
3. Comic character toys
4. Disney anything
5. Cast iron toys and banks
6. Dime store toy soldiers from the 1930s and 1940s
7. Small cars and trucks by Tootsietoy and others
8. Standard-gauge electric trains
9. Marklin windup toy trains
10. Tin scale models of 1950s cars made in Japan
11. Children's pedal cars made before 1950
12. Battery-operated toys and robots from the 1950s and 1960s
13. Santa Claus toys

Send an accurate description, including dimensions, and say whether the item is complete and working. Note all damage, rust, repairs, repainting, and so on. "I buy many of my items sight unseen but always insist that I may return something if it does not match the description. A good clear photo along with the description usually assures proper identification and a solid offer from me."

OLD TOYS

Gary Darrow
Chick Darrow's Fun Antiques
1174 2nd Avenue
New York, New York 10021
(212) 838-0730

Gary Darrow has been buying and selling "fun antiques" for nearly three decades and has a long list of toys and other items for which he has an established clientele. He buys:

1. Comic character toys, watches, and clocks
2. Early and fine-quality French and German wind-up toys
3. Robots of all kinds
4. Mechanical and still banks, especially cast iron
5. Early Erector sets
6. Battery-operated toys
7. Magic lanterns and other projectors and optical devices
8. Pedal cars, steel trucks, and miniature vehicles
9. Toy aeroplanes
10. Movie and movie star memorabilia
11. Anything to do with magic
12. Rock 'n' roll memorabilia
13. Gum ball machines
14. Advertising ashtrays, signs, and clocks
15. Steam engines and accessories
16. Model (not toy) soldiers from all makers
17. Board games related to TV shows

"I want all sorts of unusual things," Gary writes. "Send me detailed facts about what it is, what it looks like, and the condition it is in." A photograph is helpful, and he requests that you tell him "a price range of what you want for the item."

TIN WINDUP ROBOTS AND SPACE TOYS

Edy J. Chandler
P.O. Box 20664
Houston, Texas 77225
(713) 668-7864 or 527-8402

Edy Chandler wants tin windup robots and space toys, especially those made in Occupied Japan.

The items she seeks include not only robots but also flying saucers, ray guns, space ships, rocket ships, Star Wars toys, alien creatures, and Buck Rogers and Flash Gordon toys.

Describe carefully, noting whether the toys still operate. Be careful not to overwind. She will make you an offer.

TOY SEWING MACHINES

Arthur Chodrof
2805 Motor Avenue
Los Angeles, California 90064

For four years, Art Chodrof has been collecting toy sewing machines. He owns approximately 175 machines from eight different countries, but "will buy old and unusual ones, regardless of condition, as I also repair them." Provide him with the name of the machine, the model number, the color, the condition, and your asking price. He will make offers if you give sufficient information.

AIR RIFLE ADVERTISING

Bill Bramlett
P.O. Box 1105
Florence, South Carolina 29503-1105
(803) 393-2604 after 7 p.m.

Bill Bramlett expresses no interest in buying BB guns or air rifles, but he does want a wide range of paper advertising items pertaining to pre-1930 air rifles, including signs, calendars, posters, banners, letterheads, envelopes, and other paper ephemera.

Describe what you have thoroughly, including all colors. Condition is important in advertising pieces, so mention all tears, soil, stains, etc. Bill will make offers for items he can use.

BOBBING HEAD AND INCLINE TOYS

Dale Jerkins
1647 Elbur Avenue
Lakewood, Ohio 44107
(216) 226-7349

Dale Jerkins wants two distinctly different types of toys:

1. Paper-mache sports dolls with heads on a spring so they bob around. Any sports figures or personalities are wanted.

2. Plastic incline toys that walk down ramps. Made in the 1950s by Louis Marx, they came in a wide variety of styles.

Describe the figure or toy, including the colors of both the uniforms and the caps. Note any defects in condition. A good sketch would be helpful when describing incline toys. He will make offers, although he prefers you to set the price you want.

PLASTIC AND WOODEN MODEL KITS

Robert L. Geller
Kit Collectors International
P.O. Box 38
Stanton, California 90680
(714) 826-5218

Bob Geller collects and deals in old plastic and wood models in kit form that are complete and unassembled, including all types of kits for making aircraft, automobiles, vehicles, ships, figures, buildings, animals, and science fiction creatures and characters. He is especially interested in models of airliners, civilian and military transports, commercial ships, and products manufactured by Convair or General Dynamics.

"I will also buy (or accept donations of) kit manufacturers' catalogs, both U.S. and foreign, which date before 1970. These are for use by the KCI library for reference services." Bob describes himself as seeking one "non-model" item, a board game called Assembly Line, which features a miniature automobile assembly line and small plastic auto parts. If you have one of these, especially if it is complete, he is most eager to hear from you.

You must provide him with the name of the kit manufacturers; the kit or item number; and a brief description including any damaged, missing, or painted parts. Set your price, although he will make offers.

Bob has been extremely active in model building for twenty-eight years, edits a newsletter for kit collectors ($1.50 for a sample copy), is the author of the Kit Collector's Pricing Guide, and travels around the country promoting modeling.

PLASTIC MODEL KITS

John W. Burns
Kit Collector's Clearinghouse
3213 Hardy Drive
Edmond, Oklahoma 73034
(405) 341-4640

John Burns buys plastic model construction kits for just about anything: aircraft, ships, tanks, automobiles, trucks, and science fiction space ships, vehicles, and figures.

If you have the original box, he wants to know the manufacturer and the model name and number. Indicate whether all parts are present and tell him what is missing.

John is the author of Collector's Value Guide and Handbook of Kit Collecting, and is editor of a newsletter for collectors of models. He will make offers on items you have, if properly described.

TIN MECHANICAL TOYS

H. Bart Cox
11305 River View Road
Ft. Washington, Maryland 20744
(301) 292-1333

Bart Cox buys U.S. or foreign mechanical tin toys made before 1935.

"I prefer spring-wound toys such as, but not limited to, representations of cars, boats, airplanes and airships, animals, and people. The more colorful the tin lithography the better." In some cases,"broken toys will definitely be considered," but he prefers all parts to be present and in at least restorable condition.

If you want him to price what you have, you must provide a clear photograph, a self-addressed stamped envelope, and a $10 money order for each item appraised. "If I can use the toy, I will offer to buy it, and any fee charged will be returned if my offer is accepted."

TIN AND IRON TOYS AND BANKS

Mark Suozzi
P.O. Box 102
Ashfield, Massachusetts 01330
(413) 628-3241

Mark Suozzi buys antique American and European toys and banks made between 1840 and 1940. "Mechanical penny banks from the Victorian era are a particularly important aspect of our collecting," he explains.

"We buy many different kinds of toys," Mark says, and notes that he favors iron horse-drawn vehicles, automobiles, boats, and aeronautical toys; tin comic characters, trains, and vehicles, especially those that wind up. "My wife also collects figural iron doorstops," he adds.

Both scarcity and condition play a role in determining the value of a toy, according to Mark. Make certain to mention any repairs, replacement parts, repainting, missing pieces, or damage. Photographs are helpful, especially when you include the dimensions. Indicate whether a mechanical toy or bank still works. Describe your items well and Mark will make you an offer.

TOYS, TRACTORS, AND OTHER THINGS

Chester and Pauline Ashby
2232 East Maple
Enid, Oklahoma 73701
(405) 233-5532

Chester and Pauline Ashby are collectibles dealers who feature, and hence want to buy tractor repair and maintenance literature; cast iron and tin wind up toys; old fishing reels and plugs; Daisy BB guns with wood stocks; railroad items; old spurs and horse bits.

The information required varies according to what you have to sell. In general, tell what you have, its size, and its color. Include any dates, maker's marks, or patent information. Make certain to tell the Ashbys if it is not the original paint. When describing toy vehicles, always make certain to tell what the wheels are made of. No matter what you are describing, an accurate statement of condition is a must. They will make offers on what you have.

RADIO PREMIUMS AND DISNEY

Tom Tumbusch
P.O. Box 2102
Dayton, Ohio 45429
(513) 299-3785

Tom Tumbusch specializes in premiums given away by sponsors of various radio programs during the 1930s and 1940s. He can provide you with a long list of shows, but he's "interested in any and all."

Tom is the author of the price guide to radio premiums, and notes, "I will buy single items, whole collections, or quantities of an item to obtain trading material. I will pay more than book price for items I need for illustrations in my books."

You need to describe what you have and indicate condition and quantity available.

Tom also wants to purchase all items copyrighted by Walt Disney, Walt E. Disney, Walt Disney Enterprises, or Walt Disney Productions that were made before 1957.

KALEIDOSCOPES AND OPTICAL TOYS

Lucille Malitz
Lucid Antiques
P.O. Box KH
Scarsdale, New York 10583
(914) 636-5171

Lucille Malitz is in the market for antique brass and wood kaleidoscopes, preferably signed and on stands. Her shop, Lucid Antiques, also carries, hence wants to purchase, other unusual optical toys such as megalethoscopes and polyrama panoptiques.

If you have optical toys for sale, she wants to know what they are made of, the color, and the condition. A sketch or photograph is almost essential and will be returned if you request. Lucille is highly likely to request that you ship what you have on approval. She will repay your postal costs if she does.

Lucille doesn't want appraisals, nor will she make offers on unpriced items. Since you are required to price what you have, some research is suggested, because many of these early toys are worth more than $100.

VIEW-MASTER REELS

Robert F. Gill III
3934 Fulton Avenue
Seaford, New York 11783
(516) 781-8741

Bob Gill buys View-Master reels and packs made by Sawyer's Inc., GAF Corporation (its successor), and any of the European companies that make compatible stereo reels. The latter include Stereorama in Italy, Stereoscope Lestrade in France, Stereofilms Bruguiere in France, and View-Master International Group in Belgium.

In addition to the finished reels, Bob also wants View-Master 3-D cameras, accessories, film cutters, projectors, library boxes, and focusing viewers. He does not want children's cartoons and stories issued after 1955 and is not interested in titles issued after 1970.

He would like a list of reels for sale, including the title, reel number, and copyright date. Note the condition of the reel, including whether the colors are still good (some fade or undergo color shift to red). Bob will make offers on reels or other equipment that he would like to buy.

TEDDY BEARS

Ted Smith
Fun House
724 Fillmore Street
San Francisco, California 94117
(415) 864-6386

Ted Smith is a dealer who has specialized in teddy bears (among other things) for the past ten years. He will buy early fully jointed teddy bears made by Steiff, related teddy bear items such as books and postcards, and bears and other pre-1945 stuffed animals on wheels.

He requires a "very good description," including a photograph and a statement of condition. He can provide a wants list, prefers items to be priced, and will make offers.

TEDDY BEARS AND STUFFED ANIMALS ON WHEELS

Olive "Polly" Zarneski
5803 North Fleming
Spokane, Washington 99208
(509) 327-7622

Teddy bears that are jointed (have movable heads and limbs), are stuffed with straw and covered with mohair, and have glass or shoe-button eyes will find a welcome home with Polly Zarneski, even if they aren't in perfect condition.

So too will "teddy bear related" items, including children's books, post-cards, pin trays, and photographs of children holding teddy bears.

Bears are not the only stuffed animals she will buy. Horses, cows, sheep, dogs, donkeys, elephants, and just about anything else on four legs is also wanted if it is stuffed and has cast iron wheels. Animals can be made of mohair, wool, or stretched animal hides, and the wheels may be attached to the feet or to a wooden platform upon which the animals stands.

Polly also wants early wooden toys that are covered with lithographed paper. Although alphabet and puzzle blocks are the most familiar form, there are also paper-covered animals, Noah's Ark, dollhouses, and games.

Polly wants an accurate description including dimensions of all items. Give thorough construction details of all stuffed animals. She will make offers for what you have. Although the items listed above are her specialties, you may also inquire about other early, fine-condition toys.

SCHOENHUT AND OTHER WOODEN TOYS

Robert W. Zimmerman
The Schoenhut Newsletter
45 Louis Avenue
West Seneca, New York 14224
(716) 674-6657

Bob Zimmerman wants a variety of toys, models, and advertising material from manufacturers of wooden toys:

1. Toys and memorabilia from the A. Schoenhut Company, especially rarer pieces such as bread wagons, trains, dollhouses, etc.

2. Material, especially oral history and primary source data, about Nelson B. Delavan, "the toymaker of Seneca Falls"

3. Model assembly kits by the Strombeck-Becker Company, especially mint in box, but including built-up models and partial sets

4. Catalogs, advertisements, mock-ups, blueprints, and other research material related to these and other manufacturers of wooden models and toys

"I would prefer that sellers include the condition of the item and their best price. On major items, I would appreciate a photograph. If there is any known historical background on the toy, or a story connected with it, I would like to know that also. Return privileges are assumed, although in ten years I have only had to return one item."

TROLL DOLLS

Karen Dellinger
Route 3, Box 379
Harrisonburg, Virginia 22801
(703) 434-4374

"I want to buy troll dolls in any size, shape, or condition."

Karen Dellinger explains, "These are the little guys (or sometimes girls) who stand two inches to 12 inches tall, with their hands and feet out, and long, brightly colored hair, either dressed or undressed. Most go by the brand names Wishniks, Lucky Schnooks, or Dam Things. Although there are modern ones still being produced, Karen wants dolls and related ephemera from the 1960s and early 1970s. Besides dolls, there are also prize-machine trolls, troll animals, paper dolls, outfits, pencil tappers, jewelry, and other things.

Since Karen now deals in, as well as collects, trolls, condition is important. Please send a description, including dimensions, and the price you would like. She will also make offers.

DOLLS, TEDDY BEARS, AND SEWING PATTERNS

Jack and Sherri Dempsey
Dempsey Dolls and Antiques
4142 Pine Avenue
Erie, Pennsylvania 16504
(814) 825-6381

For more than ten years, the Dempseys have operated a shop specializing in dolls.

Jack and Sherri want to buy dolls and doll parts that are bisque, china, or composition (perhaps best thought of as papier-mache with a varnish finish). They also want jointed teddy bears made prior to 1950 and out-of-print dolls' clothes patterns from commercial pattern companies such as Simplicity and McCalls.

It should be no surprise that doll restorers also want to purchase quantities of old lace and ribbon, "in pieces at least a yard long, please."

You might also inquire with them if you have fine-condition old toys, especially windups, made by Marx, Lehman, Bing, or Unique Art.

Like most other collectors, the Dempseys are most concerned with your accurately describing condition. Does the toy work? Is the doll cracked? Are patterns complete? Wear, stains, spots, cracks, scratches, and the like must be mentioned if you expect an offer without actually shipping on approval.

BEAR MEMORABILIA

Marguerite Cantine and Elizabeth Kilpatrick
American Teddy Bear Club
P.O. Box 798
Huntington, New York 11743
(516) 271-8990

These active collectors especially want to buy teddy bears (1903 - 45) from the original owners or from people who can trace the history back to the original owner.

"We do not sell the bears we purchase," Marguerite notes. "They are tagged with their provenance and put into exhibits at antique shows, toy shows, libraries, etc." The folks at the Teddy Bear Club are genuinely concerned with preserving the story of various bears for future bear-loving historians.

In addition to bears, they buy teddy bear books, (1903 - 25), other bear-related paper items (pre-1930 only), and teddy and Roosevelt bear pottery.

"When we find a bear we like, the seller is instructed to ship the bear for inspection, after which a proper price will be offered. If the price is unsatisfactory for any reason, the bear is shipped back. We pay postage both ways."

CHEAP COMPOSITION AND BISQUE DOLLS

Sybil Wallender
Sybil's Dolls & Supplies
3147 West 110th Street
Inglewood, California 90303
(213) 672-0284

Sybil Wallender is a relatively new dealer in dolls who has "two tiny shops." She specializes in reasonably priced dolls in a number of categories:

1. Less expensive, usually unmarked, German bisque-head dolls, with paper-mache, composition, or kid leather bodies
2. Cheaper, unmarked, composition dolls from the 1920s and 1930s
3. Rubber dolls from the 1940s
4. Hard plastic dolls from the 1940s and early 1950s

Among particular wants are Luvums by Effanbee, the bisque-head Rock-a-Bye-Baby by Armand Marseille; and the large "mama"-sized composition dolls, which are more than twenty inches long.

"Since I'm known to sell my dolls at good prices and for giving my customers a very fair deal, I expect the person I'm buying from to understand and price dolls accordingly if they wish me to buy their dolls." She prefers you to set the price wanted, including shipping costs, but she will help by making offers.

Sybil will buy dolls with minor damage, but she wants to know the exact condition, including all damage, repairs, defects, and imperfections before she buys. She requests that you identify "what guarantee the seller will give me if I buy sight unseen."

NODDER DOLLS

Roxanne Toser
4019 Green Street
Harrisburg, Pennsylvania 17110
(717) 238-1936

Roxanne Toser collects nodder, or bobbing head, dolls.

These are dolls with heads attached by springs, so that they bob up and down or back and forth. They were popular a few years back and commonly seen in the rear windows of automobiles. She wants only those that are not sports-related, and prefers people dolls to animals.

A general description will do, she says, and notes that dolls with cracks or pieces missing are of no interest. She asks that you set the price wanted for these relatively inexpensive collectibles, but is willing to discuss the matter.

RAGGEDY ANN AND ANDY

Andrew Tabbat
333 West 57th Street, Apt. 203
New York, New York 10019
(212) 582-0027

Andy Tabbat wants to purchase Raggedy Ann and Andy dolls, or dolls of other characters from their stories such as Beloved Belindy (a black mammy), Uncle Clem (in kilts and mustache), Policeman, Pirate, etc. "All are rag dolls with striped socks," he informs us.

He is especially interested in those with real shoe-button eyes, a wooden heart, or black outlines around the nose. He buys dolls made by Volland, Mollye, Exposition, or Georgene Novelties, but does not want those made by Knickerbocker. "Homemade versions are welcome too," he notes, "the more primitive the better."

All other pre-1960 Raggedy Ann and Andy merchandise is of interest as well, including books, dishes, greeting cards, and the like. He buys Schoenhut ducks marked "Quacky Doodles" or "Danny Daddles," because they were created by Johnny Gruelle, the man responsible for Raggedy Ann. "Any other Johnny Gruelle work is also desirable to me," writes Andy.

He requests a full description, including size, colors, condition, and whether the item is complete and original, especially the clothing. If the item is tagged or marked, the maker and last copyright date are very important. If it is a book, the name of the publisher and the date of publication should be listed. All rips, stains, missing pages, and missing pieces of clothing should be mentioned. Photographs are always preferred, and Andy agrees to return them.

You may price your items for sale, or request an offer. If you are definitely selling, not just looking for free information, you may call collect.

BABY DOLLS

Shirley Jane Hedge
Route 2, Box 52
Princeton, Indiana 47670
(812) 385-4080

Shirley Hedge is an avid paper doll collector who also buys American and foreign baby dolls manufactured between 1920 and 1950.

Describe the doll fully, providing its manufacturer's name, if known. Indicate any markings you can find (often hidden on the back of the neck under the hair or on the back), its size, age, and condition. Note whether it has its original costume and box.

Shirley also wants to locate photographs of little girls posed with their dolls, especially those from before the turn of the century.

MADAME ALEXANDER DOLLS

Gary Green
Madame Alexander Doll Museum
711 South 3rd Avenue
Chatsworth, Georgia 30705
(404) 695-2412

Gary Green buys and sells Madame Alexander dolls, old and new, with emphasis on discontinued singles and series.

If you know the name and issue date of your Alexander, make certain to identify it. Since Alexanders were made in more than one size, the height of the doll is important as well. If there have been modifications to the costume, you should tell him exactly what they are. Note whether the original box and all original labels are still present.

Although he would like you to set the price wanted for your Alexanders, he will assist amateur sellers upon request. Gary is well qualified to set a fair price, as he is the editor and publisher of the doll magazine, Collectors United.

DOLLS AT CHRISTMAS

Audrey Lovell
St. Nicholas
1675 Orchid
Aurora, Illinois

Audrey Lovell wants old or antique dolls, dollhouses, stuffed animals, paper dolls, toys, doll books, 19th-century children's magazines, and fine items associated with Santa Claus and Christmas.

Always include measurements, color, and a statement of condition with your offer. You must include a return privilege statement, allowing her to return the doll or other item to you for any reason. She prefers you to set the price but will assist amateur sellers. There is a fee for written appraisals.

Audrey is the publisher of the monthly Doll Times (now in its fifth year), a show promoter, and mail-order dealer with more than ten years' experience.

ORIENTAL AND MIDDLE EASTERN DOLLS

Karen Kuykendall
P.O. Box 845
Casa Grande, Arizona 85222
(602) 836-2066

Karen Kuykendall describes what she wants: "Good-quality Oriental and Middle Eastern dolls. They must be between six and fourteen inches tall, have nicely sculpted and painted faces, be handsomely costumed, and in excellent condition. I prefer unusual types such as kings, queens, musicians, dancers, and peasants.

"Dolls must be realistic adult figures which look like real people in miniature. Dolls should be posed in realistic positions, not standing limply with the arms hanging at the sides. Clay or composition is preferred for hands and faces."

She does not want cloth-faced dolls with painted or embroidered features, plastic dolls, sleepy-eyed dolls, dolls that look like babies or children, Siamese dancers, or any doll from Korea or the Philippines.

Some of these dolls can be valuable, so good close-up pictures are a must. State the height of the doll and the material from which it is made. She requests that you tell whatever you can about the doll's age and history. Dolls do not need to be old, she notes, as quality is more important than age.

"Please state price in first letter," she requests. If you are a real beginner attempting to dispose of one of these dolls, this twenty-five year veteran collector may be willing to assist you in pricing.

DOLLHOUSES AND ACCESSORIES

Robert V. Dankanics
The Dollhouse Factory
157 Main Street
Lebanon, New Jersey 08833
(201) 236-6404

Robert Dankanics wants to buy old and antique dollhouses, doll furniture, and dollhouse accessories, especially those constructed on the scale of one inch to one foot.

Describe what you have, what it is made of, and its dimensions. If there are maker's marks, tell him, along with any known history of the piece. "The more information, the better," he says. A photograph is important when dollhouses are offered.

He will make appraisals and purchase offers.

CRISSY DOLLS

Judy McNece
1703 Sherman Place
Long Beach, California 90804

Judy McNece is a new collector who wants to buy the entire collection of Crissy and her family, a modern doll by Ideal.

These dolls were manufactured in both brown and white skin tones, with different-colored eyes, and under more than two dozen names. They are recognized by the "growing hair" feature, which permits their hair to be adjusted to various lengths. In addition to the dolls themselves, which preferably should be in mint condition in their original box, she also wants to purchase clothing and accessories created for them.

Judy wants to know the condition of the doll, whether any of the hair has been cut off, and if its outfit is original. She will make offers on dolls she can use for her collection or for trading with others.

DOLLS AND RELATED ITEMS

Ronald F. Thomas
Yesteryears Museum Collectors Shop
Main and River Streets
Sandwich, Massachusetts 02563
(617) 888-1711 (May-October)
(617) 888-2088 (November-April)

The people at the Yesteryears Museum Association operate one of the most popular doll museums in the country. They are always eager to find new items for their collection or for their resale shop.

Their wants are broad within the field of dolls. Early fine-condition dolls, dollhouses, dollhouse miniatures, and "related items" are all wanted.

Founder Ron Thomas charges $5 for written appraisals but is willing to make offers on items genuinely for sale. You must provide a complete description, including mention of any restoration or defects. A photograph would be helpful. If you have a price in mind, please indicate it.

Ron is a veteran of forty years' collecting, a member of numerous doll associations, and someone capable of being helpful when you would like to sell dolls.

AKRO AGATE CHILDREN'S DISHES

Larry D. Wells
12701 West County Line
Roanoke, Indiana 46783
(219) 672-3543

Larry Wells wants children's dishes made during the 1920s and 1930s by the Akron Agate Co. of Clarksburg, Virginia.

He says he will buy in any quantity from one piece to several thousand, in either the round or octagonal shape, and in any of the more than twenty different colors in which these dishes were manufactured.

If you have any of these for sale, Larry would like to know the size, color, shape, pattern, number of each type of piece, condition, and the price you would like. He will assist you to price the dishes if you have no idea of current market value.

CRIB AND DOLL QUILTS

Pat Beall
Braemar Collectibles
3003 Lake Shore Drive
Michigan City, Indiana 46360
(219) 872-0230

Pat Beall buys crib and doll-size quilts made before 1950.

"I am not interested in crazy quilt patterns, silk or velvet quits, or sunbonnet patterns. I want hand-quilted, not tied ones, but some machine work is acceptable, particularly on the bindings. I prefer quilts that have a border around the pattern, and am partial to Amish quilts, but all pieced and appliqued types are acceptable (except as listed above)."

Condition, age, color, pattern, and proportion are important considerations, so make certain you fully describe your quilt, sending a photograph whenever possible. If you know the material from which it is made and can identify the maker, please do so. "It is always nice to have the history of a quilt," she writes.

This longtime collector and elementary school teacher will not do appraisals, but is willing to make offers on unpriced quilts you would like to sell.

SUNDAY FUNNIES

Carl J. Horak
1319 108 Avenue
Calgary, Alberta
Canada T2W OC6
(403) 252-0870

"I am willing to purchase full Sunday comic sections and individual pages, but daily comic strips interest me only if you have at least a full month's run of them. Individual daily strips or daily pages are virtually worthless."

Carl Horak's interests are primarily in the adventure strips rather than the humorous ones. He will send a wants list of specific strips and dates he is seeking.

When writing about strips, give the name of the newspaper, the date, the number of pages, the dimensions, and any flaws such as tears, discoloration, and the like. Describe your items well and Carl will make offers. He is editor of Strip Scene, a quarterly fan publication devoted to comic strips.

COMICS

Frank Verzyl
The Batcave
1670-D Sunrise Highway
Bay Shore, New York 11706
(516) 665-4342

Frank Verzyl owns Long Island's biggest comic and pop magazine store, and he can always use quantities of fine-condition:

1. Old or recent back issues of comic books, any brands, any titles, and in any amounts. He mainly wants Marvel and DC superhero titles, or horror, science fiction, and superhero titles from the 1940s and 1950s

2. Quantities of single copies of recent superhero comics

3. Mad magazine

4. Horror and science fiction magazines, such as Creepy, Conan, Vampirella, Eerie, etc.

5. Magazines devoted to horror and science fiction movies such as Famous Monsters, Starlog, Fangoria, and Cinefantastique

Send him a list of the titles and issue numbers of the comics or magazines for sale, and "a rough idea of what price you would like, so I can judge whether we're in the same range before I spend a lot of effort." Frank cautions that he is interested only in comics or magazines with complete covers and contents.

COMIC CHARACTER MERCHANDISE

Dennis' Books
P.O. Box 99142
Seattle, Washington 98199
(206) 622-8868 days
(206) 283-0532 eves

Dennis' Books buys and sells pre-1962 merchandise related to comic or funny paper characters. Although Disney character items from the 1930s are premium goods, no Disneyland or Disneyworld souvenirs are wanted. Items of interest include:

1. Books or magazines that feature comic characters. Both hardcover and soft, U.S. and foreign, are wanted, including children's paint and coloring books, cutout or punch-out books, scrapbooks, linen books, pop-ups or Waddle books by Blue Ribbon Press, and others
2. Original art and animation models used to make Walt Disney cartoons. This includes painted celluloids, concept drawings, model sheets, story sketches, backgrounds, and any other original drawings
3. Original artwork for World War II combat insignia designed by the Disney studio
4. Disney movie and cartoon posters
5. Celluloid or tin windup toys
6. Disney character dolls from the 1930s made by Richard Krueger Company, Charlotte Clark, Knickerbocker, or Steiff
7. Bisque figurines of Disney and other comic strip characters, especially those five inches or higher
8. Sheet music picturing any comic character who ever appeared in the Sunday funnies or in a comic book
9. Figurals from Fantasia made by Vernon Kilns
10. Mickey Mouse and Donald Duck lamps made in the 1930s

When selling something to Dennis' books, you must include: whatever information is printed on the label or on the item; the dimensions and color(s) of the item; a description of what the character is doing; details on all defects and repairs; and an indication that you will mail the item for inspection if Dennis' Books pays postage and insurance both ways.

They prefer that you set your own price, but if you are not familiar with pricing on comic character items some research is in order, since a number of pieces are worth $100 or more. They will make offers, but only after inspecting what you have to sell. Include your telephone number with any correspondence.

COMIC BOOKS AND POP CULTURE

James Furfferi
Empire Comics
1176 Mt. Hope Avenue
Rochester, New York 14620
(716) 442-0371

For ten years, Empire Comics has been serving buyers and sellers all over the country. Jim Furfferi purchases for resale: comic books; pulp magazines; Big Little Books; movie material; comic or science-fiction-related items; baseball cards; Maxfield Parrish art prints; and original comic art.

Comic books should date before 1960, other items before 1940, to be of much interest.

Jim wants the title, issue number, and condition. Describe what you have accurately or take a good photo or photocopy. He wants you to set your own price, but says, "We offer a price guide to people who need one."

POP CULTURE

Colonel Ralph A. Eodice
Nevermore
161 Valley Road
Clifton, New Jersey 07013
(201) 742-8278

Ralph Eodice has been buying nostalgia and pop culture items for his shop for nearly fifteen years. He wants:

1. Comic character toys of all sorts, 1930 - 50
2. Playsuits of cowboys, indians, spacemen, and the like from the 1930s to the 1950s. No Halloween costumes, please
3. Movie nostalgia from the 1930s and 1940s, especially clothing or costumes worn in films. No press books or lobby cards
4. Disney toys or other items pre-1950
5. Unusual or attractive items of trivia or nostalgia from the 1930s and 1940s

Send a description, preferably accompanied by a nonreturnable snapshot. He would appreciate a brief history of the item. "I will not answer any mail that is not accompanied by an SASE," he says emphatically. He will make offers on items he wants for resale or for his own collection.

THE COMICS AND PULPS

Claude Held
P.O. Box 140
Buffalo, New York 14225

Claude Held buys four kinds of items:

1. "I want runs of Sunday comic sections, in the 1930s to 1960s, not just one or two pages. Pages must be in good condition, not all brown and brittle." Name the newspaper, the dates included, and some of the comic strips featured.

2. Comic books in nice condition between 1930 and 1945, but some issues to 1960. List titles, numbers, and condition.

3. Edgar Rice Burroughs first editions marked on the spine as published by H.F. Hall. Those marked "Burroughs" on the spine, and Burt or Grosset reprints if they have fine dust jackets, are also purchased. Make a photocopy of the dust jacket and the title page.

4. Pulp magazines printed between 1900 and 1945. No sports or romance titles. Give title, number, date, and condition.

Claude has been dealing through the mail in these items since the early 1940s. He prefers you to set the price wanted, but is willing to assist amateur sellers.

COMIC BOOKS AND PULPS

Hugh O'Kennon
2204 Haviland Drive
Richmond, Virginia 23229
(804) 270-2465 after 6 p.m.

After nearly fifteen years in business, Hugh O'Kennon is one of the country's largest dealers in comic books and pulps through the mail.

He wants to purchase comic books dating between 1930 and 1965, Big Little Books prior to 1948, and most science fiction and adventure pulp magazines.

All he needs to know is the title of the book, the issue number, and the condition. He will be pleased to make you an offer. Hugh reports that he was a special adviser to The Comic Book Price Guide by Robert Overstreet.

POP CULTURE

Theodore L. Hake
Hake's Americana
P.O. Box 1444
York, Pennsylvania 17405
(717) 843-3731 weekdays

Ted Hake is the country's longest-established mail-order auctioneer of pop culture collectibles. He will purchase an extensive list of fine-condition items suitable for resale, including:
1. All comic character items from 1896 to 1950
2. All depictions of Disney characters from the 1930s
3. Radio and cereal premiums and giveaways featuring Tom Mix, Buck Rogers, Little Orphan Annie, and other popular folks
4. Items tied in with movie or TV shows, including posters, lobby cards, games, gum cards, buttons, premiums, etc.
5. Advertising giveaways, particularly small items such as pin-back buttons, pocket mirrors, watch fobs, etc.
6. Political pin-back buttons prior to 1964
7. 3-D items related to celebrities or famous people
Identify what you have and the material from which it is made. Provide a complete description, including all damage or missing paint or pieces. Indicate the dimensions. He prefers you to set the price, but will help amateurs to properly price what they have. He will not, however, make offers without actually seeing your items.

POP COWBOY CULTURE

Larry Maddy
2529 South 12th Street
Irontown, Ohio 45638

For twenty-five years, Larry Maddy has been a collector and dealer in various types of pop cowboy culture.

He wants pre-1965 comic books (especially westerns); pre-1970 TV Guide magazines; lobby cards and posters from cowboy movies 1940 - 54; "any western paperback books;" and other items related to the heroic cowboys of film and fiction.

He can supply you with a detailed single-page wants list of comic books he seeks, almost all of them westerns. All comics and other items must be complete and in good or better condition. He guarantees to pay 50 percent or more of Overstreet (a standard comic reference work).

POP CULTURE

Ken Mitchell
Mitchell Books
710 Conacher Drive
Willowdale, Ontario
Canada M2M 3N6
(416) 222-5808

Ken Mitchell has been buying and selling pop culture memorabilia for twenty years and has an established clientele for a large number of items:

1. Comic books, "1900 - 69, all companies, all sizes, duplicates"
2. Other comic-book-like publications, pre-1960
3. Big Little Books, 1935 - 50, all types, all titles, but in perfect or near-perfect condition only. No missing pages
4. Sunday funnies sections and pages, 1931 - 59, but will consider earlier and later. Average decent condition okay
5. Movie magazines, 1900 - 69. No missing pages
6. Radio and comic give-aways and mail premiums, 1930 - 59
7. Walt Disney items, 1929 - 59, books, games, toys, etc.
8. Song magazines that contain words only (Hit Parade, etc.)
9. Adventure pulp magazines from the 1930s and 1940s
10. Pop music and radio programs, magazines, and catalogs, 1920 - 69
11. Original comic art for newspapers or comic books
12. Cards of all types: gum, baseball, candy, tobacco, cigarette
13. Edgar Rice Burroughs hardcover books, pre-1960s
14. TV collectibles, games, toys, books, etc., 1948 - 69

"I can never use any item that is in poor condition, has missing pages, is dirty, soiled, or brittle, so please don't send them requesting an offer." Mails are reliable to Canada, Ken says, and he encourages you to send fine-condition items on approval, but only after writing him. He makes offers based on the quality of the merchandise after inspecting it.

POP CULTURE

The Reverend Morris Hamasaki
1341 College View Drive
Monterey Park, California 91754
(213) 264-3523

The Reverend deals through the mail in a number of pop culture items:
1. Movie memorabilia including magazines from the 1930s and 1940s; Dixie cup eight-by-ten-inch movie star picture premiums; souvenir movie program books; colored ads from the movie trade magazines; personally autographed movie star photos; lobby cards from 1930s and 1940s musicals and Greer Garson films; movie publicity packets, and some similar items
2. Party masks from the 1930s and 1940s featuring Disney characters or movie stars of the period
3. Books or sheets of paper dolls of movie stars, Disney or comic characters, and various celebrities. Newspaper paper dolls from Chicago Tribune and St. Louis Post-Dispatch
4. Advertising cutouts of Buster Brown, Red Goose, Howdy Doody, teddy bears, and other interesting figures
5. Punch-out or cutout books of Disney or comic characters
He requests "description of item, condition of item, date of publication (if possible), and your asking price. Please include your phone number."

VARIOUS GAMES AND CIRCUS TOYS

James A. Conley
4101 Shuffel Drive
North Canton, Ohio 44720
(216) 497-1500

"Board games, action games, target games, almost any game in excellent condition which pre-dates 1920," is how Jim Conley describes his wants, but suggests that he will buy later games as long as their condition is nearly perfect.

He also wants circus sets, toys, games, animals, clowns, including Royal Circus by Hubley. He also wants pre-1940 windup, mechanical, or lever-action amusement park toys such as roller coasters, merry-go-rounds, and Ferris wheels.

Some of these can be moderately valuable, so Jim is willing to help you in pricing, but it is important to include good clear photographs. Dimensions and any manufacturers' names or marks would be helpful. Condition of paint, fur, and paper is important, so describe all defects carefully.

Jim also buys large, intricate, three-dimensional valentines. "The pullout kind," he explains.

CARTOON BOOKS

Gordon Sack
10914 Shawnbrook
Houston, Texas 77071
(713) 944-0313

Gordon Sack is an M.D. who believes laughter to be the best medicine and therefore buys hardback and paperback collections of cartoons, old or modern.

Books can be by a single cartoonist or collections of the works of many. Cartoons may be humorous, political, or editorial. He does not want comic books, he emphasizes.

Provide him with title, date, and statement of condition. This veteran of more than twenty-five years of collecting will make an offer for what he can use.

BOARD GAMES

Lee and Rally Dennis
The Game Preserve
110 Spring Road
Peterborough, New Hampshire 03458
(603) 924-6710

The Game Preserve is a museum and gift shop devoted to early American board games.

Lee and Rally Dennis are always eager to purchase pre-1930 board games. Duplicates of those already in the museum are sold in the gift shop to other antique game fanciers. "We are especially interested in large McLoughlin Brothers games and all games with bright lithographed covers with interesting subject matter."

They want to know the name of the game, its manufacturer, whether all the parts are still there, the dimensions, what is pictured on the top, and any dates that can be found. Price what you have; but if you send a complete description and a photograph, you can expect them to make an offer.

NON-SPORTS GUM CARDS

Roxanne Toser
Non-Sports
4019 Green Street
Harrisburg, Pennsylvania 17110
(717) 238-1936

Roxanne Toser is one of the country's largest mail-order dealers of gum cards, but only those that are not of sports figures.

She buys individual cards, stickers, wrappers, unopened packs and unopened boxes of gum cards issued between the late 1930s and 1974. Some particular wants are: Addams Family, Beverly Hillbillies, Hogan's Heroes, Gilligan's Island, Dark Shadows, Lost in Space, Voyage to the Bottom of the Sea, Mars Attack, Outer Limits, Monsters, Land of the Giants, Three Stooges, Star Trek, and many others, especially short-lived trial series of cards.

"My business is conducted through the mail and my customers expect to receive mint or near-mint cards with sharp corners, no creases, and no tears in wrappers. Cards from the 1930s and 1940s may have slight damage, but no major creases." It is not necessary to list every card you have. Tell her how many are in each set and the condition, especially of the worst ones. She will make offers in accordance with latest price guides.

PUZZLES

Jerry Slocum
Puzzles
P.O. Box 1635
Beverly Hills, California 90213
(213) 275-1276

Jerry Slocum buys mechanical puzzles of all types.

Although he is not interested in jigsaw puzzles, he does want take-apart and put-together puzzles; sliding block puzzles; puzzle rings; peg jumping puzzles; cast metal puzzles; string and wire puzzles; wood burrs; anchor stone puzzles; glass-top dexterity puzzles; and catalogs, books, and pamphlets that contain mechanical puzzles, anamorphic art, illusions, and optical puzzles.

He can provide you with an illustrated wants list. You must give him a detailed description including a sketch or photograph. Indicate the materials used and the condition of the puzzle as well as its box. If you know the manufacturer or the date it was made, tell him. Although he prefers puzzles to be priced by you, he will make offers.

MAH-JONGG

Joe Scales
Mah-Jongg Sales Company
P.O. Box 255721
Sacramento, California 95865
(916) 965-0749

Joe Scales is a fairly recent, but very active, persuer of things Mah-Jongg.

Pre-1940 ivory Mah-Jongg sets and miscellaneous Mah-Jongg ivory items such as sticks, ming, and dice are a particular interest. So too are intricately carved Mah-Jongg boxes, rosewood racks, and old Mah-Jongg playing cards. He also wants "unusual items" such as Mah-Jongg tea sets and Mah-Jongg items with advertising. His interest does not stop with ivory sets, however, as he also seeks a jade set and will purchase fine-quality bone and bamboo sets in nice boxes.

He asks you to note: "There are thousands of old Mah-Jongg sets of bone or synthetics believed to be ivory. Even dealers get confused. I will buy every old ivory set and can help you distinguish ivory from other materials."

In addition to game pieces and boxes, Joe will buy old Mah-Jongg score pads, score cards, and other paper Mah-Jongg ephemera.

A complete description is required, including the number of tiles, the number of counting sticks, a list of other items, and a description of the box. Note whether instructions or other papers are included. "I would appreciate knowing anything of the set's history, if the seller knows.

"The best way to sell me a set is to mail me two carved tiles, one counting stick, and a photograph of the set, and I will evaluate them and return with an offer. Mah-Jongg sets vary so greatly that each one needs to be judged individually."

ANTIQUE MARBLES

Erv Austin
1534 North Saginaw Street
Flint, Michigan 48503

If you have anything old, odd, or different in the way of antique marbles, Erv Austin is interested.

He also wants swirls and sulphides of all types, but especially sulphides made of colored glass and swirls with gold stripes. He also wants old marbles in their original boxes, marble games, old drawstring marble bags, pictures of children playing marbles, and magazine or newspaper articles pertaining to marbles.

Please describe your item fully and include a photograph whenever practical. "Instant reply guaranteed with SASE."

VARIOUS GAME DECKS

Dave Greenwald
302 West 78th Street
New York, New York 10024
(212) 496-8007

Dave Greenwald's specialty is strategy, educational, and other unusual decks of cards.

Any old or unusual card games might be of interest, even if the deck is incomplete. Dave also buys fine-condition board games and sliding block puzzles.

When describing decks and games, tell him if the set is complete, whether the original box is complete and in good condition, and whether the rules are included. Describe the condition of the pieces and what the more unusual ones look like. A sketch is sometimes helpful, but a photocopy of a few of the cards (front and back) and of the top of the game box is a good idea. Dave will make offers for items he can use.

BOOKS ABOUT CHECKERS

Don Deweber
Checker Book World
3520 Hillcrest, Apt. 4
Dubuque, Iowa 52001

Don Deweber wants to buy books on the game of checkers or draughts. He also wants to buy older general books on games that have sections in them dealing with checkers.

Tell him the title, author, copyright date, number of pages, publisher, and condition of the book. A photocopy of the title page is recommended.

Don prefers you to set the price, but will make offers. He can send a large wants list of books he will buy. Not only does he buy for his own collection, he operates a free library service to readers all over the world who want books on checkers.

BOOKS ABOUT CARD GAMES

Bill Sachen
927 Grand Avenue
Waukegan, Illinois 60085
(312) 662-7204

Bill Sachen seeks any books or magazines on bridge, whist, or other card games, especially bridge and whist magazines published prior to 1960 and books on bridge and whist that were privately printed by less well known authors.

He also wants to buy early nonstandard decks of playing cards.

"I answer all letters if an SASE is enclosed, but am not responsible for returning unsolicited items," he states. He also affirms a willingness to make offers on unpriced items.

PAPER DOLLS

Loraine Brudick
5 Court Place
Puyallup, Washington 98371

Paper dolls of all types, cut and uncut, are one of Loraine Burdick's fascinations. She buys, sells, and collects paper dolls, has written or published twelve books about paper dolls, belongs to two paper doll clubs, and for seventeen years has published Celebrity Doll Journal while writing for other publications.

She will buy cut and uncut paper dolls, especially mint-condition early celebrity dolls and movie star dolls from the 1940s.

When describing paper dolls, pay particular attention to condition and list all cuts, tape, bends, breaks, wrinkles, and tears. Loraine assures that she will buy paper dolls that have been cut out, but says, "I must know their condition. Downgrading is necessary when feet or hands are off or any pieces are taped." A photocopy would be greatly appreciated. She does not do appraisals but will make offers on desirable paper dolls.

PAPER DOLLS

Shirley Jane Hedge
Route 2, Box 52
Princeton, Indiana 47670
(812) 385-4080

Among numerous other items, this twenty-year veteran collects paper dolls of all kinds, cut and uncut. Among Shirley Hedge's special interests:

1. Paper dolls from the Chicago Tribune, any kind
2. Sets of dolls printed between 1930 and 1950 from any source, including paper doll books, boxed sets, etc.
3. Paper dolls created for advertising purposes
4. Foreign paper dolls of all types and periods
5. All paper doll reference materials such as books, magazines, or newspapers featuring paper dolls from any period
6. Current magazine or newspaper ads that utilize paper dolls as part of the illustration

When describing paper dolls, tell her whether they are cut or uncut, the publishing company, the date published (if you know), the title of the book or boxed set, the condition (noting all tears, creases, bends, tape, glue, soil, etc.), and the number of pieces that are available.

Shirley will make offers, but warns, "I will send a reply only to those who enclose a self-addressed stamped envelope, unless it is a priced offer to sell me something I want."

PAPER TOYS

Barbara and Jonathan Newman
The Paper Soldier
18 McIntosh Lane
Clifton Park, New York 12065
(518) 371-9202

This husband and wife collector-dealer team buys "all types of paper toys including paper dolls, soldiers, theaters, buildings, ships, airplanes, and so on, both American and foreign, antique or modern.

When corresponding, list the date, publisher, size, condition, and price. "If in doubt as to price, items can be sent on approval. We do not like to make an offer for paper toys without seeing them, since so much of their value depends upon condition.

A large illustrated catalog of paper toys for sale may be ordered for $2.

PAPER DOLLS

Fran Van Vynckt
6931 Monroe Avenue
Hammond, Indiana 46324
(219) 931-2196

Fran Van Vynckt wants pre-1960 paper dolls, "either celebrities or ordinary people." She does not especially want those printed in newspapers but will consider them.

When you write, describe your dolls by including the number of pieces, type of dolls, size, and the like. Indicate whether they are cut or uncut, and the date they were printed, if you know.

She prefers you to set your asking price, but will make offers. Fran is a very active collector of more than ten years' experience.

PAPER AND CELEBRITY DOLLS

Lois Shearer
P.O. Box 250
Prospect, Kentucky 40059

Lois Shearer collects celebrity dolls, both three-dimensional and paper, along with other paper ephemera related to celebrities.

She is most interested in obtaining dolls, paper dolls, books, posters, lobby cards, and "standees" of Shirley Temple, Jane Withers, and Judy Garland. In addition, she also buys a general run of antique dolls with bisque or china heads.

Make a photocopy of paper goods. When describing dolls, indicate any maker's marks on the head or body. "I will make offers on items of particular interest, but prefer to have items priced."

TOYS, CHINA, AND OTHER THINGS

Heinz Mueller
Continental Hobby House
P.O. Box 193
Sheboygan, Wisconsin 53081
(414) 693-3371

Heinz Mueller is a veteran dealer who seeks a variety of rare items in fine condition for resale:
1. Antique toys and trains
2. Antique European toys (in any condition)
3. Old children's pedal cars
4. Cylinder and disk music machines
5. French and German procelain
6. Items made of gold
7. Fine pocket watches

He requests simply that an accurate description be provided, including any defects. In all cases, he would prefer a picture if you are asking him to quote a price. You may find his wants list helpful.

SUPERMAN

Danny Fuchs
209-80 18th Avenue
Bayside, New York 11360
(212) 225-9030 eves.

Danny Fuchs buys any rare, odd, or unusual Superman collectible that dates from 1938 to 1960.

This includes toys, games, figurines, pebbles, coloring books, button banks watches, puppets, advertising material, premiums same period. However, if somebody comes up with a really unusual Superman item produced after 1960, "I'll probably be interested. I prefer items related to the Superman comic book character, but I also collect Superman items from the TV series, movie serials, radio programs, etc.

"I appreciate it when the first letter accurately, honestly, and carefully describes the item(s), noting any tears, defects, markings, copyright dates, and the like. I prefer to be quoted a price, but I will make a reasonable offer on unpriced items. It someone writes for help or has anykind of question about Superman, an SASE is requested."

VENTRILOQUISM MEMORABILIA

Kenny Warren
1250 Ocean Parkway, 2M
Brooklyn, New York 11230
(212) 252-1876

Kenny Warren collects "anything relating to the art of ventriloquism," including books, photographs, posters, playbills, and old professional ventriloquists' dummies. He is particularly eager to locate items associated with the more prominent ventriloquist teams, such as Edgar Bergen and Charlie McCarthy or Paul Winchell and Jerry Mahoney.

"Please describe your item and its condition, and state the price you want in your first letter to expedite the transaction." Ken does not wish to make offers. If you are describing a dummy, note if there are any visible markings indicating the maker or date of manufacture. It would be helpful to describe the material from which the dummy is made and the mechanism(s), if any, for creating movement.

BRITISH FIGURAL BISCUIT TINS

Bonnie Bizzarro
678 South Wellwood Avenue
Lindenhurst, New York 11757
(516) 957-6905

Bonnie Bizzarro wants to buy figural tin containers used by British companies, primarily for biscuits.

British biscuit tins were intended to be used as toys; as a result, they were made in the shape of automobiles, buses, trucks, locomotives, golf bags, volumes of books, carousels, houses, and many other interesting shapes. Names of manufacturers such as Huntley Palmer, Victory V, Lyons, Barringer, Wrights, Crawford, and W. Dunsmore & Sons can usually be found somewhere on the tin.

When describing condition, "specify every dent, flake, chip, or faded spot." She claims to pay "the highest prices" for figurals, and agrees to make offers on good unpriced items.

4
Glass, China, Pottery and Utensils

ART GLASS, CHINA, AND ORIENTALIA

Howard Farber
200 West 79th Street, 8K
New York, New York 10024
(212) 580-9475

Howard Farber has been in business for more than ten years and requests a wide range of quality items:

1. Nippon marked vases, chocolate sets, plaques, bowls, etc.
2. Noritake china and accessories
3. Goldsheider figures
4. American and European art glass
5. Art Deco figurines
6. Cut glass
7. European porcelains and china, including Doulton, Sevres, Meissen, Royal Worcester, Royal Doulton, R.S. Prussia, R.S. Germany, Dresden, and others--vases, cups, saucers, ewers, chocolate sets, unusual items
8. Orientalia of all sorts, including Chinese watercolors, Chinese reverse paintings on glass, textiles, rugs, and "any other items."

Howard has a priced and illustrated wants list that he will forward in exchange for your long SASE. When writing him, describe what you have, paying attention to size, color, shape, markings or names, and its history, if you know it. Condition is critical and must be described accurately, as items for resale cannot be cracked, chipped, or defective in any way except in the case of minor hurts to valuable pieces. He will make offers for what you have. A great number of these items can have value in excess of $1,000 and must be handled and packed very carefully.

CARNIVAL AND OTHER GLASS

Tom Burns
Burns Auction Service
RD #1
Bath, New York 14810
(607) 776-7942

Tom Burns is one of the country's more important glass auctioneers. He is also an avid collector who buys a wide range of glass and china.

1. Carnival glass, from single pieces to $100,000 collections, especially rare patterns and colors, opalescent pieces, pitchers and tumblers, punchbowls and cups, whimseys, and unusual pieces

2. Nippon china, but only humidors, wall plaques, large vases, large "blown out" high relief pieces, and other unusual items

3. RS Prussia china, especially those decorated with portraits, scenics, or pearlized florals

4. Mandarin red glassware by Fenton Glass Co.

5. Noritake china with Art Deco designs

6. Human and animal figures made by Noritake

7. Victorian colored pattern glass

8. Sculpted "cameo glass" by the Phoenix Glass Co.

9. Early figural oil lamps, especially in colored glass.

Please check all glass and china for chips and cracks, espcially around the base, the rim, and around the lid. Make certain to mention every defect no matter how small.

If you are not confident of your ability to accurately identify the maker and the name of the pattern, a photograph is highly advisable. When describing glass, size and color must be mentioned, as well as any markings or signatures which might be on the bottom, hidden in the pattern, or found under a lid.

You may set the price or ask Tom to make an offer. Amateur sellers will find him quite helpful, but you must include your phone number along with an SASE. If your glass meets certain standards of value and condition, Tom will buy it outright or suggest auctioning it for you during one of the many carnival glass auctions he conducts around the country.

WILLOW OAK PRESSED GLASS

Audrey V. Buffington
AVB Collectibles
2 Old Farm Road
Wayland, Massachusetts 01778
(617) 358-2644

In the 1870s and 1880s, a Pittsburgh glass company named Bryce Brothers manufactured a pattern called Willow Oak in a variety of colors, including clear, amber, blue, and vaseline (a greenish yellow). A very busy pattern, it includes an oak leaf, a star, an acorn, a thistle, and other design elements.

Audrey Buffington wants to buy undamaged pieces of Willow Oak in blue and vaseline. The latter color is very scarce, so she urges you to contact her even if you have only one item.

Tell her what pieces you have, their size and color. Note every chip, flake, or crack. You may set the price wanted or ask Audrey to make an offer.

ART NOUVEAU GLASS

Oscar Merber
Merber Enterprises, Ltd.
2700 Virginia Avenue NW
Washington, D.C. 20037
(202) 337-0862

Oscar Merber is a veteran dealer in fine art glass of the Art Nouveau period.

He buys American art glass by Tiffany and Quezal, and French and English cameo glass by Galle, Daum-Nancy, D'Argental, Legras, Webb, and Stevens & Williams.

He requests that a color photograph accompany your description. Note where on the piece the signature appears and give appropriate dimensions. He asks that you set the price, but he is willing to make offers. Since much of this glass is quite valuable, research is in order before you attempt to price items on your own. Oscar is an experienced appraiser and can be of help.

QUALITY GLASS AND CERAMICS

Dorothy-Lee Jones
The Jones Gallery of Glass and Ceramics
The Gallery Shop
East Baldwin, Maine 04024
(207) 787-3370

The Jones Gallery of Glass and Ceramics is a nationally known museum of glass with nearly 4,000 fine pieces on display, a continuing lecture series, and constantly changing exhibits. Two curators are in residence to assist with questions in the museum or large research library on glass, which is open to the public. In addition, they operate a gallery shop that offers antiques (especially glass), cards, and other gifts to help support the museum's activities.

The gallery wants to buy fine-condition quality glass and ceramics of all origins (American, English, and Continental) and all types, including plates, dinnerware, figurines, whimseys, and art glass. They buy some "modern" glass and ceramics, including interesting art pottery, Depression glass, Fenton, Heisey, and other dining room glass. Oriental ceramics of all periods are also purchased. "All goods submitted should be in excellent condition and of substantial interest."

A thorough description is necessary. Include the type of object, maker (if known), dimensions, identifying marks, colors or decorations, and statement of condition noting all cracks, rim chips, and base chips. "A photograph which shows the objects well is highly preferable," say gallery experts. If you have a selling price, please state it in the first letter. If not, they will make offers on good items they can use.

CARNIVAL GLASS

Singleton Bailey
P.O. Box 95
Loris, South Carolina 29569
(803) 756-7495

Singleton Bailey is seeking certain types of carnival glass: Millersburg patterns such as Peacock at the Urn, Big Fish, and Trout and Fly; carnival glass in red, Vaseline, or pastel colors; carnival glass in rare shapes, especially whimseys.

He wants to know the type of item you have and the name of the pattern, the color, and the quality of the irridescence. Indicate whether there are any nicks, cracks, or other signs of damage. Singleton is a member of half a dozen glass collectors' clubs and has been buying carnival glass for more than fifteen years.

PAPERWEIGHTS

Charles W. Stutsman, Sr.
5013 Old Boonville Highway
Evansville, Indiana 47715

Charles Stutsman buys and sells a wide range of collectible items, but specializes in glass paperweights, American and foreign, old or new. "I especially like to find weights by lesser-known glass workers," he says.

"Weights that are in perfect condition are preferred," he says, "but I will consider weights with repairable defects such as scratches or small chips." He wants to know the size, pattern or design, colors, markings or signatures, and name and location of the maker (if known). Since weights are fairly valuable, he indicates that in many cases he will want to inspect the weight before purchase. You may price your weight, or ask him to. Charles is very active in the world of contemporary weight makers and considers many of them close friends.

PAPERWEIGHTS

George Kamm
P.O. Box 254 W
Lititz, Pennsylvania 17543
(717) 626-2338 eves.

George Kamm buys and sells paperweights, both antique and better-quality contemporary ones.

All the famous makers are sought, including Baccarat, Clichy, St. Louis, Bacchus, Sandwich, and others, as are all types of patterns and designs in weights. The only restriction? No lucite!

Identify the maker and date if you can. Otherwise, an accurate description of the design and condition must suffice. Note the exact diameter, please. George will make offers when sufficient information is provided.

MISCELLANEOUS ITEMS MADE OF GLASS

Stanley A. Block
P.O. Box 51
Trumbull, Connecticut 06611

Stan Block wants to buy an assortment of fine items made from glass:
    1. All types of marbles made prior to 1930, including stone and mineral spheres (sometimes called "bowls")
    2. Antique glass paperweights
    3. Blossom bottles, small blown perfume bottles made in Germany during the Depression
    4. Agate items, including boxes, letter openers, button hooks, pens, etc., trimmed with natural agate
    5. Glass canes with colored twists of glass within the cane
    Describe what you have, including its size and condition. He requests that you include your phone number and your asking price, but neither is absolutely essential. He will make offers on fine items. Stan is founder and executive director of the Marble Collectors Society of America.

GREENTOWN GLASS

Jerry D. Garrett
Jerry's Antiques
1807 West Madison Street
Kokomo, Indiana 46901
(317) 457-5256 eves.

Jerry Garrett buys glassware pressed by the Indiana Tumbler & Goblet Company in Greentown, Indiana, from 1894 to 1903.
    Commonly called Greentown glass, it was pressed in nine different clear and opaque colors, including milk glass, and in a large number of patterns. The company produced many specialty items such as hen on the nest, bird with berry on nest, cat on the hamper, dog and child mug, dog's head toothpick holder, and other distinctive bowls, creamers, vases, pitchers and the like. Jerry wants any of these novelty glass pieces as well as salt-and-peppers, tumblers, goblets, wines, cordials, and other stemware.
    If you have any Greentown but don't know exactly what it is or what it is worth, you may make arrangements with Jerry to ship on approval. When you contact him, include a drawing of the pattern, describe the color, and "tell me the true condition of the item" (don't disregard chips and flakes no matter how small). Once Jerry knows what you have he will make an offer. Jerry is coauthor of the 1982 Greentown Glass Price Guide.

COLORED GLASS INKWELLS

Jeffrey Dane
2639 Batchelder Street
Brooklyn, New York 11235
(212) 644-9247

Jeff Dane has been collecting colored glass inkwells for nearly fifteen years.

He buys inkwells of colored glass, and he prefers cut or patterned pressed glass. All colors are sought, as are all shapes and styles.

He wants to know the color of the glass from which the inkwell is made; the inkwell's shape, dimensions, approximate age and condition; the components of the piece (does it have a lid, hinges, etc.); and a firm price.

Jeff has written about inkwells and the difficulties of collecting.

GLASSWARE OF THE DEPRESSION

Nadine Pankow
Nadine Pankow's Glass
207 South Oakwood
Willow Springs, Illinois 60480
(312) 839-5231

Nadine Pankow has been a collector and dealer of Depression-era glass for nearly fifteen years.

She buys American-made colored and crystal glass dinnerware of the 1930s and 1940s, "both handmade and tank-made." She needs to know the maker, he pattern name, and the size in inches. "A flat piece will photocopy nicely," she says, enabling identification in some cases.

All items must be priced, as she will not make offers. She does encourage you to do research through your local library, since the glass of that era is well documented. Some pieces have fairly good value, so it is worth the time.

STANGL POTTERY AND DEPRESSION GLASS

Fran Jay
Popkorn
P.O. Box 1057
Flemington, New Jersey 08822
(201) 782-9631

Fran Jay's shop, Popkorn, specializes in Stangl pottery, a heavy red decorated earthenware once manufactured in New Jersey. She buys dinnerware, bird figures, and other pieces of this distinctive pottery, often recognized by its Pennsylvania Dutch motif.

In addition, the shop handles all manufacturers and patterns of Depression glass, "from the best to the worst," according to Bob, Fran's partner.

They would like to be contacted if you have any fine-condition Stangl or Depression glass. Provide them with the name of the pattern marked on the bottom of your Stangl. If you don't know the glass pattern, make a photocopy of a saucer or do a good sketch, rubbing, or tracing.

Indicate what pieces you have, their dimensions, and the quantity of each. Do not count damaged china or glassware. Fran or Bob will be happy to make you an offer for pieces they can use.

COLLECTOR'S PLATES

Adam Selesh and family
Tiffany Steven's Collectibles
478 Ward Street Extension
Wallingford, Connecticut 06492
(203) 265-1722

The Selesh family operates a central exchange for plate collectors around the world. They publish Plate-O-Holic (an investment-oriented newsletter), perform appraisal services (for a fee), accept consignment sales, provide expert figurine repair, and have an extensive catalog of items for sale.

In addition, Adam, Terry, and their children are all involved in buying collector's plates and other limited-edition collectibles, expecially M.I. Hummel and Sebastian figurines.

They may purchase your item outright or they may advise consignment sale, but only after you tell them exactly what you have, its markings, colors, serial numbers when appropriate, and whether its original box and certificates are there. "We will not answer mail that does not include an SASE."

LENOX AND OXFORD CHINA

Jacquelynn G. Ives
Jacquelynn's China
4770 North Oakland Avenue
Milwaukee, Wisconsin 53211
(414) 962-7213

Jacquelynn Ives wants to buy discontinued patterns of Lenox and Oxford china.

Selling to her is simply a matter of telling her the pattern name and number. If you don't know it, a good sketch or a photograph or photocopy will help. When describing condition, note all cracks, rim chips, bottom chips, pattern wear, and knife scratches.

Send a self-addressed stamped envelope and she will make an offer for what you have.

SALEM SQUATS

Charles McDonald
Old Bottle Museum
4 Friendship Drive
Salem, New Jersey 08079
(609) 935-5631

Charles and Lee McDonald have been active collectors of bottles for more than fifteen years.

They are particularly interested in obtaining "Salem squats" (a local soda bottle) and any other bottles, fruit jars, or paper goods that originated in Salem, New Jersey.

When writing, let the McDonalds know what you have, its condition, and the quantity available. They will make an offer for items they can use.

WILLOW PATTERN CHINA

Lois K. Misiewicz
6543 Indian Trail
Fallbrook, California 92028
(619) 941-1944

The most popular design ever to grace dinnerware, blue willow has been around for three centuries and has been made in China, Japan, England, America and in small amounts elsewhere. Lois Misiewicz will consider various manufacturers but is particularly interested in pieces by Allerton, Ridgeway, and Doulton.

In addition to willow ware, she wants unusual pieces of Pennsylvania pattern glass made by the U.S. Glass Co. in Pittsburgh, as well as ladies' gold watch chains and slides.

A complete description must include a reproduction of all marks and writing on the bottom of the china. Give dimensions and a statement of condition. She will make offers on pieces she can use, but you must include an SASE. Lois assisted in the willow ware sections of two major price guides.

EARLY BOTTLES AND HISTORICAL FLASKS

Burton Spiller
300 White Spruce Boulevard
Rochester, New York 14623
(716) 424-6400

Burt Spiller buys "better-quality early American bottles and historical flasks such as those listed in American Glass by Helen McKearin. I also want figural bitters bottles and ink and medicine bottles with pontil marks on their bases as evidence the bottles were blown in molds. I will also buy colored, round milk bottles and any of the less commonly found fruit jars complete with original closures.

"Of course, I seek all these items in fine condition with no cracks, chips, or stains in the glass. I want the person to fully describe the item as to condition, measurements, and all wording shown on their bottle, flask, or fruit jar." Burt will make offers on good-quality items he can use.

HAVILAND CHINA

Barbara C. Berger
The China Corner
P.O. Box 7745
Colorado Springs, Colorado 80933
(303) 578-9882

For about ten years, Barbara Berger has run a matching service for china, dinnerware, and household decorator items marked "Haviland & Company," "Theodore Haviland," "Charles Field Haviland," or "Jonathan Haviland."

Tell her the manufacturer and the name and number of the pattern, if you know it. If you do not, make a photocopy or photograph of the pattern and a copy of any markings on the bottom. List the number and types of pieces you have for sale. Do not count any with cracks, chips on the rims or bottoms, pattern wear, or obvious knife scratches. Items must be in like-new condition, or she isn't interested. Barbara will make offers on unpriced items.

HAVILAND CHINA MATCHING SERVICE

Eleanor B. Thomas
Auld Lang Syne
7600 Highway 120
Jamestown, California 95327
(209) 984-3474

Eleanor Thomas runs a Haviland china matching service and regularly keeps about 750 patterns on hand. She wants to buy a wide range of Haviland pieces, both American and European.

She is particularly eager to locate hard-to-find pieces such as egg cups, salts, candleholders, and waste jars. Dora and Bird & Butterflies are two patterns she would especially like to find.

A photocopy of the pattern and the marks on the bottom is helpful, but a good clear sketch will do. Indicate all colors and make certain to copy all names, numbers, and marks from the bottom of plates or the underside of lids. Tell her how many pieces you have and what you would like to receive for them. Research is advised, since she does not make offers.

FINE CHINA AND STEMWARE MATCHING

Sophia Papapanu
Sophia's China & Crystal
141 Sedgwick Road
Syracuse, New York 13203
(315) 472-6834

Sophia Papapanu operates a major matching service, specializing in American-made china such as Castleton, Flintridge, Lenox, Franciscan, Haviland, Syracuse, Gorham, Stangl, Iriquois, and Pickard. In addition, some pieces of Wedgwood, Royal Worcester, Spode, Royal Doulton, Minton, and Denby are stocked.

She also specializes in American-made stemware by Fostoria, Gorham, Franciscan, Tiffin, Cambridge, Duncan, Imperial, Stuart, Royal Doulton, and others.

"We buy china and crystal on a continuing basis. If you have china for sale, let us know what you have. Items must be in excellent condition. Since we do not bid on china, please tell us your sale price."

Sophia also buys glass and china company catalogs or related material helpful in identifying the products of various glass companies.

FINE CHINA MATCHING

Dirck and Sjoeke Meengs
P.O. Box 578
Woodland Hills, California 91365
(818) 341-9641

The Meengs operate a china matching service specializing in pieces by Castleton, Flintridge, Franciscan, Spode, and Royal Worcester. They purchase complete or partial sets in fine condition.

They also purchase selected patterns of Franconia, Gorham, Haviland, Lenox, Minton, Noritake, Oxford, Rosenthal, Royal Doulton, Syracuse, and Wedgwood. "Our personal collection is of Plateel, an Art Nouveau earthenware produced in and near Gouda, the Netherlands, prior to 1939."

Give names of the manufacturer and the pattern; if you don't know them, send photocopy showing the pattern. List the quantity of each item, plate and bowl sizes, and condition.

Provide a drawing of any marks on the bottom and a color photograph or snapshot. The Meengs will make offers.

ROSENTHAL CHINA

Mary Helen Zawaski
Vintage Patterns Unlimited
3571 Crestnall Drive
Cincinnati, Ohio 45211

"We sell a variety of discontinued fine china and crystal," writes Mary Helen Zawaski, "but we specialize in Rosenthal china and crystal." The latter is no surprise to friends who know that Mary spent five years on the road as a Rosenthal sales rep.

If you have any Rosenthal for sale "at realistic prices," tell her the name of the pattern, the number of pieces available, and the condition, noting every crack, chip, and spot of wear. If you don't know the name of the pattern, make a photocopy of one of the plates and indicate the colors.

She charges a $25 fee for providing the current market value of what you have, but she is willing to assist you to set the price when you sell to her.

CASTLETON, FRANCISCAN, AND FOSTORIA

Judy Giangiuli
Back Door Antiques
RD 6, Box 152
New Castle, Pennsylvania
(412) 924-9052

Back Door Antiques provides a matching service for selected items.

Judy Giangiuli will buy full or partial sets of Castleton China dinnerware (a prestigious local brand used in the White House), Masterpiece china from Franciscan, and Fostoria stemware. Fostoria is a maker of etched, cut, or decorated crystal as well as colored glassware and table accessories.

List all the pieces you have, including dimensions, since pieces can be rare in one size, common in another. Condition is critical. Glass that is chipped or cracked is not wanted, although incomplete sets are bought. "We prefer no bidding," so they require you to price what you have for sale.

NORITAKE CHINA

Kenneth W. Kipp and Gloria Munsell
Allenwood Americana
P.O. Box 116
Allenwood, Pennsylvania 17810
(717) 538-1440

The Larkin Company of Buffalo, New York, distributed various patterns of Noritake china for thirty years. Ken and Gloria specialize in buying and selling two of those patterns, Azalea and Tree in the Meadow, and want to buy all the pieces of it they can find, especially children's-size pieces.

They also want to buy Larkin Company catalogs, advertising, sales literature, and other ephemera.

A simple description is sufficient, but make certain to note all chips, cracks, and worn gold. They don't want damaged pieces. List the number of pieces in each pattern and style. They prefer that you price what you have but will make offers on unpriced china.

FLYING TURKEY AND PHOENIX BIRD CHINA

Ruth L. West
P.O. Box 252
Roseland, New Jersey 07068
(201) 228-9491

For more than a decade, Ruth West has been buying all the pieces she can find of two Japanese china patterns, Flying Turkey and Phoenix Bird. The patterns are blue and white, feature the birds and vines, and generally have a blue-and-white border.

She no longer needs cups, saucers, or bread-and-butter plates, but continues to seek hard-to-find pieces such as children's sets, serving pieces, and accessories.

She would like to know which pattern you have, the type and number of pieces, the shape and size of the pieces, and the condition. Make certain to list every crack, chip, or heavy wear mark. If you want an offer for your china, you must include your phone number and a self-addressed stamped envelopes.

FINE CHINA MATCHING

Margaret Roe and Sons
Old China Patterns Limited
1560 Brimley Road
Scarborough, Ontario
Canada, M1P 3G9
(416) 299-8880

Margaret Roe and her sons operate a china matching service, now in its nineteenth year.

They buy out-of-production dinnerware patterns "from a restricted range of manufacturers" that include:

1. American makers Lenox, Castleton, Syracuse, Oxford, Franciscan, and Haviland

2. German maker Rosenthal and some patterns in Royal Beyreuth

3. English makers Wedgwood, Royal Doulton, Spode, Minton, and Royal Worcester, and some pieces and patterns from seventeen other manufacturers

4. French Haviland and work of a half-dozen others

When describing china, include everything that is written on the bottom. If you know any of the history of the dishes, particularly when and where they were originally purchased, make certain to provide that information. Dishes must be in excellent condition, free of all chips, cracks, crazing, pattern wear, or dishwasher damage.

The Roes will make offers on items you have for sale, but remember that postage from Canada to the U.S. is high, so include fifty cents in coin instead of an SASE when requesting information or offers.

NORITAKE CHINA

Edith "Dee" Berry
31 White Oak Circle
St. Charles, Illinois 60174

Edith Berry buys Noritake china, but only in one pattern, Merle.

A Merle plate can be recognized by its white center surrounded by a wide yellow band. Three multicolored bouquets can be found evenly spaced within this band around the center. The outside rim of Merle is characterized by a series of fine yellow, bittersweet, and gold bands decorated with tiny white flowers.

Tell her what pieces you have, since she claims, "I want any and all pieces available." Describe the condition and set the price you'd like. If you have no idea what the value or your china is, you may ask her to make an offer on items actually for sale.

FLO BLUE ORIENTAL CHINA

Bonnie Bizzarro
678 South Wellwood Avenue
Lindenhurst, New York 11757
(516) 957-6905

Flo blue is the name given to an English china made for export to the United States during the 19th century. It is a white china recognizable by its blue patterns, which were usually smeared or runny-looking.

"There are approximately twenty different flo blue patterns," she writes, "but I collect only the Oriental patterns known as Temple, Manilla, Hong Kong, Formosa, Oregon, and Shapoo. I want very dark and runny pieces especially."

Tell her the name of the pattern if you know it, otherwise a sketch will do. Make certain you indicate every chip and hairline crack. She will make an offer for what you have.

AMERICAN ART POTTERY

Duke Coleman
Nothing New
P.O. Box 714
Silver Spring, Maryland 20901
(301) 587-7921 eves.

Duke Coleman buys American art pottery dating between 1880 and the 1930s, particularly early and artist-signed pieces of all types by Rookwood, Newcomb College, University City, Cowan, Pisgah Forrest, Van Briggle, Marblehead, Niloak, Robineau, Weller, Roseville, and Grueby.

He also buys "selected lines and patterns" of some commercial or production pottery. "These include typical beginner items frequently overpriced by dealers who don't specialize in pottery. I buy them only when very reasonably priced," he warns.

A thorough description should include the object's size, type of glaze (shiny, matte, etc.), coloring (including decorations), and maker's marks, cyphers, numbers, and signatures that appear anywhere. Coleman prefers being offered only perfect pieces because "even very slight damage or imperfection detracts seriously from its value." Photos are welcome.

DISCONTINUED TABLETOP ITEMS

Betty and Warren Roundhill
Patterns Unlimited
P.O. Box 15238
Seattle, Washington 98115

The Roundhills want to buy discontinued patterns of all tabletop items, including dinnerware, glassware, silver, and silverplate from all manufacturers.

"We buy anything people eat from or eat with," Warren says, but no "fancies" such as candleholders, ornate vases, or elaborate bowls.

Tell them the name of the manufacturer, the pattern name, and provide a facsimile of all backmarks on the china. List the types and sizes of all the perfect pieces and the quantities available. Price what you have, please, as they do not make offers. They state that "there are many books available at libraries that cover china, crystal, and tableware," and encourage you to research what you have.

DECORATED AMERICAN STONEWARE

Alvin H. Behr
3 Behrs
RD 8, Horsepound Road
Carmel, New York 10512
(914) 225-4747

From single pieces to entire collections, Al Behr wants to buy blue and gray decorated American stoneware jugs, crocks, jars, pitchers, churns and the like, but only pieces with unusual or elaborate designs such as birds, animals, dates, bouquets of flowers, and other configurations.

He also wants American stoneware specialty items such as spittoons, matchsafes, flasks, bottles, and banks. Redware pottery marked "Bell" and Pennsylvania stoneware marked "Cowden & Wilcox" are also sought.

Describe what you have, including its capacity, markings, and design. Examine condition carefully. Slight damage is acceptable, but mint-condition pieces bring the highest prices. He prefers items to be priced but will make offers on desirable unpriced pieces. Al does not do appraisals by mail.

NOTE: Pankow caters to the serious collector and says "We sell about 10,000 pieces per year. All that stock has to come from somewhere...and you are where it comes from. Check others for the amount of their inventory."

AMERICAN ART POTTERY

Thomas Turnquist
P.O. Box 256
Englewood, Colorado 80151

"I'm looking for American art pottery," writes Tom Turnquist, author of more than twenty articles and one book on the topic.

He wants Cowan figurals and work by Glen Lukens, Natzler, Laura Anderson, Harrison McIntosh, Eugene Deutsch, Jalan, Vivika and Otto Heino, Charles Abott, Von Tury, Carlton Ball, and Robineau.

He wants to know the type of pottery and all marks thereon. Describe the shape, colors, patterns, and condition. You are encouraged to set your own price, but Tom will make offers.

CHINA PAINTED BY LELL FRANKS

Ruth A. Arch
919 SE 6th Street
Forest Lake, Minnesota 55025

Lell Franks painted and taught painting in Cedar Rapids, Iowa, from about 1890 to 1940. Ruth Arch, her granddaughter, is now collecting her work.

"This lovely lady painted dresser sets, vases, jardinieres, entire sets of table china, porcelain plaques, mugs, bowls, and such a variety of things." Flowers are most common, but elves, fairies, and geometrics are also found. All work is marked with capital letters "L F" (which touch at the middle of the "F") or with the name "Franks," but the marks are often interwoven into the design.

Describe what you have and how you know it is a piece of her grandmother's work. You may set a price, or Ruth will be pleased to make offers.

SHAWNEE POTTERY

Mark Supnick
8524 NW 2nd Street
Coral Springs, Florida 33065
(305) 755-3448

Mark Supnick wants Shawnee pottery, either corn or figural, and all types of Hull's Little Red Riding Hood kitchenware.

He asks only that you provide a description and "your best price." He will make offers, but no damaged pieces, please. Mark is the author of Collecting Shawnee Pottery, available from him for $11.

ROSEVILLE AND OTHER AMERICAN ART POTTERY

Muriel Dexter
15748 Ranchland Drive
Redding, California 96001
(916) 243-7611

For nearly a decade, Muriel Dexter has been buying and selling American art pottery, with special emphasis on Roseville. In addition, she buys catalogs, advertising, and other paper ephemera related to American potters and pottery manufacturers.

When describing what you have, include dimensions, colors, marks or signatures, and the maker if known. "Sellers should be aware that not all pottery is marked. So if you have one of these unknown pieces, send me a photograph and whatever information is available on the bottom and I will be happy to attempt an identification for you. Don't forget your SASE."

Muriel prefers you to set the price wanted, but since a few of these items can have value over $100, it is advisable to take advantage of her offer to assist you in arriving at a fair price.

FIGURAL POTTERY

Edy J. Chandler
P.O. Box 20664
Houston, Texas 77225
(713) 668-7864 or (713) 527-8402

Edy Chandler wants to buy three-dimensional figural objects made of pottery, porcelain, pewter, or wood.

If they are the appropriate subject matter, she will buy statues, figurines, mugs, tea pots, coffee pots, tobacco jars, and jugs. Subject matter includes mythological beasts of all types (devils, gargoyles, elves, trolls, mermaids, griffins, dragons, unicorns, wizards, fairies, Pegasus, etc.), robots, witches, dinosaurs, and the Schmoo. In particular, she would love to locate the Wizard coffee pot and the King Kong mug, both made by Jim Rumph, as well as works by Martin Brothers and Jason Christobel.

Describe the item, giving all colors and markings. Make certain you note any chips or missing paint. She will make offers.

COLLECTIBLE PLATES AND FIGURINES

Philip Hershkowitz
Hershy's
8642 20th Avenue
Brooklyn, New York 11214
(212) 266-5225

After specializing in Royal Doulton figures and mugs for five years, Hershy's has recently expanded to carry other collector's plates, figures, and items "at discount prices."

Philip Hershkowitz wants to purchase figures, figurines, and mugs for resale, especially discontinued ones by Royal Doulton, Lladro, and Hummel. He also would like to know about "all kinds" of collector's and limited edition plates for sale.

He wants to know the name of the maker and the figure, mug, or plate. Give the height of figures, the diameter of plates and both dimensions when describing mugs. Condition is critical, so make certain to note every chip, crack, or imperfection. He asks that you price what you have, but he is willing to make an offer if you are in amateur seller and so request.

TORQUAY POTTERY

Jerry and Gerry Kline
604 Orchard View Drive
Maumee, Ohio 43537
(419) 893-1226

Jerry and Gerry Kline are among less than two dozen serious collectors of Torquay pottery, a hand-painted terra-cotta produced by a dozen or more makers in the southwestern English coast community of Torquay between 1869 and 1962.

Cream-colored Devon motto ware, with its hand-painted cottages and mottoes, is the best-known type of Torquay. Plates, urns, vases, and animal figures were also made, and in a wide variety of boldly painted patterns. The Klines especially seek very large or very small pieces, the unusual, and the rare.

They would like to know the dimensions, the potter's mark (if any), the motto (if any), and the design. When examining your pottery, note all chips, cracks, glaze flakes, etc. If there is any such damage, the piece is not salable. They prefer you to set the price but will make offers.

HEUBACH PORCELAIN AND BISQUE

Frances V. Sandra
5624 Plymouth Road
Baltimore, Maryland 21214
(301) 254-6177

Fran Sandra buys porcelain and bisque cups, plates, paintings, miniature portraits, religious items, trays, children's dishes and "anything unusual" bearing one of the Heubach marks (which often include a capital "G" and "H" intertwined).

In your description be certain to include a drawing of how the piece is marked, its color(s), and size. Send a photograph when possible. Please set the price you want, although Fran will make offers.

After twenty-five years, Fran's own collection is unsurpassed, but she is always eager to buy or to learn about Heubach items unfamiliar to her. If you own anything made by Gebruder Heubach, even if not for sale, Frances wants to know about it because she is compiling a catalog of every item known to have been manufactured by that company.

BUFFALO POTTERY AND CHINA

Violet Altman
Vi & Si's Antiques
8970 Main Street
Clarence, New York 14031
(716) 634-4488

The Altmans want all sorts of pottery and china made by Buffalo Pottery or Buffalo China - "the same company," Vi assures us.

The company produced Deldare Ware, Emerald Deldare, Abino Ware, railroad china, hotel china, commemorative plates and mugs, blue willow, gaudy willow, a series of pitchers, and much more. They want these, and anything else you can find, from the Buffalo Pottery (or China) Company.

Make certain you copy the marks on the bottom accurately, including all numbers and names. Describe what your item looks like. No damaged, cracked, or chipped pieces are wanted. Violet is the author of The Book of Buffalo Pottery and a series of price guides, so is well qualified to assist a beginner who has no way of knowing what items are worth.

POPE-GOSSER AND CLARUS WARE

Carlyle and Hilda Roderick
27858 TR 31
Warsaw, Ohio 43844
(614) 824-3083

The Rodericks collect Pope & Gosser china (but only that with a unicorn mark) and all china marked with the name "Clarus Ware," a Pope & Gosser line of china.

Pieces sought include water or cider sets, chocolate sets, pitchers, spittoons, berry bowls, mugs, cracker jars, calendar plates, portrait plates, vases, and similar household functional and decorative objects.

Their first priority is the mark, so copy it exactly. Then describe what you have, including color(s), size, and decoration. If you describe carefully, they will make you an offer. No damaged pieces, please.

DAMAGED PORCELAIN FIGURINES

Dave Rubin
Berkley, Inc.
2011 Hermitage Avenue
Wheaton, Maryland 20902
(301) 933-4440

Dave Rubin, owner of Berkley, Inc., specializes in repairing fine-quality porcelain figurines that have been damaged.

He especially wants figures by Hummel, Lladro, Cybis, Boehm, B&G, Royal Copenhagen, and Royal Doulton.

He will repair your figurine or buy it from you outright and resell it to someone else once it has been restored. He must actually see the extent and nature of the damage before he can give estimates of the value of the damaged piece or the cost of restoration. Contact him before shipping, please.

DEVON MOTTO WARE

Barbara H. Shenton
5 Merryweather Drive
Cambridge, Maryland 21613
(301) 228-8543

Barbara Shenton has been buying Devon motto ware for more than a decade.

There are many different patterns of terra-cotta ware, the most common featuring a cottage. It was produced by a number of makers in the Torquay region of Devon, England, so wide variations in motto ware can be found. She wants "any items such as plates, hatpin holders, matchsafes, candlesticks, whimseys, and so on."

She wants to know what the item is, what motto is has, and what the pattern is. Three of the most common patterns are named Cottage, Sailboat, and Cock of the North. Examine the condition carefully, as she does not want chipped or cracked items. You are urged to set your price, but she is willing to make offers.

OCCUPIED JAPAN AND M.I. HUMMEL FIGURINES

Sharon Mohammed
P.O. Box 2561
Glen Ellyn, Illinois 60138
(312) 495-0182 eves., and weekends

For more than six years, Sharon Mohammed has been buying and selling collectible small items of various types. She particularly wants:

1. Good-quality items marked "Occupied Japan," including, but not limited to, figurines, cups and saucers, bowls, steins, decanters, and small vases

2. M.I. Hummel figurines, "old marks only," in any quantity

3. Goebel items such as Friar Tuck monks with the "old mark"

She requests details about what you have, its size, and its coloring. Include any numbers on Goebel items especially. Markings are important, she emphasizes. A self-addressed stamped envelope is necessary for a reply. Offers will be forthcoming on pieces genuinely for sale.

STERLING SILVER FLATWARE

Helen Cox
As You Like It
3929 Magazine Street
New Orleans, Louisiana 70115
(504) 897-6915

For a decade and a half, Helen Cox has operated As You Like It, a matching service for sterling silver dinnerware and serving pieces.

If you have sterling silver tableware to sell, she wants to know the name of the maker and the pattern, the number of pieces, and whether the pieces are monogrammed. If you have serving or utility pieces to sell, it is best to take a photograph if you do not know the name of the maker and the pattern.

Helen prefers that you establish the price wanted, but she is willing to make offers if she believes she can resell what you have.

COIN SILVER FLATWARE AND HOLLOWWARE

Alan R. Kossack
Chamberlain Road
RD 2, Box 172
Barre, Massachusetts 01005
(617) 355-2061

Alan Kossack has twenty-five years of experience buying marked early American-made coin silver.

Simply describe what you have, its marks, and its condition. If there is a pattern on the silverware, it can often be copied by a photocopy machine. Make certain to mention if the pieces are monogrammed.

You may set your price or request an offer.

SILVERPLATE

Grace Friar
The Silver Chest
12 Grafton Street
Greenlawn, New York 11740
(516) 261-2636

The Silver Chest is a mail-order silver matching service. As a result, Grace Friar is always in the market for silver-plated flatware and serving pieces, from one piece to a complete service for twelve, especially obsolete ornate patterns with leaves, flowers, grapes, and scrolls.

She also buys catalogs and other promotional literature that depict the product lines of various silver manufacturers.

Send the name of the maker and the pattern, along with a count of each type of piece available, and Grace will make you an offer. If you don't know the maker or pattern, make a pencil rubbing or a drawing and list those marks you are able to find. Wear on tines or bowls is acceptable if not excessive, but she does not want pitted bowls or bent tines.

ENGRAVED OR EMBOSSED PEWTER

Albert J. Phiebig
P.O. Box 352
White Plains, New York 10602
(914) 948-0138

This distinguished and well-known dealer wants to purchase rare and unusual pieces of antique American and European pewter that are "illustrated" with engraving or embossing.

He is not particularly interested in ordinary round plates but in more unusual figurals, lamps, religious pieces, and the like.

Mr. Phiebig buys primarily from dealers and expects them to set the price wanted when they contact him with a description of the item for sale. If you are an amateur private party, you may ask Mr. Phiebig for assistance in pricing. You should be aware that these items can have substantial value.

Albert Phiebig is listed in Who's Who in the East.

SILVER-PLATED FLATWARE

L.C. Fisher
Fisher Silver Exchange
P.O. Box 680042
Houston, Texas 77268-0042
(713) 353-4167

The Fisher Silver Exchange buys and sells silver-plated flatware or hollow-ware, especially old grape patterns, 1847 Rogers, Community and Holmes & Edwards brands.

Mr. Fisher also will purchase sterling tableware in discontinued patterns or in unusual serving pieces. The prices he pays are influenced by the current retail value set by silver manufacturers for comparable pieces. He says that you "will always get more than scrap prices for sterling from me."

You may request his substantial illustrated wants list, which provides examples of patterns he seeks. The Silver Exchange does not do mail appraisals but will make offers. "We need to know exactly what you have for sale, how many pieces, whether they are monogrammed, and in what condition."

The Silver Exchange has been in business more than twenty-five years and is listed in Dun & Bradstreet.

SILVER-PLATED FLATWARE AND HOLLOWWARE

Carol J. Bennett
Bennett Silvermatching
417 Marina Boulevard
Suisun City, California 94585
(707) 425-2994

For twelve years, Carol Bennett has operated a matching service for people buying or selling partial or complete sets of silver-plated flatware and hollowware "in popular patterns."

Active, inactive, or obsolete patterns may be of interest as long as they are in excellent condition and not monogrammed.

Carol wants to know the name of the manufacturer, the name of the pattern (if you know it), and a description of the number and types of pieces you have to sell. Make certain to mention any monograms, damage, or missing parts on serving pieces.

You may request a priced wants list, an appraisal, or her offer on what you have to sell. Carol regularly maintains an inventory of approximately three hundred thousand pieces and keeps extensive wants files on other buyers.

STERLING SILVER FOLDING FRUIT KNIVES

David A. Culpepper
D.A. Culpepper Mother of Pearl Co.
P.O. Box 445
Franklin, North Carolina 28734

For ten years, David Culpepper has been collecting sterling silver hallmarked fruit knives, generally the folding styles. He also buys fancy or unusual bowie knives and pocketknives.

He requests an "in-depth description" and photographs whenever possible. A photocopy machine is suggested as an easy alternative since it registers items in their exact size and pictures most engraving and design very well. Record any names, numbers, or silver hallmarks on the knives.

He prefers to have you set the price, but will make offers on desirable items. Dave's company sells mother-of-pearl and other shell for restoration of knives and other antiques.

5

The World of Work

GASOLINE PUMP GLOBES

Scott Benjamin
161 Canterbury Road
Elyria, Ohio 44035
(216) 365-6975

Scott Benjamin collects gasoline pump globes, specializing in those that are made of one piece or those with metal frames surrounding the glass inserts. He does not want later plastic globes or those with glass frames.

A good description of the type of globe and the wording on it is sufficient. Pictures are not required.

He expresses willingness to answer all inquires about buying or selling globes. You may set the price you want or ask him to make an offer.

FIRE DEPARTMENT MEMORABILIA

John Blessing
15 Park Circle Road
Middletown, Pennsylvania 17057
(717) 944-1077

John Blessing is a captain in a major Pennsylvania fire department and a serious collector of virtually anything having to do with fire departments.

Among his wants, he lists leather helmets and buckets; parade torches, lanterns, capes, belts, and the like; alarms, gongs, and indicators; badges, trophies, and awards; extinguishers and grenades; books and other fire-related paper goods; and advertising for fire apparatus, including trade cards.

He especially wants pieces marked with the name and location of a fire company. When describing, make certain to include any brand names, patent dates, serial numbers, and other identification. A photocopy of paper items is recommended. He will make offers on things he would like to purchase.

FIRE DEPARTMENTS AND FIRE INSURANCE

Ralph N. Jennings, Jr.
301 Fort Washington Avenue
Fort Washington, Pennsylvania 19034
(215) 646-7178 eves.

Ralph Jennings wants an extremely wide range of items related to fire departments and fire insurance, including, but not limited to: leather helmets, leather buckets, leather parade belts, early glass grenades, parade hats, parade capes, lanterns, lamps, torches, fire marks, fire insurance advertising signs, fire engine builders' plates, decorative panels from fire engines, badges, speaking trumpets, presentation items, books, photographs, postcards, nozzles, alarm equipment, toys, tin fire extinguishers, uniforms, uniform buttons, and "anything related to any of the above."

He requests a complete description and photograph whenever possible. He asks that you set the selling price, but will make offers if you prefer. It is difficult to authenticate pieces without actually seeing them, and shipment on approval will sometimes be necessary.

MILITARY, POLICE, AND FIRE DEPARTMENT

Jacques Noel Jacobsen, Jr.
Collectors Antiquities, Inc.
60 Manor Road
Staten Island, New York 10310
(212) 981-0973

Collectors Antiquities, Inc., buys and sells a broad range of law-and-order memorabilia:
  1. Military uniforms dating between 1776 and 1945
  2. Civil War relics of all types, including photographs
  3. Fire department collectibles, including badges, helmets, photographs, trumpets and apparatus
  4. Police department uniforms, badges, daysticks, medals, books, and photographs

If you have any of these items to sell, Jacques Jacobsen wants "an accurate description, preferably with a clear photograph or a detailed drawing." If it is a uniform, provide the color or colors of all parts. Although he has been in business for thirty years and is the author of more than fifty monographs on these collectibles, Jacques insists that you set the price. He does appraisals only for a fee. Collectors Antiquities, Inc. offers a handsomely illustrated catalog; sample copies can be ordered for $1. Perhaps they will help you price what you have.

FIRE INSURANCE

Glenn Hartley, Sr.
2859 Marlin Drive
Chamblee, Georgia 30341
(404) 451-2651

Glenn Hartley wants a selection of items related to fire insurance and fire departments, including:
  1. Nontechnical books about fires, fire insurance, or fire departments
  2. Badges, medals, or ribbons associated with fire departments or fire insurance
  3. Fire marks (metal plaques affixed to buildings to indicate that insurance was paid) and
  4. Stamps, first day covers, or cacheted (decorated) envelopes with fire-department or insurance-related themes.
  Describe thoroughly anything you wish to sell. A photocopy is recommended for decorated envelopes. Glenn will make offers.

FIRE MEMORABILIA

J. Matt Grimley
P.O. Box 244
Oakland, New Jersey 07436

Matt Grimley has a long list of fire-related items that he buys: firemen's trumpets, nozzles longer than three feet, early hand fire engines, early steam fire engines, nameplates from fire engines, fire engine lights, lanterns, elaborate helmets, presentation items or trophies, New York fire department badges, alarm equipment (including gongs with oak cases), early photographs, catalogs of fire equipment, early photographs, postcards, advertising featuring firemen, toy fire engines or firehouses, candy molds of fire engines, books on fire department history, prints, paintings, posters, and you name it.
  He requests a "complete description, photo if possible, and your telephone number." He can supply you with a wants list, and will make offers.

BARBERSHOP MEMORABILIA

Robert Blake Powell
P.O. Box 833
Hurst, Texas 76053
(817) 284-8145

Bob Powell may be the largest collector-dealer of barbershop memorabilia in the country. What he doesn't buy for his enormous collection, he will accept on consignment and sell to other collectors.

His extensive wants include virtually any good-quality item associated with barbering or barber shops: shaving mugs, barber bottles, bowls, shaving soap containers, shaving paper vases, waste jars, trade cards, photographs, catalogs, wall posters and signs, moustache curling irons, moustache wax molds, straight razors, razor sets, razor boxes, razor racks, razor strops, tokens, tools, safety razors, razor blades, and what have you.

He wants barber supply catalogs and items from the following companies: Koken and Boppert, Koken, Kochs, Kern, Melchior, Archer, Hanson, Buerger, and Berninghaus.

Your description should include all colors, words, marks, and defects. Photocopies or photographs are strongly suggested for best offer.

BARBER BOTTLES AND MUGS

Burton Handelsman
18 Hotel Drive
White Plains, New York 10605
(914) 428-4480

Burt Handelsman wants to buy pre-1920 barber bottles and shaving mugs that are adorned with the name of the previous owner and a picture of his occupation or hobby.

He also buys barbershop shaving mug racks and old barbershop catalogs that contain pictures of mugs.

He requests a thorough description of the design on the mug, preferably with a close-up color slide. Make a sketch showing what is taking place in the design on the mug. Include the owner's name and a drawing of any marks or names on the bottom of the mug. Make certain to describe the condition of the name, the design, and the cup itself. Note all wear, fading, or chips.

Burt has been collecting for thirty years, is president of the Shaving Mug Collectors Society, and will make a fair offer for what you describe well.

DRUGSTORE

Matt James
2068 Hampton Hill Drive
Memphis, Tennessee 38134
(901) 386-4733

Matt James is a pharmacist who collects items related to his profession.

Although he does buy a number of advertising displays and signs, he expresses particular interest in the various types of fancy glass once so popular in drugstores, including show globes, show jars, glass-stoppered apothecary bottles, large perfume bottles, and other bottles, jars, and related equipment. You may request his illustrated wants list if you are uncertain about what you have.

Provide him with a sketch, indicating the overall dimensions. Describe the color(s) and identify all trademarks, numbers, maker's marks, or other writing or embossing. You must set the price wanted.

DRUGSTORE AND MEDICAL ITEMS

Charles G. Richardson
Richardson's Antiques
710 King's Lane
Fort Washington, Maryland 20744

Charles Richardson collects all types of drugstore (apothecary) items, including tools and implements of the pharmacist, drugstore glassware, pill machines, scales, leech jars, health care items sold by the pharmacist for home use, doctors' medical bags, and other medical and surgical items.

Send him a complete description, including the material from which your item is made, dimensions, and condition. He does not have a wants list and does not make offers. If you want an item appraised, there is a fee and you must include a sharp close-up photograph.

THE WORLD OF WORK

BOOKS ON EYES

Dr. James P. Leeds
2470 East 116th Street
Carmel, Indiana 46032
(317) 253-1479

Books related to the eye, optics, or vision are a natural for someone in practice as an optometrist for nearly forty years. Dr. Leeds wants fiction and nonfiction, as long as it is "even remotely" related to the eye or vision.

Provide him with standard bibliographic information: title, author, publisher, place of publication, and date. You may set the price or ask him to make an offer.

MEDICINE

Barry Wiedenkeller
The Printers' Devil
1 Claremont Court
Arlington, Massachusetts 02174
(617) 646-6762

Antique medical books and instruments are Barry Wiedenkeller's interest.

Since he includes medical books, ephemera, instruments, artifacts, photographs, artwork, and coins and medals among items he is willing to buy, you might try him with anything old related to medicine.

Tell him what it is, and its dimensions, condition, and price. He expects any items purchased to be returnable if he's not satisifed.

Barry has published reprints of two early books on medical instruments, and is a member of numerous groups including the American Association for the History of Medicine.

BOOKS ABOUT MEDICINE

G.S.T. Cavanagh
Old Galen's Books
P.O. Box 3044
Durham, North Carolina 27705
(919) 489-6246

G.S.T. Cavanagh wants books, documents, and instruments related to medicine and its history before 1900.

As curator of a major university medical library and a dealer in medical miscellany for nearly fifteen years, he is well able to assist you in identifying what you have and its value.

Provide him a complete description or standard bibliographic information as necessary.

CHIROPRACTIC

Mel Rosenthal, D.C.
507 South Maryland Avenue
Wilmington, Delaware 19804
(302) 994-0874

Mel Roenthal is a practicing chiropractor, and for nearly ten years has been building a historical library of books and memorabilia of his profession. He is particularly interested in obtaining items from before 1940.

Provide him with a photocopy of the title page and a description of condition. If you cannot have a copy made, accurately write down the author, title, name and location of publisher, and all copyright and printing information found on the front or back of the title page. If the book has illustrations, give him a rough count. Describe or sketch memorabilia you have to sell.

Mel can provide a wants list, and he is willing to make offers on unpriced items for sale.

ARCHITECTURE

Robert M. Des Marais
618 West Foster Avenue
State College, Pennsylvania 16801
(814) 237-7141

Bob Des Marais buys a wide range of items connected with architecture:

1. Architecture, building, structural engineering, and carpentry books; catalogs, manuals, pattern books, and guides
2. Biographies of architects and their works, and general histories of architects and architecture
3. Early American drawing and watercolor instruction books
4. Popular magazines (1800-1920) containing features on architecture, designers, and construction
5. European books in any language on these topics
6. Architects' drawings, renderings, and specifications
7. Early brass and wooden drafting instruments

"A short description of the item is sufficient, as long as you indicate size, date, author, number of pages, illustrations, and condition and completeness of the item. Some incomplete items can still have value." Include an SASE and he will respond to all inquiries. He wants the seller to set the price, but reserves the right to offer more or less than the asking price.

AUTOMATIC SPRINKLER HEADS

Warren H. Pine
RFD 1, Box 284
Buskirk, New York 12028

"I collect automatic sprinkler heads that were, and still are, used to put out fires in many large buildings," writes Warren Pine.

According to Warren, brass and chrome-plated sprinklers have been used to protect against fires in public buildings since the late 1870s. From the beginning, each sprinkler head has been marked with the name of the maker, the date of manufacture, and the temperature at which it was set to go off.

That's the information Warren wants, along with a sketch. If you know whether it was intended to hang up or hang down, tell him. "The older heads are the most interesting," he notes, but he will be glad to make offers on any head that is well described, and pictured.

WOODEN PRINTER'S TYPE

Nancy and Irving Silverman
Nancy Neale Typecraft
P.O. Box 40
Roslyn, New York 11576
(516) 621-7130

Nancy Neale Typecraft sells antique wooden printer's type and is always in the market for type, from an entire shopful to a single letter in an unusual font (type face).

The Silvermans also want selected items of pre-1940 printer's memorabilia, such as fancy initials, copper and zinc engravings, lithographic stones, decorative wooden borders, dingbats, printer's advertising, old trade posters, type specimen books, and other ephemera.

If you know your way around a print shop, Irving asks that you make an inventory and pull proofs of sample material. If you don't, do the best you can and include your telephone number. The Silvermans describe themselves as the country's largest buyers of printing ephemera, are pleased to send you a wants list, and will make offers for good items.

PRINTING AND BOOKBINDING

Frank D. Walsh, III
Yesteryear Book Shop, Inc.
256 East Paces Ferry Road, NE
Atlanta, Georgia 30305
(404) 237-0163

Antique printing presses and "anything" to do with the art of printing or bookbinding are of possible interest to Frank Walsh.

"Anything" includes wooden type, foundry type, litho stones, engraving plates, engraving presses, book presses, embossing tools, and all the other smaller tools of the trade. "I am particularly interested in purchasing 19th-century Washington hand presses. These can be rather large and weigh upwards of 1,000 pounds. I am also interested in buying a vast variety of other old styles of printing presses."

He point out that presses can range from small table-model card presses that look like children's toys to giant old-time Washingtons.

"Please correspond or call if you have anything you think I would be interested in buying. I will sometimes commit to buy on the basis of just a good clear photograph." It would be better, though, to send the manufacturer's name whenever possible, the size of the printing surface, and any other information appearing on the press. Give the approximate weight and describe its mechanism if you can.

Frank will make offers and arrange for pickup of larger items. The First National Bank of Atlanta (Atlanta, Georgia 30302) is cited as a reference.

SURVEYING

Michael S. Manier
P.O. Box 100
Houston, Missouri 65483
(417) 967-2777

Mike Manier is a civil engineer and land surveyor seeking antique items of his profession.

His wants include brass or wood compasses, theodolites, levels, circumferentors, transits, and wire like-type measuring chains. He is particularly interested in American makers and in anything out of the ordinary. He is also interested in compasses or transits with solar attachments.

"A photograph is most helpful, along with basic dimensions, any markings, numbers, etc. Is the item in a box? Are there any trade cards affixed to the case, inside or outside? Of course, the more detail, the better."

EXPLOSIVES

George G. Kass
P.O. Box 541
Spring Arbor, Michigan 49283
(517) 750-1011

George Kass wants to buy dynamite and blasting cap cans and boxes from any country in the world.

His collecting specialty for many years has been small arms ammunition, so he is always in the market for single specimens or entire boxes of unusual or obsolete ammunition, including rimfire, centerfire, and shotshells. He also collects empty boxes from small arms and shotgun ammunition. All catalogs, advertising, and other literature pertaining to dynamite, blasting caps, or ammunition is of interest as well.

Kass wants you to provide a sketch of the box or can, noting the colors, size, and condition. If you have ammunition or casings, he wants to know the markings on the base, the case material, and the dimensions. Everything should be priced, as he does not make offers on items through the mail.

GOLD MINING MEMORABILIA

Richard and Susan Sisti
Ramapaugh Trading Company
P.O. Box 363
Newfoundland, New Jersey 07435

Rick and Susan Sisti collect the history and artifacts of gold mining in the eastern United States and Canada.

Their interests include popular and technical books, pamphlets, maps, claim deeds, letters, stock certificates, and photographs pertaining to gold mining east of the Mississippi.

When describing books, you should include the title, author, publisher, date and place of publication, and information about the type and number of maps and illustrations. If any other paper good is offered, a photocopy is almost essential.

Rick and Susan will provide you with a wants list upon request, and will make offers on unpriced items they can use.

MINER'S LAMPS

Ron Bommarito
Genoa Museum
P.O. Box 114
Genoa, Nevada 89411
(702) 782-3893

For display in this museum of mining and western artifacts, Ron Bommarito wants to buy early underground miner's lamps, including candlesticks, oil cap lamps, candle lanterns, frog lamps, French tunnel lamps, carbide lamps, and safety lamps.

He would like you to send him a good sketch that shows the dimensions. If a maker is indicated, or if there are other dates or numbers, make certain to tell him. Describe the condition accurately.

Ron would prefer that you set the price you want, but he will make offers to amateur sellers.

LABOR UNION MEMORABILIA

Scott Molloy
P.O. Box 2650
Providence, Rhode Island 02907
(401) 461-0900

Scott Molloy is a longtime collector of items associated with labor unions.

Wanted items include pins, badges, ribbons, books, pamphlets, magazines, and virtually all other paper material that discusses unions and union activities.

Describe what you have carefully and include a photocopy whenever possible. He will make an offer for items he can use, although you are welcome to price what you have.

PADLOCKS

John L. Kosiba
RD 5
Amsterdam, New York 12010
(518) 842-4046

John Kosiba buys old and unusual padlocks, locking mechanisms, handcuffs, leg irons, and balls and chains. "No repros," he warns, and all items must be at least one hundred years old.

He wants a photograph or good sketch to accompany a description, including whatever you know of the item's history. Include an SASE and John will make an offer.

GLASS INSULATORS

Claude A. Wambold
H & W Antiques
450 Perkiomenville Road
Perkiomenville, Pennsylvania 18074
(215) 234-8413

Claude Wambold asks for glass insulators, both threaded and threadless.
"A complete description of the item is necessary. A good clear photo would be best, but equally useful is a drawing which includes measurements, description of all markings and embossing, color, and notation of any damage."
Claude has more than a decade's experience with insulators and will be pleased to identify what you have and make an offer. You may wish to write for his wants list.

GLASS INSULATORS

L.L. "Len" Linscott
Line Jewels
3557 Nicklaus Drive
Titusville, Florida 32780
(305) 267-9170

Len Linscott is a collector-dealer of glass telephone and telegraph insulators. He wants to obtain both threaded and threadless insulators that are embossed, especially those made of milk glass or those in shades of cobalt blue, amber, or purple.
If you have insulators for sale, Len encourages you to obtain Marion Milholland's Most About Glass Insulators from your local library and describe them according to numbers assigned in that book. If you can't do this, make the best sketch you can, noting all words and numbers. Tell whether it is threaded or threadless, its color, and its height and diameter.
Len is willing to appraise or make offers on clearly described insulators for sale.

MILK AND DAIRY MEMORABILIA

Ralph S. Riovo
686 Franklin St.
Alburtis, Pennsylvania 18011
(215) 966-2536

Ralph Riovo claims to buy "almost anything" marked with the words "milk" or "dairy," but shows particular interest in bottles used by corporations or institutions that bottled their own milk.

He also wants colored or unusually shaped milk bottles, bottles with patriotic slogans, pictorial bottles, milk bottle miniatures used as toys or salt-and-pepper shakers. restaurant creamers, and home cream separators. He also wants caps, calendars, tokens, trays, thermometers, signs, and trade cards that were given away or used by dairies, especially Borden's.

Describe the item, including dimensions and wording. Note all damage. It is suggested that a photograph would be useful when selling colored items. Tell Ralph the price you want, although he will make offers.

BEEKEEPING

Anthony J. Zalvis III
P.O. Box 51
Wellesley Hills, Massachusetts 02181
(617) 881-5108

Anthony Zalvis collects all types of beekeeping and honey tools and equipment, including old bee skeps (the domed straw hives), pottery hives, swarm boxes, and other bee containers. "No new woodenware, please," he says, but small tools and gadgets, especially the unusual, are always of interest.

Honeypots of glass, tin, crockery, "or anything else" are wanted, as are books, catalogs, magazines, prints, photographs, and paintings that depict tools or hives.

Describe everything completely, including all dates. Photocopies and photographs are always helpful. State condition, listing defects such as cracks, chips, rust, rot, abrasions, and missing parts. "I do not want junk, but some items are still acceptable even if not in perfect condition." He goes on, "Please keep the item in the condition you find it. Do not try to clean or polish an item." He will make offers.

STOCKS, BONDS, AND CHECKS

Phyllis L. Barella
Buttonwood Galleries
P.O. Box 1006, Throggs Neck Station
New York, New York 10465
(212) 823-1523

A relatively new dealer in fiscal paper, Phyllis Barella wants ornate pre-1930 stocks, bonds, and checks, especially those from railroad, mining, oil, and automobile companies, as well as the banking industry.

When writing, tell her the name of the company and the date of issuance. If you have more than one item, let her know the quantities available. Make certain to describe the pictorial vignettes.

She is a member of more than half a dozen organizations related to money and paper collecting. She has no wants list but will make offers if you include a photocopy of your stocks or other item(s).

BUSINESS CARDS

Steve Collins
Bizcards, International
P.O. Box 721632
Houston, Texas 77272

Steve Collin wants business, name, and calling cards, especially the old and unusual. He writes, "The majority of business cards are common and ordinary, and do nothing but expand the quantity of my collection. Older cards are harder to come by and therefore command a higher price. Cards that seem fancy, foreign, unusual, or humorous to you may not be to me, so everything that is sent is judged subjectively. When in doubt, inquire."

He is not interested in postcards or greeting cards, but says, "Occasionally some business cards take that form or size." He buys duplicates and multiples of cards, but only at a substantially reduced price unless they are rare.

He would like a photocopy and your price, if you have one in mind. He warns, "A seller should not hope to get rich from a dozen cards. Business cards do not have the value of baseball gum cards."

ILLUSTRATED LETTERHEADS

E. Scott Pattison
2382 Mangrum Drive
Dunedin, Florida 33528
(813) 734-3285

Scott Pattison wants business letters and invoices (bills) from before 1920 that have illustrations engraved on the letterhead, such as rural scenes, equipment, animals, ships, etc. He does not want to buy ordinary letterheads without pictorials. The contents of the letter are not important, but the illustration should be well engraved or lithographed.

Scott has been collecting for nearly fifteen years. He will make offers if a photocopy is sent or will pay postage if items are shipped on approval.

STOCK CERTIFICATES

Ken Prag
P.O. Box 531
Burlingame, California 94010
(415) 566-6400

Ken Page is a full-time collector-dealer in obsolete stock and bond certificates. He seeks pre-1920 certificates with elaborate vignettes or engravings.

He also buys and sells railroad timetables and passes from before 1950; stereoviews of California and other western states; and Wells Fargo checks, letters, and other financial documents.

Send a photocopy of what you have. "Please include your phone number so that I may call and find out the information I need."

CHECKS AND OTHER FISCAL PAPER

Neil Sowards
A-Z Coins & Stamps
548 Home Avenue
Fort Wayne, Indiana 46807
(219) 745-3658

Checks are Neil Soward's chief interest, although he also buys a wide range of other fiscal paper: bills of exchange, drafts, cashier's checks, promissory notes, ration checks, salesmen's samples of checks, canal paper, steamboat paper, stocks, and bonds, among other items.

Make certain to include an SASE and a photocopy if you want an answer from this veteran of fifteen years' collecting. He will make offers.

Neil wrote the Handbook of Check Collecting, now out of print.

CHECKWRITERS AND CHECK PROTECTORS

William Feigin
Dualoy, Inc.
45 West 34th Street
New York, New York 10001

William Feigin buys checkwriters and check protectors, machines that perforate or print numbers on checks or otherwise mark or deface them to prevent fraud. Unless it is something very unusual, only those from 1900 or before are wanted.

"I also buy very old office equipment such as fasteners, date stamps, etc."

He requests a complete description accompanied by a sketch or photograph. Indicate whether it appears to be working, whether it is in its original container, and whether there are any dates, patent numbers, or other lettering. He will make offers.

CASH REGISTERS

Kenneth Konet
119 Powdermill Road
Morris Plains, New Jersey 07950
(201) 267-1075

Ken Konet buys antique brass, wood, or cast iron cash registers in any condition, since broken or damaged machines can be used for parts.

He also wants "amount purchased" signs that once occupied the tops of cash registers, and any cash register advertising or memorabilia. He prefers early wooden registers with inlaid cabinets, dial-type registers, registers that ring only to $1, and large multi-drawer cash registers.

Describe your register, giving brand and model name when available. Make certain to mention all defects, and include your phone number when you write. Ken typically makes arrangements to pick up registers he buys.

BRASS CASH REGISTERS

Lt. Col. B.A. Gill
P.O. Box 381
Clifton Park, New York 12065
(518) 371-6035

For thirty years, Colonel Gill has been collecting brass cash registers and related items, including sample registers, salesmen's literature and catalogs, awards given to cash register salesmen, and photographs of registers in use in stores. He also wants paper goods and other ephemera related to the National Cash Register Company (NCR).

He would like to know the brand name and the model or serial number of the machine. Describe it well, including a sketch or a good clear photograph. He will pay all shipping expenses if he buys your machine, but under most circumstances he requires you to be responsible for crating. Everything is negotiable, including the price. National Commercial Bank on State Street in Albany is cited as a reference.

In addition to cash registers, Colonel Gill buys memorabilia of Irving Berlin, including pictorial sheet music.

TYPEWRITERS AND MEMORABILIA

Paul Lippman
1216 Garden Street
Hoboken, New Jersey 07030
(201) 656-5278

Office and portable typewriters made in the U.S. before 1920, including "what laymen may regard as toy typewriters," are his main interest. Paul Lippman also buys typing accessories and "almost anything relating to typewriters of that period," such as user's manuals, advertising, repair and servicing tools, typing tables (especially those resembling sewing stands), typewriter business magazines, typewriter ribbon tins, and typing textbooks printed before 1910.

He also expresses interest in related pre-1925 office equipment such as devices for duplicating, adding, or calculating.

If you have a typewriter or other early machine to sell, supply its name and any model designation that appears. Indicate whether it has a case, base, or lid. Say whether it works or doesn't work, is complete or incomplete, is clean or filthy, and whether there is any rust. If you supply this information, he says a photo isn't necessary. If you have anything else to sell, a "reasonable description" is considered adequate, but make certain to note all defects. Include an SASE, and "please don't try to tell me how old or valuable it is." Paul knows value (or lack of it) and will make offers accordingly.

EARLY ELECTRICAL DEVICES

William F. Edwards
State Road
Richmond, Massachusetts 01254
(413) 698-3458

Bill Edwards wants pre-1900 electrical devices manufactured by Stanley Electric, Edison General Electric, Thomson Houston, Sprague, and Westinghouse.

Items he buys include small open frame bipolar motors and generators, electric fans with brass blades, carbon arc street lamps, switchboard voltmeters and ammeters, transformers, watt-hour meters, and circuit breakers. He also wants paper ephemera related to the companies and devices listed.

"I would like," he advises, "all nameplate data including patent dates and numbers, the size or weight of the item, its condition, and a short description or photograph. All letters will be answered and photographs will be returned. Please price what you have."

TYPEWRITERS

Joel G. Andrews, Jr.
206 Sycamore Drive
Florence, South Carolina 29501

Joel Andrews has been a collector for more than fifteen years and "will consider" all makes of pre-1925 typewriters except Corona, Royal, or Underwood.

He also wants old books on the industry and inventions, and U.S. Patent Office Gazettes.

When describing a typewriter, give him the name, the model number, the date if you know it, the number of keys, and an idea of condition. If any parts are damaged or missing, let him know. For books, the title, author, year printed, number of pages, and condition are required.

Include an SASE and Joel will make offers.

6
Advertising Signs and Packaging

CRACKER JACK

Wes Johnson
P.O. Box 10247
Louisville, Kentucky 40210
(502) 776-2481

Wes Johnson buys items associated with Cracker Jack, including toys, premiums, point-of-sale incentives, packages, stationery, and other older marked pieces.

Most items are relatively inexpensive and financially not worth a great deal of your fuss. There are a few that are quite good, however, so it could pay to ask.

It is suggested that if you have items for sale, you contact Wes, then ship on approval. He will send a check for what your items are worth.

AUNT JEMIMA

Ted Smith
Fun House
724 Fillmore Street
San Francisco, California 94117
(415) 864-6386

Ted Smith is a ten-year veteran collector-dealer who wants to buy store displays or oversize boxes featuring Aunt Jemima. He also wants black mammy cookie jars and original boxes of Aunt Jemima Pancake Mix.

Send him a photocopy or snapshot plus an accurate description, especially regarding condition. He will make offers, but requests you tell him how much you want.

WEST VIRGINIA GROCERS

Tom and Deena Caniff
1223 Oak Grove Avenue
Steubenville, Ohio 43952
(614) 282-8918

Tom and Deena Caniff want bottles, jars, tins, tip trays, pottery water coolers, and advertising from the following West Virginia grocery companies: J.W. Hunter Co., Exley Watkins & Co., McMechen's Co., Flaccus Bros., E.C. Flaccus Co., Flaccus & Elliott Co., and any other Wheeling food packing company.

"These companies advertised extensively and sold widely throughout the East and even on the west coast, packing their mustard, catsup, pickles, and other foodstuffs in fancy containers such as gunboat covered dishes, stag- and dog-topped covered dishes, pottery mugs, pottery water coolers, Uncle Sam figural bottles, and fancily embossed jars made in clear, emerald green amber, and milk glass."

When writing them about an item for sale, please include:
1. The type of item: bottle, jar, labeled tin can, etc.
2. The size, dimensions, and capacity
3. Description of any labels, exact wording of embossing
4. What it's made of: glass, tin, pottery, etc.
5. Color of glass, lettering, etc.
6. Condition of the item, including all cracks, chips, stains, missing lids, scratches, etc.

"We will attempt to answer all questions to the best of our ability, and if we are unable to help will attempt to forward questions to someone in the bottle or jar hobby who can help." The Caniffs are available for appraisals and will make offers on unpriced items you might wish to sell.

TIN ADVERTISING

Burton Spiller
300 White Spruce Boulevard
Rochester, New York 14623
(716) 424-6400

Burt Spiller buys advertising signs, trays, and tip trays manufactured of tin before 1925.

The advertising can be for beer, soft drinks, whiskey, smoking tobacco, or patent medicine. He also wants tin cans and boxes used for tea, coffee, smoking tobacco, candy, coconut, peanuts, and peanut butter.

"I want the seller to fully describe the item as to condition, measurements, and all wording and colors that are part of any bottle, flask, fruit jar, or advertising. The asking price would be helpful." He will make offers, though.

CAMPBELL SOUP, MORTON'S SALT, AND THE PILLSBURY DOUGHBOY

Linda Woodward
6720 Crest Avenue
Riverside, California 92503
(714) 687-0868

Linda Woodward wants specific advertising ephemera from three prominent advertisers and their campaigns:
1. The Campbell Kids and other Campbell Soup items
2. The umbrella girl and other Morton's Salt items
3. Pillsbury Doughboy signs, ads, statues, containers, etc.

Linda also wants books, toys, paper dolls, and the like that feature Dolly Dingle.

When you describe any of these, make a sketch showing the main pictorial features and the major lettering. Photocopies are helpful. Give the dimensions and estimate the age. She can provide you with a wants list, and will make offers.

DEL MONTE CANNED FOODS

Harvey Halpin
1141 Verdemar Drive
Alameda, California 94501
(415) 521-0840

Harvey Halpin wants anything associated with the Del Monte canned food operation, including advertising, cans, photographs, labels, booklets, articles, and ledgers.

In the past, the company was also known as California Packing Corporation and California Fruit Canners Association, and ephemera under those names is also sought. In general, Harvey is most interested in very early items, and almost nothing after 1940.

If you are offering ads, he wants the exact date of the magazine and would prefer that you send a photocopy or good sketch. Describe other items appropriately. He will answer all mail accompanied by an SASE and will make offers, but prefers that you price what you have.

TIN AND MISCELLANEOUS ADVERTISING

Andy and Irene Kaufman
4th Dimension Collectibles
P.O. Box 383
Manchester, New Hampshire 03105
(603) 622-7404

The Kaufmans buy and sell pre-World War I tin advertising, tin signs, tin boxes, tin trays, dye cabinets, syrup dispensers, string holders, china, trade cards, and paper and cardboard signs with colorful pictures and designs.

All items must be in perfect or near-perfect condition. They prefer that the product being advertised also be pictured, but it is not necessary.

The Kaufmans want you to describe the graphics and the colors involved. A slide would be greatly appreciated on more valuable items. Also state the dimensions, the material(s) from which the item is made, and the condition. "Write first, before shipping any items to us," Andy warns.

DIXIE CUP PICTURE LIDS

Stephen A. Leone
94 Pond Street
Salem, New Hampshire 03079
(603) 898-4900 eves.

Steve Leone saves Dixie cup picture lids of movie stars, cowboys, presidents, circuses, war scenes, and the like produced and franchised by the Individual Drinking Cup Co. of Easton, Pennsylvania, later known as the Dixie Co.

Steve is also interested in premiums, advertising, and literature from Dixie, and selected lids and items from other makers of paper cups.

Provide him with the diameter of the lid, its color, wording, and picture. Note whether the tab is missing. Describe condition carefully. Send photocopies whenever possible. He will make offers for lids that he can use or trade with other collectors.

C.D. KENNY CO.

Paul D. "Kenny" Waclawski
8823 Blairwood Road B-2
Baltimore, Maryland 21236
(301) 256-4775

Paul Waclawski wants anything given away by the C.D. Kenny Co., a dealer in coffee, tea, and sugar between 1872 and 1934.

The Kenny Co. was a great believer in promotional items, so it gave away tip trays, toys, kitchen gadgets, match holders, toothpick holders, trade cards, pocket mirrors, small games, tin plates, paper fans, calendars, buttons, banks, china figurines, dolls, and many other items. Waclawski wants these, plus signs, tins, cans, boxes, or other items manufactured or used by the C.D. Kenny Co.

Include the size, material, and condition in your description. A photograph or photocopy is suggested, but a good sketch will do. Condition is very important, and only mint or near-mint items are wanted.

STATE FARM INSURANCE CO.

Ken D. Jones
100 Manor Drive
Columbia, Missouri 65201

Ken Jones wants memorabilia from the State Farm Insurance Co. but only that dating between 1922 and 1952.

Items wanted include brass bumper and radiator emblems, signs, watch fobs, mechanical or bullet pencils, pocketknives, banks, belt buckles, tape measures, thermometers, match holders, ashtrays, and other items.

"The older bumper and radiator emblems are colored gold, black, and red. They read 'Protection-Service, State Farm Mutual Auto Ins. Co' and have a picture of an old Buick in the center. That was replaced by the three-oval emblem, which pictures a car, a fire helmet, and a cornucopia. I don't want the emblems that just have words."

Ken asks for a complete and accurate description of the item for sale, including its condition. "I feel it is the sellers' responsibility to tell me what they want for an item. I'd rather not make offers."

COLT FIREARMS CO.

Dr. Johnny Spellman
10806 North Lamar
Austin, Texas 78753
(512) 258-6910 eves.

Johnny Spellman wants to buy any advertising or other memorabilia related to the Colt Firearms Co. or any of its subsidiaries, such as Noark, Coltrock, Autosan, and Baxter Steam Engine. Any item marked "Colt" is likely to be of interest, including archery equipment, knives, handcuffs, tobacco humidors, holsters, and other products.

In addition, he wants memorabilia associated with Sam Colt, including photographs, autographs, documents, etc.

When offering books or other paper items, it is extremely helpful if you send a photocopy. He prefers that you price what you have, but in some instances will make offers.

7
Sports, Cards and Gambling

POKER CHIPS

Dale Seymour
P.O. Box 10888
Palo Alto, California 94303
(415) 948-0949

Dale Seymour buys antique poker chips made of ivory, mother-of-pearl, bone, or clay. "I don't want plain chips, plastic chips, or paper chips," he emphasizes.

If you want to sell chips, send him a sample. If you prefer, you may send a good rubbing or photocopy. Indicate the number and color of chips you have. Don't forget to describe the box or the holder, if there is one.

Dale can provide an illustrated wants list of poker chips, and he is willing to make offers.

SLOT MACHINES

Joel Gilgoff
G.A.M.E.S.
18701-10 Hatteras Street
Tarzana, California 91356

Coin-operated machines, especially slot machines, have been Joel's passion for more than a decade, and he claims his store is "the world's largest buyer and seller of antique slot machines."

The folks at G.A.M.E.S. want to know the brand name and model number, as well as all damage, missing parts, etc. It is advisable to send a clear photograph along with your inquiry.

Joel prefers that you establish what you would like for your machine, but indicates that he will make offers on unpriced machines.

SLOT AND OTHER COIN-OPERATED MACHINES

Ted Salveson
P.O. Box 602
569 Kansas SE
Huron, South Dakota 57350
(605) 352-3870

Ted Salveson buys slot machines, jukeboxes, pinball machines, gumballs, and person-weighing scales. Better machines do not need to be operating or complete, because he also buys parts and supplies for all coin-operated machines.

"Coin-operated collectibles can range anywhere from an old $50 gumball machine to a perfectly restored 1946 Wurlitzer Model 1015 jukebox worth $8,000."

Ted has more than thirty years' experience working with coin-ops, as collectors call them. He is the publisher of an information-packed monthly newsletter about jukeboxes and slots.

Give him a complete description and an indication of whether it works. Whatever names and identifying marks you can find should be included. Send photos if possible. Offers can be requested.

SLOT MACHINES AND OTHER COIN-OPS

Fred Ryan
The Slot Closet
7217 North Jersey
Portland, Oregon 97203
(503) 286-3597

Fred Ryan is primarily interested in slot machines, but will purchase most coin-operated machines and amusement park devices, regardless of condition, if priced reasonably.

He will consider arcade machines, vending devices, pintables, jukeboxes, gambling equipment, carnival devices, and parts, catalogs, manuals, magazines, literature, or promotional material for any of these. Fred also buys photographs of any of these in use, especially saloon interior photos with gambling devices on the counter.

Describe what you have as completely as possible, including an estimate of size and weight. A photograph or good sketch is important. "I will answer all mail and will provide a fair and reasonable offer. I furnish shipping instructions and pay all shipping expenses, of course."

PUNCHBOARDS

James Akers, Jr.
5182 Phantom Court
Columbia, Maryland 21044
(301) 730-7788

Jim Akers buys punchboards made before 1960, especially those dating from before 1930.

"Desirable items include boards with mutoscope pictures, boards with the actual product prizes still on them, and boards showing product pictures. Punchboards should not be punched."

Provide the name of the game (if it has one), a description of the face of the board, its dimensions, age, and condition. "Be specific," he requests, "as to any damage, soil, or defects." If the board has prizes on it, please describe them. Also indicate whether the writing on the back of the board was done by ballpoint or ink pen. It is advisable to take a good clear photograph or make a photocopy of any board you wish to sell. He will make offers.

PLAYING AND TAROT CARDS

Stuart R. Kaplan
U.S. Games Systems, Inc.
38 East 32nd Street
New York, NY 10016
(212) 685-4300

Stuart Kaplan buys pre-1900 playing, Tarot, and fortune telling cards and books on cards, in English or any other language.

When writing, indicate how many cards are in the deck and the name of the card manufacturer (if it can be found). Include a description of any tax stamp on the package. A statement of condition is essential. A photocopy of a few cards, showing the back of one, and the face of a variety of aces and picture cards, is advised.

Book descriptions should include author, title, publisher, date, and notation of illustrations. Indicate all wear or damage to pages, covers, or binding.

He has an extensive wants list available. He prefers you to establish an asking price, but will make offers when complete information is supplied.

PLAYING CARDS

Edy J. Chandler
P.O. Box 20664
Houston, Texas 77063
(713) 668-7864 or 527-8402

Edy Chandler buys complete mint-condition decks of playing cards that contain designs on the front or the back of Uncle Sam and patriotic themes, especially World War II; supernatural and mythical creatures; space and science fiction; women's rights; pin-up art; Art Deco women; airlines; blimps; motorcycles; Planter's peanuts; Oriental art; Felix the Cat; and various specific fairs and exhibitions. Write for her wants list.

She also wants cards that have black faces with red and white or yellow suits instead of the normal black and red on white. Decks that incorporate the suits into a design on the face of the card are also desired.

In addition, she would like decks of cards with backs painted by Erte, Leyendecker, Dali, Szyx, Rockwell Kent, Don Blanding, Vasarelly, Peter Max, Artzybashev, Vargas, Petty, and Escher.

OLD PLAYING CARDS AND GAMBLING

Gene Hochman
Full House
29 Hampton Terrace
Livingston, New Jersey 07039
(201) 992-0084

Single decks or enormous collections, Gene Hochman has been buying old playing cards for thirty-five years.

He also wants pre-1940 books on cards or gambling, gambling-related memorabilia, and gambling devices other than coin-operated machines. Trade catalogs or any advertising for playing cards, gambling items, and cheating devices are also wanted.

Send brief description, accompanied by a photocopy of the face of the ace of spades and a picture card or two, "That, and an SASE if you want an answer," he advises.

Gene is the author of numerous books and articles on playing cards and has been conducting five mail auctions each year of cards and gambling devices.

GREEN BAY PACKERS PROGRAMS

Larry Setaro
6 Concord Road
Danbury, Connecticut 06810
(203) 743-4094

Larry Setaro collects programs, schedules, yearbooks, posters, press guides, and other historical paper memorabilia from the Green Bay Packers football team.

"My seventeen-page trade and wants listing gives a complete, updated look at my current needs as well as those items I have available for trade." His wants are extensive but specific, so it is advisable to write if you have more than a few Packer items. He is mostly interested in things from the 1940s and 1950s, although any Green Bay football items predating the Packers are also considered.

Specify the names of the teams represented, the date (including day, month, and year), the game site (when applicable), and the condition of the item. Set a price or request an offer. Let him know if you would be interested in trading for other similar football items.

BOXING MEMORABILIA

Jerome Shochet
6144 Oakland Mills Road
Sykesville, Maryland 21784
(301) 795-5879

Jerry Shochet has been one of the world's largest dealers in boxing material for forty years, and is always seeking boxing memorabilia of all types.

He lists books, magazines, posters, programs, tickets, autographs, photographs, scrapbooks, films, and "anything else having to do with boxing" as his wants. He can supply a detailed list of more than fifty books on boxing he will buy.

Send "a general description of the item, its age, condition, and price." He will make offers on items he can use.

BASEBALL MEMORABILIA

Robert Sevchuk
Baseball Card Collectors Exchange
P.O. Box 234
Centereach, New York 11720
(516) 822-4089 days

Bob Sevchuk runs a specialty shop devoted to baseball memorabilia, so he buys the following items for resale:
  1. Baseball cards, from the 19th century to 1975
  2. Paper memorabilia such as guides, programs and autographs
  3. Three-dimensional baseball memorabilia, including statues, pins, buttons, uniforms, "and almost anything related to baseball"
  4. Advertising pieces featuring baseball, including signs, product labels, testimonials, magazine ads, etc.
He wants a description of the item, accompanied by a photocopy whenever practical. He would like to know the year it is from and the exact condition it is in. If you can, he requests that you place a value on what you have and offer it priced. He will make offers, however.

BASEBALL, FOOTBALL, AND BOXING

John Buonaguidi
738 Daffodil Way
Concord, California 94518
(415) 827-3707

"I buy a multitude of items related to baseball, football, and boxing. I pay premium prices for 19th-century items, but collect 20th-century items as well."

Among the items John Buonaguidi most wants are display posters showing athletes doing testimonials for various products; early baseball cards; fight posters; early photographs and autographs; and equipment, uniforms, and other apparel worn by early professional players.

John has been buying baseball items through the mail for nearly three decades. He asks for a complete description and the condition. "If possible, I would like to know how much the person would like for the item, although this is not mandatory, as I will still make a fair offer." Include an SASE, please.

OLYMPIC GAMES MEMORABILIA

John and Virginia Torney
P.O. Box 417
Los Alamitos, California 90720
(213) 430-9261

The Torneys want Olympic memorabilia from all summer and winter games.

They are interested in medals, pins, badges, documents, flags, uniforms, books, programs, tickets, porcelain and glassware, photographs, autographs, first day covers, official publications, ornaments and decorations, souvenirs, and what have you.

Please send a photo, illustration, or rubbing along with your description. Include measurements, color, material from which it is made, condition, and asking price. They do not make offers.

John (a college professor) and Virginia (a high school teacher) have been collecting for twenty years and own the country's largest private collection of Olympic memorabilia.

ARCHERY

David C. Sterling
The Toxophilite Collector
57 Spring Glen Drive
Granby, Connecticut 06035
(203) 653-3319

Dave Sterling buys and sells antique bows, arrows, crossbows, thumb rings, and other archery equipment. He also deals in books, catalogs, pamphlets, advertising, prints, photographs, correspondence, and just about any other printed ephemera (in English or a foreign language) that has to do with archery.

Describe equipment as best you can, including a sketch when necessary. Include any brand or model names, and the date and place of origin, if known. A photocopy of a page or two of printed matter is helpful. When describing books, include the author, title, publisher, date and place of publication, number of pages, type and number of illustrations, and type of binding. The latter is important because Dave collects variations in binding of archery books as well.

Dave is available for appraisals and will make offers on items he can use for his collection.

TENNIS MEMORABILIA

Sheldon D. Katz
211 Roanoke Avenue
Riverhead, New York 11901
(516) 369-1100

Sheldon Katz's specialty is tennis memorabilia, including statues, trophies, stamps and first day covers, postcards, gum cards, tobacco cards, buttons, books, china, magazine covers, dolls, and "knicknacks of all sorts," especially those from before 1940.

He does not want to buy tennis rackets, programs, autographs, or photographs.

He would like to see a detailed description, including an identification of the item, its size, coloring, materials, age, condition, and place of origin. A purchase offer may be requested, although he prefers you to set the price. "I'll buy any quantity of reasonably priced items," he says.

He would also like to purchase pieces of Haviland china in Butterfly pattern for his own collection.

SKATING MEMORABILIA

Tom Kuo
Skatiques
P.O. Box 450154
Atlanta, Georgia 30345
(404) 634-7009

Tom Kuo seeks "outstanding and unusual" antique ice skates, especially "those with high curved prows, swan-headed skates, bone skates, combination ice and roller skates, and those with bronze runners. Absolutely, no common, cheap, clamp/club metal skates wanted!"

He also buys (1) miniature ice skater's lanterns with colored globes; (2) old skating figurines made of bronze, porcelain, and the like; (3) old books, prints, and cards featuring skating; (4) early skate catalogs; and "other skating collectibles." No hockey or speed skating, please.

A photo or sketch that shows the blade is needed, plus a statement of condition. He prefers the seller to set a price, but will make offers. Tom is an engineer whose love of figure skating has led to owning "one of the top ten" skating collections.

THOROUGHBRED HORSE RACING

Gary L.Medeiros
1319 Sayre Street
San Leandro, California 94579

For nearly thirty years, Gary Medeiros has been collecting the memorabilia of throughbred horse racing.

Among items he wants are old racing programs, books, trophies, magazines, games, prints, photographs, postcards, and any other items related to thoroughbred racing.

A complete description "is very helpful," he says, and he asks that you include a photograph or photocopy whenever possible. Examine and report the condition of items carefully, please.

Gary is owner of one of the largest collections of horse racing programs and is pleased to make offers for items he can use.

DAN PATCH MEMORABILIA

Donald W. Sawyer
40 Bachelor Street
West Newbury, Massachusetts 01985
(617) 363-2983 eves.

Dan Patch was as turn-of-the century trotter that captured the public fancy with his record-breaking performances.

Enormous amounts of Dan Patch memorabilia were produced, including stopwatches, watch fobs, postcards, trade cards, photographs, advertising, and more. In 1911 a Dan Patch automobile was offered in newspaper ads for $525 ("Does anyone have one of these?" Don Sawyer asks plaintively.) Watches marked "Jockey Club," "Hambletonian," "The Racer," and similar names are wanted, especially those depicting horse heads on the case. Don is a dealer in horse and carriage memorabilia.

It is suggested that you include a photocopy or good close-up photo of what you have. You may price it or ask him to make an offer.

MISCELLANEOUS SPORTS MEMORABILIA

Joel Platt
Sports Immortals Museum
Clark Building, Suite 2317
Pittsburgh, Pennsylvania 15222
(412) 232-3008

Joel Platt is a collector of enormous range who is always looking for first-class or unique mementos from famous athletes and games in all major sports.

Wants include old World Series and All Star Game programs and press pins; old uniforms; trophies and medals from famous athletes; old baseball and cigarette cards; all museum-type sports artifacts and collectibles.

He asks that you send him a description, photograph (or photocopy), date, any other necessary information, and a statement of condition. You may request offers and appraisals from this forty-year veteran collector.

HUNTING AND FISHING

Bruce Rayeske
816 Columbia Avenue
South Milwaukee, Wisconson 53172
(414) 762-8848

Bruce Rayeske purchases a variety of items related to hunting and fishing:

1. Books about hunting or fishing
2. Catalogs of fishing and hunting equipment
3. Old fishing reels and wooden bait
4. Indian artifacts
5. Books about Indians (nonfiction only)
6. Items produced by or for the Iver Johnson Arms and Cycle Works (including guns, catalogs, signs, calendars, etc.)

Author, title, date, and condition should be supplied for books, says Bruce, and "a reasonable description of anything else." Bruce, who is the Iver Johnson company historian, will make offers for items he can use.

FISHING TACKLE

Robert B. Whitaker
2810 East Desert Cove Avenue
Phoenix, Arizona 85028
(602) 992-7304

Bob Whitaker is interested in antique and pre-1940 fishing tackle, including:
1. Bamboo fly rods, especially those by Leonard, Orvis, Payne, Thomas, Heddon, Montegue, Gillum, Winston
2. Fishing reels by Meek, Milam, Sage, Snyder, Talbot, Vom Hofe, Heddon (early), Shakespeare (early), and others
3. Creels, nets, and wooden lures
Tell him what you have, the name of the manufacturer (when possible), any marks or numbers, and its condition. He asks you to include your phone number; he prefers buying over the phone so he can ask about what you have. He would appreciate your setting the price you want, but will discuss value with you.

FISHING TACKLE

Hugh H. Williams
10643 SE 29th
Bellevue, Washington 98004
(206) 455-3217

Hugh Williams collects old fishing tackle, especially reels and plugs.
Both baitcasting and fly reels are wanted, and he can list nearly thirty brands of particular interest. A few of the makers he seeks are Billinghurst, Bogdan, Chubb, Clerk, Follet, Fowler, Hardman, Hardy, Kosmic, Krider, Leonard, Meek, Noel, Orvis, Redifor, and William Shakespeare Jr.
Bass, muskie, and salmon plugs by another thirty makers are of interest, including lures made by Algers, Bing's Bite-em-Bait, Creek Chub, Charmer, Chippewa, Hungry Jack, K & K , Manco, Michigan Lifelike Minnows, Pflueger, South Bend, and Winchester.
He would like you to include the name of the maker if you can, the model name or number when available, and any other markings on the reel or lure. Provide a general description of condition, noting any obvious surface blemishes, worn spots, or damaged or missing parts.

TRAPS

Boyd W. Nedry
728 Buth Drive
Comstock Park, Michigan 49321
(616) 784-1513 after 5 p.m.

"I buy all types of traps."

Boyd Nedry buys "old traps, unusual traps, inventor's models of traps, hand-forged traps, no matter how large or small, from bear traps down to mouse-sized. I want rat, mole, gopher, hawk, fly, roach, literally anything in the way of a trap, with or without teeth, from this country or abroad." Boyd will also purchase important broken traps for parts.

In addition to traps, he buys fur house catalogs, trapping method books, and other paper ephemera related to trapping.

He needs to know the brand name of the trap, its size, and its condition. He will make offers for items he can use.

DUCK DECOYS

Joe Engers and Jeff Williams
Decoy Magazine
P.O. Box 1900, Montego Bay Station
Ocean City, Maryland 21842
(301) 524-0989

"We are not collectors ourselves, but publish the only magazine devoted to decoy collecting. As a result we have a network of contacts who are always searching for new birds to add to their collections."

They ask that you send a description of the decoy, including its species, maker, condition, and asking price. Good photographs are a must. The editors of Decoy pledge "We can link you with a buyer for a 10 percent commission. We can also offer you a classified ad which will bring response from around the world." If you know nothing about decoys, have good clear pictures taken, record all marks, and ask for help. Remember to send an SASE with all requests.

8
The World of Transportation

HORSE AND CARRIAGE

Donald W. Sawyer
West Newbury Wagon Works
40 Bachelor Street West
Newbury, Massachusetts 01985
(617) 363-2983 eves.

One of the largest and most informative illustrated wants lists you are likely to see can be obtained from this specialist in hard-to-find horse and carriage memorabilia.

The list has eighteen pages of lamps, watches, carriage tools, wheels from carriages, hubs, life-sized animal heads, harness makers' stuffed or wooden horses, carriage salesmen's samples, picnic baskets, carriage horns, wagon wrench sets, barn tools and brackets, harness hangers, children's wagons, wagon robes, carriage clocks, and cast hitching posts, among other items.

Donald Sawyer also wants books, catalogs, and promotional literature from any product or device related to carriages, wagons, and carriage horses and their care. Copies of any issue of The Hub, a carriage makers' magazine, are sought.

A photocopy of small items and a photograph of larger ones is recommended. A good sketch with all dimensions and names, dates, or patent information is useful. Any historical information you have about the item(s) would be helpful. Provide a statement of condition, and "a reasonable price," and Don will make offers for items he can use for resale or for his collection.

RAILROAD MEMORABILIA

Scott Arden
Antiques & Artifacts
20457 Highway 126
Noti, Oregon 97461
(503) 935-1619

A collector since the middle 1950s, Scott Arden is today the largest dealer in railroad memorabilia in the country.

He seeks every kind of item imaginable, as long as it's marked with the name of a railroad or express company. He includes a very lengthy list, including china, lanterns, silverware, badges, pocket watches, railroad telephone and telegraph items, and much more.

High-interest paper goods, according to Scott, include most books and booklets published by Simmons-Boardman or the Railway Gazette, early annual passes, menus, calendars, posters, and more. Scott notes that he also buys "high-grade steamship, bus, stage, and other transportation matter."

He wants a general description, markings, age if known, and a statement of condition with details of damage or defects. If the item is heavy, he wants to know the weight. He prefers to have you set the price, but will make offers.

ILLINOIS ELECTRIC RAILWAYS

Steve Hyett
1440 Royal St. George Drive
Naperville, Illinois 60540
(312) 357-3538

Steve Hyett wants to buy "anything from the Chicago , Aurora & Elgin Railroad, or the Aurora, Elgin & Chicago Railway, and related trolley, interurban, and streetcar lines of northern Illinois."

Steve points out that he is not interested in steam railroads, but in the various electric railways that plied Chicago and northern Illinois. His interest extends as far as buying complete streetcars, but he also wants more mundane minutia including maps, tickets, timetables, photographs, and stock certificates. Hardware such as badges, locks, lanterns, china, and headlights is very desirable.

Your description should include dimensions, any dates or maker's marks, and the exact spelling of railroad names. When describing condition, make certain to point out every defect, stain, tear, fold, wrinkle, rust spot or dent. You may request his wants list. Steve will make offers.

THE SWITCHBACK RAILROAD

Robert C. Gormley
Brownsburg Road, RD 2
Newtown, Pennsylvania 18940

For a decade and a half, Bob Gormley has been buying souvenir and paper items associated with eastern Pennsylvania's once famous Switchback Railroad, which wound through coal country. Billed as the oldest railroad in America, it was a popular tourist attraction for three-quarters of a century.

The most desirable items are those from the railroad itself, such as timetables, passes, and ticket stubs, but photographs are wanted, as are engravings, snapshots, home movies, souvenirs of all sorts and everything else, " except postcards."

Tell him what you have, its shape and dimensions, whatever scenes are depicted, and its condition. Please set the price you want, but he will make offers if you prefer.

DIRIGIBLES AND ZEPPELIN MEMORABILIA

Joseph L. Rubin
Jody Stamp Studio
6001 Riverdale Avenue
Riverdale, New York 10471
(212) 796-6550

Joseph Rubin is a stamp dealer by profession, but his hobby is collecting zeppelin and dirigible memorabilia. He wants to buy just about anything that is from or features the giant gas bags, foreign or domestic. Among items he buys are stamps, coins, and medals that depict dirigibles; envelopes, postcards, and letters featuring dirigibles; books about dirigibles; pins, china, and uniforms used on dirigibles; tickets to, or photographs of, dirigibles; models or games featuring or depicting dirigibles; dirigible parts, especially propellers.

Send a full description of what you have to sell. Make a photocopy of smaller items and all paper goods whenever possible. Take a photo of larger pieces. Joseph will sometimes request that you send your item registered and insured. He will make an offer, and if you do not accept it, he will return your item the same way it was sent.

TELEGRAPH AND THE RAILROADS

Charles B. Goodman
5454 South Shore Drive
Chicago, Illinois 60615
(312) 753-8342

Charles Goodman wants large or small quantities of fine-condition items in three seemingly unrelated categories:

1. Railroad dining car china, silverware, glassware, linens, etc.
2. Telegraph instruments, keys, sounders, and related items
3. Memorabilia and souvenirs of Northwestern University or the University of Chicago, especially Wedgwood and Spode plates.

He wants you to tell him about all markings on the item(s) and to give him an accurate statement of condition. Please price what you have and indicate that it is returnable if unsatisfactory.

RAILROAD MEMORABILIA

Fred N. Arone
The Depot Attic
377 Ashford Avenue
Dobbs Ferry, New York 10522
(914) 693-5858 eves.

"Anything from or about railroads may be of interest," sums up the wants of this veteran, thirty-year collector-dealer.

Paper, china, badges, silverware, stocks and bonds, posters, calendars, books (both fiction and nonfiction), depot signs, advertising...items the list goes on and on.

He wants a general description of the item, its age if you know it, the name of the railroad involved, and a statement of condition. As to pricing, "Include your price if you have one, otherwise I will make an offer."

COMMERCIAL AVIATION

Charles C. Quarles
204 Reservation Drive
Spindale, North Carolina 28160
(704) 245-7803 eves.

Commercial airline pilot and stewardess uniform wings and hat emblems from United States carriers, 1930s to the present, are Charles Quarles's main collecting interest. He also wants complete stewardess uniforms from the 1940s through the early 1960s. No military insignia, please, or later uniforms.

Charles also buys travel-agent-type display models of airliners.

A photocopy of any insignia is recommended. When offering uniforms or models, a complete description accompanied by a photograph is ideal. He will make an offer depending upon the rarity and desirability of what you have.

AIRPLANE MODELS

Robert L. Keller
P.O. Box 38
Stanton, California 90680
(714) 826-5218

Everyone admires those models of commercial airliners that seem to zoom through the skies as they sit in the travel agent's window or, in the case of the smaller models, on her desk. If you have one or more of these eye-catchers, Bob Keller might buy them.

Please describe it well, especially the dimensions from nose to tail and from wing-tip to wing-tip. Note any damage. He will be pleased to make you an offer.

TRANSPORTATION TOKENS

Lee Schumacher
10609 Eastern
Kansas City, Missouri 64134
(816) 761-1550 eves.

Lee Schumacher buys all types of transportation tokens, including tokens good for one ride, toll, or trip from a hotel to a depot. Bridge crossing tokens and all others pertaining to transportation are usually of interest. Other selected tokens, such as merchants' trade tokens "good for " a product, service, or discount, are also sought. He does on occasion purchase paper tranfers, tickets, passes and the like.

Photographs of old transit systems, bus lines, streetcars, or street scenes showing these vehicles in operation are also wanted. And Lee buys a variety of old medals from fairs and expositions, and a wide range of foreign medals.

"I have been a collector of these items for nearly forty years and will pay top dollar for any material I can use," he says. In you decription include size, type of metal, what both sides of the coin look like, and any dates. Lee will make offers.

LICENSE PLATES

George Chartrand
149 Ellen Street
Winnipeg, Manitoba
Canada R3A 1A2
(204) 943-0119

George Chartrand is a veteran, twenty-year collector-dealer of license plates who has some unusual and specific wants:

1. All license plates, any place, any date, if in perfect, unused mint condition
2. Plates dating after 1920, but only in large quantities
3. All fine-condition Australian, Mexican, South American, Caribbean, African, or Asian plates
4. United States plates only if pre-1915, unless in large quantities
5. All good condition motorcycle plates before 1950
6. Any fair condition motorcycle plates before 1920
7. Any North American Indian tribe license plates

George requests you list the date, place, material, type of license, quantity, condition, and price of your license plate(s). It is not necessary to list the number unless it is unusual. Since a few early, unusual, or foreign plates can have values in excess of $100, some research on your part is advisable. George does not make offers and insists that all items be priced.

LICENSE PLATES AND MEMORABILIA

Dr. Edward H. Miles
888 8th Avenue
New York, New York 10019
(212) 765-2660

Dr. Miles' specialty is license plates in a variety of forms.

He buys old and unusual automobile license plates, but also Disabled American Veterans key chain license plates, B.F. Goodrich key chain license plates, windshield stickers, dashboard registration disks, chaffeurs' badges, license plate gum cards, and other "auto-related" items.

He wants to know the year of origin, the state, the numbers or letters, the condition, and your asking price. He will assist you to price earlier license plates, a few of which can have substantial value.

MOTORCYCLE MEMORABILIA

Chris Kusto
Antique Cycle Supply
Cedar Springs, Michigan 49319
(616) 887-0812

For more than a decade, Chris Kusto has been buying "anything relating to antique (pre-1950) motorcycles."

He lists books, brochures, fobs, medals, pins, old photographs, trophies, manuals, toys, and miscellaneous mementos as typical of wanted items.

Your description should include a photo if possible, a statement of condition, and the price. He does not have a wants list, does not make offers, and does not do appraisals.

FORDS, MERCURYS, AND SCHWINN BIKES

"Gus" R. Garton, Jr.
Garton's Auto
5th and Vine
Millville, New Jersey 08332

"We buy and sell 1932-70 Ford and Mercury automobiles and parts. We specialize in new and old stock fenders, grilles, bumpers, chrome, ornaments, and all mechanical items. We will purchase one item or an entire dealer lot.

"We also collect, buy, and sell classic era (1935-60) bicycles, and are especially interested in 1949-60 boys' twenty-six inch Schwinn bikes in excellent condition."

Send a full description of the item(s) you have for sale. Items should be priced, but Gus Garton will make appraisals for a fee.

THE SEA AND SHIPS

William W. Hill
Cross Hill Books
P.O. Box 798
Bath, Maine 04530
(207) 443-5652

William Hill wants "anything relating to the sea and ships, including early voyages, sailing ships, shipbuilding, whaling, fishing, piracy, shipwrecks, steamships, the Arctic, and the Antarctic. I am particularly interested in anything dealing with Maine shipbuilding (especially in Bath, Maine), and 19th- century sailing ships." Books about yachting and small boat voyages are a personal hobby.

Wants include books, photos, original log books and papers, and other items. He also buys steamship memorabilia.

For books and other printed matter, he requests the author, title, place and date of publication, and edition number. For photos and other material, a photocopy is helpful. "Accurate description of condition is important." If items are properly described, he will make offers.

NAUTICAL ANTIQUES

Fred von Wiegen
Ye Olde Ship Store
484 Kuhio Highway
Kapaa, Hawaii 96746
(808) 822-1401

Ye Olde Ship Store is Hawaii's largest dealer in marine antiques.

Its owner wants to buy nautical items of every description, particularly items dating from the 17th through the 19th centuries. Small handcrafted items are reportedly very popular with his customers, as are brass items, old charts and maps, and paper relating to nautical events. "I most like to obtain unique, one-of-a-kind items." He also purchases newly made nautical handcrafts.

Fred von Wiegen wants to know about size, general condition, dates or lettering, and approximate age. If you know the background of the piece, please tell him. A photograph is appreciated. You may price or ask him to make an offer.

GAR WOOD BOATS

Anthony Mollica
Gar Wood Society
P.O. Box 6003
Syracuse, New York 13217

Tony Mollica wants all sorts of ephemera related to Gar Wood and Chris Craft wooden speedboats.

His current wants list contains Chris Craft and Gar Wood sales literature and price lists, Gar Wood photos and other paper, and parts for the Gar Wood boats. He also buys selected boating magazines from the 1920s, 1930s and 1940s.

He asks simply for an accurate description acompanied by the price you want. This director of the Antique and Classic Boat Society will make offers for the items he can use.

OCEAN LINER MEMORABILIA

Edward C. Hill
114 Uhland St.
East Rutherford, New Jersey 07073
(201) 939-4302

Ed Hill wants "any item from oceangoing steamships as long as it has the name of the ship, the name of the steamship line, or both."

Desired memorabilia include menus, passenger lists, postcards, hat ribbons, models, napkin rings, tea strainers, deck plans, souvenir spoons, brochures, pins, etc.

As part of your description, make certain to include the name of the ship or line, the date (if possible), the condition, and your asking price. He will make offers when appropriate.

OCEAN LINER MEMORABILIA

Ken Schultz
P.O. Box M753
Hoboken, New Jersey 07030
(201) 656-0966

Ken Schultz wants a variety of items related to transatlantic or transpacific passenger ship travel, including posters, menus, deck plans, passenger lists, souvenirs, models, postcards, etc.

If you have any ocean liner relics that you wish to sell, send him a full description including the name of the ship or ship line, the date (when possible), the dimensions, the condition, and the price wanted. He will make offers on unpriced items that are for sale if he can use them for resale.

OCEAN LINER MEMORABILIA

Alan Taksler
New Steamship Consultants
P.O. Box 1721
El Cajon, California 92022

"We are the world's largest buyers of ocean liner memorabilia, especially deck plans, interior photo booklets and brochures, menus, passenger lists, log cards, and other paper ephemera," claims Alan Taksler.

Favorite ships include the Queen Mary, Lusitania, Titanic, Normandie, and the Rex, but Taksler expresses interest in all items from all ships issued before 1960.

"It is almost impossible to fairly determine the value of items without seeing them first, because value depends on so many factors." A description should include name of ship, approximate date, size, etc. A photocopy is useful. "We welcome people to send us items for approval or for our offer. There is no obligation to accept our offer," but he claims, "our offers are accepted in almost every case."

AUTOMOBILE ITEMS

Mark Shetler
Remember When
12592 Charloma Drive
Tustin, California 92680
(714) 838-4364

Mark buys and sells a variety of seemingly unrelated items:
1. Classic and antique automobiles
2. Parts for antique automobiles, especially the Lancia, Amilcar, Delahaye, Autocar, and two-cylinder Maxwell
3. Antique and mechanical dolls
4. Antique and vintage clothes (from 1900 - 1930 only)
5. Pre-1941 slot and other coin-operated machines

Please include complete description and photographs in your first letter. Mark asks that you price what you have, but he is willing to make offers.

9

Guns, Swords
and the Military

KNIVES, SWORDS, AND HELMETS

Joseph "Colonel Joe" Kelly
The Knife Trader
6415 Lankersham Boulevard
North Hollywood, California 91606

Joe Kelly is a major west coast dealer in things military. Chief among his interests are:
1. Knives, both military and civilian but only unusual ones
2. Military medals from any country, any era
3. Swords, from any nation, any period, and in any condition
4. Military helmets and headdresses of any nation prior to World War II. He particularly wants elaborate plumed or figural headdresses, and will buy pieces as far back as the 12th century.

Photographs or good accurate sketches are important. Take close-ups or make rubbings of any engraving on swords or knives, and mention whether the scabbard is present. When describing a helmet, indicate the different materials used in construction and whether all parts and decorations are present.

He will send an illustrated one-page wants list upon request, and is willing to make offers for items he can use for his collection or for resale.

ARMS AND ARMOR

Marvin E. Hoffman
Museum of Historical Arms
1038 Alton Road
Miami Beach, Florida 33139

Marvin Hoffman is a major dealer in guns, sidearms, armor, and related items. Twice a year he publishes an illustrated catalog that offers more than a thousand lots for sale. He buys and sells:
1. Antique weapons of all kinds: swords, knives, battle axes
2. Firearms made before 1889, especially muzzle-loading firearms
3. Helmets, shields, and suits of armor
4. Powderhorns and flasks
5. Japanese swords, sword guards, and other mounts
6. Restraint devices, including leg irons and handcuffs
7. Instruments of torture
8. Nautical instruments, sextants, telescopes
9. Brass surveying instruments

"Clear and sharp photos are best. In addition, we want to know any marks or names, and the overall condition, including whether anything is missing. Also, the sellers should say how much they want for it, as we do not make offers. If they wish an appraisal, they must send along $20 with their letter."

JAPANESE SWORDS AND ARMOR

Ron Hartmann
5907 Deerwood Drive
St. Louis, Missouri 63123

Ron Hartmann collects Japanese swords, daggers, spears, armor, and sword parts (such as guards and handle ornaments).

Many swords brought home as souvenirs from the Pacific theater of World War II were rare early Japanese swords, worth substantial sums today. Ron strongly urges you to make certain of what you have before giving swords away or selling them too cheaply. He will give you a free appraisal if you describe your weapon in the manner he requests.

First, he suggests, do not make any effort to clean the item, as you can hurt its value. The best way to sell your sword or other item is to leave it as is and take good clear pictures of both the scabbard and the details of the blade.

GUNS AND WAR RELICS

Ed Kukowski
Ed's Gun House
Route 1
Minnesota City, Minnesota 55959
(507) 689-2925

Ed Kukowski has been buying, selling , and trading guns through the mail for more than twenty years.

Ed likes to purchase entire collections of antique or modern weapons, but he will buy desirable single items, Gatling guns, cannons, and unusual war relics.

Guns should be described as fully as possible. Note the maker, model, and caliber, all of which can often be found on the barrel. Note any breaks, cracks, worn spots or other damage. Ed likes you to price what you have but will make offers. He advertises that he pays cash and keeps all transactions confidential. Merchants Bank, 130 Plaza East, Winona, Minnesota, 55987, is the reference he provided.

KENTUCKY RIFLES

Siro Toffolon
P.O. Box 112
Wallingford, Connecticut 06492
(203) 237-2861

If you have a Kentucky rifle for sale that is decorated with carving or engraving, Siro Toffolon would like to hear from you, whether the rifle still works or not.

The rifles he wants are characterized by an octagonal barrel, a flint lock firing mechanism (although some have been converted), a stock usually made from maple, a brass patch box built into the side of the stock, and brass or silver inlay. He wants only those guns with ornate carvings or engravings.

He asks for a clear photograph of each side of the gun. Tell him about any maker's identification you can find. Meriden Home Bank will provide references should you want them. Siro will make an offer for your gun, subject to final inspection.

CIVIL WAR RELICS

C.L. Batson
5512 Buggywhip Drive
Centreville, Virginia 22020
(703) 830-0583 (6-9 p.m.)

C.L. Batson buys a variety of Civil War artifacts for resale:
1. Official records, diaries, and Confederate histories
2. Photographs of encampments, battles, and the like
3. Uncommon bullets and field artillery projectiles
4. Buttons, badges, pins, insignia, and other decoration
5. Memorabilia and maps of Virginia, West Virginia, Maryland, North Carolina, South Carolina, or any parts of these states during the Civil War period

He wants a complete description, preferring you to refer to illustrations in standard reference books on Civil War collectibles. Batson says he wants the seller to "state price wanted in first letter," but he also indicates a willingness to make offers. You'll have to play it by ear.

MILITARY MEMORABILIA

William Seifert
Route 3, Box 243
Lebanon, New Jersey 08833
(201) 236-2062 eves.

For more than four decades, Bill Seifert has been collecting military memorabilia, including bayonets, helmets, buttons, leather goods, foreign medals, home-front items, posters, autographs, magazines, and a wide range of paper goods, including newspaper articles about wars, especially early or obscure foreign wars.

Describe your item, including all markings, designs, or insignia. Provide a detailed report on conditions, including scuffs, wear, chips, dents, tears, soil, and the like. Photocopies are very helpful. He makes offers only reluctantly, and prefers you to set "your bottom line price" when you write.

In addition, Bill would like to purchase postcards that depict the Bellewood Amusement Park in Pattenburg, New Jersey.

UNIFORMS OF WORLD WAR I

Orton Begner
290 Chestnut Ridge Road
Rochester, New York 14624
(716) 889-3389

Orton Begner is a specialist in the uniforms of World War I. He buys:

1. American uniforms from World War I, if they have shoulder patches
2. Helmets with painted insignia
3. Photogrpahs of soldiers in uniform, but only if you can see and identify their shoulder patches
4. Any item associated with black soldiers in World War I
5. Any item associated with pilots and the air service of World War I

He would like you to describe what you have. Be certain you make a careful sketch of any shoulder patches or insignia on the uniform or helmet. He will make you an offer.

MILITARY INSIGNIA

Col. Jack Britton
Quincy Sales
P.O. Box 7792
Tulsa, Oklahoma 74105

Jack Britton buys, sells, and trades anything used or worn on military uniforms, either American or foreign. This includes medals, badges, patches, insignia, armbands, daggers, and swords. He also handles Nazi-era souvenirs "with discretion."

Jack pledges to identify military items and to answer questions if you enclose a large self-addressed stamped envelope.

Please describe what you have, making sketches whenever needed for clarity. State whether you want to sell or trade (note: he pays more in trade than in cash). You may set the asking price or ask Jack to make an offer. "You can send items and we will write you giving our offer. If we cannot come to terms, we will pay return postage and insurance. Send all items to us by insured mail so that you have a receipt."

MILITARY AVIATION

Ronald J. Mahoney
Air Age Book Company
P.O. Box 40
Tollhouse, California 93667
(209) 855-8993

Ron Mahoney is a dealer in pre-1950 aviation who wants to purchase books, pamphlets, photographs, scrapbooks, World War II aviation shoulder patches, aircraft manuals, and personal letters from flyers about air combat. He will also purchase airplane recognition models and their accompanying manuals which were used to train aircraft spotters in the war.

He does not want items dating after 1950 or general works on flying, motor maintenance or weather studies.

Make certain to include author, title, date, edition, and condition if you want to sell a book or pamphlet. If you have a photograph, indicate whether it is an original, a copy, a postcard or whatever. In the case of recognition models, identifying names and numbers are usually embossed onto the plane and should be provided.

MILITARY MEMORABILIA

Steve Folio
Collectors World
5351-1 Buford Highway
Atlanta, Georgia 30340
(404) 452-7102 days

Steve Folio wants an interesting variety of military and quasi-military items:

1. Early photographs of soldiers: daguerrotypes, ambrotypes, tintypes, and calling cards

2. Confederate and Confederate veterans' items, including weapons, uniforms, letters, photographs, etc.

3. Military relics from the Vietnam War, with Vietcong and Communist Chinese items particularly wanted

4. Items related to the Ku Klux Klan, pre-1960

He requests a photocopy of any paper materials, including photographs. A sketch should accompany your description of three-dimensional items. Make certain to describe the condition of what you have. "An SASE is a must if you want a reply," he cautions. If you send one and your description is adequate, Steve will make offers.

NAZI NOTABLES

Thomas W. Pooler
P.O. Box 1861
Grass Valley, California 95945
(916) 268-1338

Thomas Pooler wants anything belonging to, or received from, notable Nazi leaders.

If you have any items that were once in the possession of Hitler, Himmler, Hess, Goering, Rohm, Ribbentrop, Rommel, or any other prominent Nazi, Tom is interested. These can be items from their family and personal life as well as military memorabilia.

He requests a detailed description accompanied by a photograph or photocopy. Note all damage, stains, missing parts or pages, and the like. He would like you to state your price range. Please include your telephone number and the time of day when it is convenient for Tom to call.

If you want Tom to make an offer for what you have, it will often be necessary to ship it to him, insured. If his offer is not acceptable, he will return your item promptly the same way. If you have Nazi items from the leaders, Tom may be able to assist you to find other buyers.

ARMY UNIT HISTORIES

Wilfred Baumann
RD 1, Box 188
Esperance, New York 12066
(518) 875-6753

Wilfred Baumann, a retired army officer, collects United States Army unit histories of all eras, but is especially interested in army histories of Vietnam and Korean and Army Air Force histories from any period.

Army unit histories are narratives of the participation of specific units in a campaign or war, although some histories begin with the founding of the unit. He also collects various unit memorabilia such as albums, guidons, scrapbooks, tour books, medals, berets, helmets, anniversary programs, shoulder sleeve insignia, and unit crests.

Tell him the exact title of the book, the name of the author and the publisher, and the publication date. An accurate statement of condition should include any damage. If the book is inscribed or autographed, make certain you mention this. You may price your book or ask Baumann to make an offer.

RECOGNITION MODELS

Paul W. Hering
350 Woodland Drive
South Hempstead, New York 11550
(516) 538-0494

Paul Hering buys all World War II ship and aircraft recognition models.

These come in a variety of scales and materials, with most being made of plastic, although metal and wood were used in whole or in part. All have data molded underneath: type, country, date, and manufacturer's coded initials (B, C, DC, S, and others).

When writing, make sure certain to provide all the identifying information molded on the bottom. As in most other things, condition is critical in determining value. He will buy those with damaged or missing parts, however, since they can often be cannibalized to help repair others.

Since Paul sells models to other collectors, he is willing to make offers on most items.

U.S. MERCHANT MARINES

George R. Canaday, Director
U.S. Merchant Marine Museum
1923 East 8th Street
Anderson, Indiana 46012
(317) 643-6305

George Canaday wants a variety or items associated with the merchant marines and the Victory and Liberty ships they sailed.

He buys World War II seaman's papers, uniforms, medals, ribbons, and documents. He also wants anything removed from Victory or Liberty ships, such as marked blankets, instruments, gauges, and other artifacts.

He requests only that you identify what you have and provide a detailed description, paying particular attention to condition. You may set a price or request an offer.

UNITED STATES MARINES

Bruce H. Updegrove
RD 5, Box 546
Boyertown, Pennsylvania 19512
(215) 369-1798 *eves.*

Bruce Updegrove has two military specialties: World War I and the United States Marine Corps.

World War I items he wants include uniforms, helmets, insignia, medals, unit photographs, and trench art.

His Marine Corps wants are broader, and include "anything pertaining to the Corps, from the earliest years up to and including World War II." Unit histories, photographs, early uniforms and insignia, medals, and other items are all sought.

He requests that you send any information you have about your item's history along with its description. Make certain you accurately describe condition. Bruce will make offers on things that he can use.

10

Art Prints,
Paintings and Objects

ART OF PETTY AND VARGAS

Reid Austin
Michael Reid, Inc.
1018 East Las Olas Boulevard
Fort Lauderdale, Florida 33301
(305) 467-3000

Michael Reid, Inc. deals in paintings, cartoons, gatefolds, and calendar art by George Petty and Alberto Vargas.

"I'd like a clear and honest description of the prints or art, with a photocopy always a good idea. I also prefer that they know the price they want, as I'd rather not make offers."

ILLUSTRATIONS BY MAUD HUMPHREY

Evelyn Poteat
Columbia Highway
Franklin, Tennessee 37064

Evelyn Poteat wants to buy books, prints, calendars, greeting and trade cards, fans, and anything else that was illustrated around the turn of the century by Maud Humphrey.

Maud Humphrey, a highly successful commercial artist and the mother of Humphrey Bogart, is best known for her portraits of Victorian children and ladies. Her work is inevitably signed, generally with her initials.

Evelyn wants a description of the item, including the dimensions and the condition. She prefers you to set the price, but requests your telephone number so that the item and price may be discussed.

ART BY PHILIP BOILEAU AND ROBERT ROBINSON

Dave Bowers
P.O. Box 1224
Wolfeboro, New Hampshire 03894
(603) 569-5095

Dave Bowers seeks artwork by two American illustrators:
    1. Sketches and paintings by Philip Boileau done between 1900 and 1917, a period in which he primarily painted attractive women for private customers as well as magazine covers, postcards, and commercial activities
    2. Artwork of all types by Robert Robinson, especially covers and illustrations, done between 1907 and 1952
    When trying to sell paintings, a good close-up color photograph is almost essential. Provide as much information as you can. The value of paintings varies greatly, so requesting an evaluation and offer is advisable if you desire to sell.

YESTERYEAR'S ILLUSTRATIONS

John and Shirley Rosenhoover
100 Mandalay Road
Chicopee, Massachusetts 01020
(413) 536-5542

The Rosenhoovers want to buy illustrated magazines and newspapers that pre-date 1925, especially Harper's Weekly, Truth, Vim, Illustrated London News, Hearth & Home, Every Saturday, Puck, New York Illustrated News, Needlecraft, Verdict, Leslies, Ballou's, Judge, Wasp, and the like.
    They also want calendars, prints, etchings, engravings, albums of trade cards, posters, paper or cardboard advertising, and pre-1925 books illustrated with color plates on all topics from children's books to western land surveys.
    Indicate the title, author or editor, publisher, date published, copyright date, size of the book, number of pages, number of color plates, artist or engraver, and condition. Also describe the subject matter of the advertising or illustration. "I usually request that items be forwarded on approval, and if I do not buy I will return the sender's postage. But do not forward items without first contacting me," John writes.

ILLUSTRATORS AND EROTICA

Charles Martignette
The Saturday Evening Post Gallery
P.O. Box 9295, JFK-Gov't. Center,
Boston, Massachusetts 02114
(617) 739-4500

Charles Martignette is a gallery owner who buys a wide range of art items:
  1. Original paintings by American illustrators, both 19th and 20th century
  2. Magazine cover and story illustration paintings
  3. Advertising, pinup, and calendar paintings, especially those by Alberto Vargas
  4. Erotica made before 1950, including bronzes, ivory, wood, bone, porcelain, bisque, postcards, and photographs
  5. Marble and alabaster statues of nudes and semi-nudes
  6. Silk lamp shades from the turn of the century
He requests "as much information as possible about the artist, size, medium, age, and asking price." This well-known expert will make appraisals and purchase offers.

PRINTS, POSTERS, AND BOOKS

Edy J. Chandler
P.O. Box 20664
Houston, Texas 77225
(713) 668-7864 or (713) 527-8402

Edy Chandler writes, "I am interested in obtaining limited edition prints, posters, and hardback first edition books containing the work of the following artists: Charles Adams, Alan Aldridge, Boris Artzybashev, Don Blanding, Philip Castle, R. Chouinard, Diane & Leo Dillon, Erte, Escher, Virgil Finlay, Brian Froud, Steve Favian, Robert Grossman, Rick Griffin, H.R. Geiger, Roger Huyssen, John Held, Rudolph Hausner, Brad Johannsen, Tim Kirk, Rockwell Kent, Michael Kaluta, Kelly/Nouse Studios, Peter Lloyd, Overton Lloyd, Peter Max, Victor Moscoso, Maxine Miller, Shusei Nagaoka, Ul de Rico, Szyx, Maurice Sendak, L. Salazar, Hajime Sorayama, William Stout, Vasarelly, Lynd Ward, Gahan Wilson, Gilbert Wilson, Patrick Woodroffe, Charles White III, and David Willardson."

Please provide an accurate description. Some of these items can be quite valuable (more than $1,000), and condition is of great importance. A good photograph showing close-up detail is advisable.

POSTERS

John Campbell
Fine Art
P.O. Box 22974
Nashville, Tennessee 37202
(615) 242-6773

John Campbell is a mail-order poster dealer, buying and selling fine examples of American and European posters.

He is always in the market for fine-condition examples of 1890-1940 posters of all types, sizes, and countries of origin.

Take a photograph of your poster or make a good sketch. Pay careful attention when describing condition, noting every crease, stain, or tear, no matter how minor. John will make offers, subject to final approval upon receipt of the poster(s).

IVORY FIGURES

Terry Cronin
1327 South Oak
Melbourne, Florida 32901

Terry Cronin is a longtime private collector of ivory, whether from elephant, hippo, walrus, whale, or narwhale.

Terry's interests are only in figures of people, animals, creatures, and the like, rather than in small trinkets or utilitarian items. But pieces are purchased from all parts of the world, including Asia, Africa, and the Arctic.

Send a photograph or photocopy of your figurine, along with dimensions and known history. Please carefully note all damage, cracks, and chips. He would prefer you to set the price range wanted, and he will make a counteroffer.

IVORY ART AND ARTIFACTS

David L. Boone
Boone Trading Company, Inc.
469 Duckabush River Road
Brinnon, Washington 98320
(206) 796-4330

David Boone is a dealer in ivory art and artifacts from Japan, China, Europe, and Africa. He's also interested in American Indian pieces, especially ancient Eskimo.

Whether netsuke, religious objects, fancy-work, knife handles, or scrimshaw, if it's ivory and nice to look at, Dave probably wants it. Artifacts of all sorts and all periods are of interest to him, as are raw teeth, tusks, skulls, animal skin rugs, and mounted heads.

Dave wants to know the dimensions, approximate age, and history of the piece. He wants to know the color of the ivory, and whether there are tiny pits on the piece. Note any cracks or chips. Make a photocopy of what you have, if possible. If the item is for sale and you include an SASE, he will make offers.

ORIENTALIA

Sandra Andacht
P.O. Box 94-W
Little Neck, New York 11363
(212) 229-6593

Sandra Andacht is a highly knowledgeable and experienced collector, dealer, and author in the field of Orientalia.

She lists among her wants antique and collectible Chinese and Japanese pottery, porcelain, cloisonne, lacquer, ivory, paintings and prints, netsuke, Inro, Satsuma, Imari, Kutani, tea caddies, tea ceremony utensils, textiles, tea bowls, sword furniture, etc.

"Items should be described with measurements, and condition stated. Photos should accompany the description and seller should list the rock-bottom price for each object. Condition need not always be perfect." Since some of these items can be quite valuable, research is suggested before amateur sellers attempt to price them.

ORIENTALIA

Lawrence E. Gichner
Adventures in Art
3405 Woodley Road
Washington, D.C. 20016
(202) 362-4393

Lawrence Gichner is a longtime collector and dealer in Orientalia.

He seeks "Japanese and Chinese works of art with emphasis on ivories, bronzes, scrolls, gongs, netsuke, and shunga. I especially want Japanese fancy-handled metal letter openers and paper slicers."

He requests only a description that will convey a general idea of the subject matter. "Seller should quote the price," he says. Since some of these items can be quite valuable, research is advisable before quoting.

11
Cameras
and Photographic Images

MOVIE LOBBY CARDS

Joe Gish
P.O. Box 1587
McAllen, Texas 78501
(512) 686-3476

Joe Gish's movie wants are specialized. He buys 11-by-14-inch lobby cards from early silent western movies, particularly those starring famous western heroes such as Bill Hart, Harry Carey, and Tom Mix.

Since the cards are relatively small, they can be photocopied easily. He asks that you set a price on the card(s) you have, and he will make a counteroffer if he feels it is too much. Joe is a well-known western artist and collector of western artifacts.

PHOTOS OF FEMALE IMPERSONATORS

Ralph S. Sullivan
346 Ivy Avenue
Westbury, New York 11590

Ralph Sullivan is in his thirty-fifth year of trying to locate photographs relevant to the history of female impersonation in the United States.

He especially wants to find photographs of Julian Eltinge, Lyn Carter, The Great Renaud, and other important impersonators. He seeks pre-1950 photographs only, please.

Describe what you have to Ralph and he will be pleased to make a purchase offer.

MOVIE POSTERS

Lloyd R. Toerpe
3389 Brookgate Drive
Flint, Michigan 48507
(313) 245-6991 2-10 p.m.

Lloyd Toerpe buys posters and other paper items associated with films, including lobby cards, still photographs, and card sets. He is particularly interested in westerns, adventure movies, and comedies.

He also buys sports-related paper, including gum cards, photographs, yearbooks, guides, record books, programs, posters, and the like from football and baseball before 1970. Gum cards other than sports are also wanted.

An accurate description should note any stains or tears. If a date or manufacturer is indicated, please say so. He requests that you set the price, but he will make offers for amateur sellers.

35MM THEATRICAL MOVIES

Tom Souder
Seventh and Pine
Millville, New Jersey 08332

Tom Souder has been an avid collector of old theatrical 35mm movies, both silent and sound, for more than thirty years. He also occasionally purchases old cameras and projectors from the silent era.

Tom wants to know the title of the films you have and whether they are complete. If you can't find a title but believe you can recognize some of the stars, let him know what you think. Condition of old film is critical. Old nitrate film can be both valuable and dangerous in any condition. If the film is marked "safety film" along the edges, then you have no worry.

If you have equipment for sale, indicate the name of the manufacturer, as well as the model name and/or number if there is one. Indicate any damage. He will make an offer for good items he can use.

GLASS MOVIE SLIDES

Glenn Ralston
276 Riverside Drive
New York, New York 10025
(212) 662-1985

Glen Ralston's primary interest is the small 3¼-by-4¼ inch glass "coming attractions" slides made between 1910 and 1950.

He also buys some 11-by-14-inch lobby cards, especially those from Paramount Studios during the 1920s and 1930s. He claims to want a few select movie projectors, but is looking for an undefinable something. If you have an early projector, you'd best take a photograph of it and price it cheaply if you hope to sell.

If you have any of these movie items for sale, tell him the title, the date (if you know), and the principal actors and actresses named. Give him the dimensions if they are other than those listed above, and describe the condition accurately. Always include your telephone number, because he prefers to buy over the phone.

If Glen wants what you have, he will be pleased to make offers.

MAGIC LANTERNS AND SLIDES

Joseph Koch
819 14th Street
Auburn, Washington 98002
(206) 833-7784

Joe Koch is a longtime advocate of the magic lantern and its slides.

He buys lantern slides, both static and mechanical, in color or in black and white, and on any subject except travel and religion. If you have travel or religious slides, however, he indicates that he will refer you to other collectors.

He also buys magic lanterns and other optical and kinetic toys and professional devices, as well as catalogs or other printed ephemera relevant to the history or sale of magic lanterns and magic lantern slides.

When describing lanterns, give the brand name, color, materials, physical measurements, type of illumination, and describe any unusual features. When describing plates, give the subject matter, country of origin, and size.

SHIRLEY TEMPLE

Frank Garcia
8963 S.W. 34th Street
Miami, Florida 33165

Shirley Temple paper dolls, figurines, glassware, postcards, toys, tea sets, films, jewelry, records, advertising, and anything else featuring the little moppet will find a home with Frank Garcia. No reproduction items are wanted.

Frank also buys items from the movie Gone With The Wind, but they must be original from the first release of the film. "Watch the dates," he warns, referring to the fact that many of the paper goods will be dated. He wants lobby cards, press books, original posters, as well as games, jewelry, and cigarette cards. Frank claims to pay especially well for uncut original paper doll sets.

Describe what you have as well as you can, note its condition, and set a price. Frank does not make offers. Include an SASE to guarantee a reply.

JAMES DEAN

David Loehr
G.P.O. Box 2153
New York, New York 10116
(212) 244-8426

If it's related to James Dean, David Loehr will probably buy it.

Among Dean items he wants, Loeher lists movie posters and lobby cards, movie stills, movie press books and programs, record albums and 45s, pins, buttons, gum cards, collector's plates and even scrapbooks assembled by other fans. Books, magazines, and newspapers with major stories about Dean are wanted, as are documents or photos he signed.

When you describe your item, make certain to include dates of clippings or magazines. You may price what you have, or David will make you an offer. After more than ten years of effort, he has become a nationally known authority on Dean and owner of the world's largest collection of Dean memorabilia.

SHIRLEY TEMPLE

Loraine Burdick
5 Court Place
Puyallup, Washington 98371

Loraine Burdick is a twenty-five year veteran collector, dealer, and researcher. Among other credits and activities, she is the founder of the Shirley Temple Collectors Club and has published thirteen books on Shirley.

If you have anything at all related to Shirley, from her public, private, or movie life, Loraine would love to hear from you.

Please describe what you have, including all tears, creases, mends, soil, or other damage. If there are other identifying marks (the printer, publisher, photographer, manufacturer, etc.), be certain to tell her. She will make offers.

FRANK SINATRA

Stan Komorowski
P.O. Box W-2254
Warminster, Pennsylvania 18974
(215) 675-1452

Stan Komorowski buys phonograph records, radio transcriptions, books, magazine articles, autographed photos, and other Sinatra memorabilia.

When describing records, make certain to include the label, the catalog number, the song title(s), and a description of condition. When selling items other than records, describe as best you can. Photocopies are helpful.

More than ten years ago, Stan became a collector, and later a collector-dealer, of items pertaining to Frank Sinatra. For the past five years, he has been conducting mail auctions of Sinatra items among other fans of "Old Blue Eyes." Stan will make offers on items suitable for his personal collection or for resale.

BETTY PAGE MEMORABILIA

John Detrick
Americana Bookshop
1719 Ponce de Leon Boulevard
Coral Gables, Florida 33134
(305) 442-1776

Betty Page was a Miami girl turned national pinup queen during the 1950s; she was especially known for her work with pinup photographer Bunny Yeager.

John Detrick is looking for photographs, postcards, magazine features —anything on Betty Page and other pinups from the 1920s to the 1960s.

What does John want to know? "Condition! Condition! Condition!" He also wants to know the size, the date, whether the item is in color or black and white, and the price asked. He will make offers.

NEWSREELS

Arthur Natale
Newsreels
P.O. Box 295
Cliffside Park, New Jersey 07010

Art Natale is building a complete collection of Castle Newsreel films made between 1937 and 1975.

He buys both 8mm and 16mm, but only in certain titles, and only in complete full-length versions. There are also some titles of "outer space films" abridged by Castle that he will buy. He has a wants list, which you are advised to request if you have a selection of these old films.

You must send him a list of titles, the catalog number (if it is on the box), the length of the film, and say whether it is silent or magnetic sound. Indicate whether your films are 8mm, Super 8, or 16mm. Tell him if there is any damage to the film or to the box. You may price these inexpensive movies or ask him for a quote.

ANTIQUE AND UNUSUAL CAMERAS

Jim McKeon
Centennial Photo
P.O. Box 3605
Grantsburg, Wisconsin 54840
(715) 689-2153

Jim McKeon buys antique and unusual cameras of all types, including subminiature cameras, panoramic and wide-angle cameras, disguised or concealed cameras, and oddly shaped cameras, particularly those shaped or named for characters such as Mickey Mouse, Charlie the Tuna, Hopalong Cassidy, and the like.

Among other items he would like are world's fair souvenir cameras, a camera concealed in a cane handle, and a cane that converts into a tripod. Catalogs that describe or illustrate cameras are also sought, as are pre-1915 photographic magazines and the British Journal Photographic Almanac from any year.

Provide him with any names and numbers printed on or inside the camera, as well as those on the ring around the camera's lens. Offers will be forthcoming if your description is clear and complete, and the item is one he can use.

OLD CAMERAS

Alan Lee Voorhees
Cameras and Such
492 Breesport Road
Horseheads, New York 14845
(607) 739-7898

Alan Voorhees is a relatively new buyer of cameras and other photographic equipment.

He is looking for a wide range of items for his rapidly expanding collection, but he has a particular interest in pre-1954 Kodak cameras, equipment, and catalogs. He will consider buying early catalogs, manuals, and other ephemera from any photographic company.

Send a complete description, including the brand name of the camera and any model numbers. Copy the numbers surrounding the lens. Mention the color of the camera and any damage, defects, or scuffs. Make a photcopy of a page or two of printed matter. A photograph of your camera is helpful, but only if it is a clear close-up. "If the item is one I need, my offer will be more than fair," he says.

STEREO AND OTHER CAMERAS

Mr. Poster
P.O. Box 1883 W
South Hackensack, New Jersey 07606
(201) 794-9606

Mr. Poster is an active buyer of a variety of cameras:
1. Stereo 3-D cameras, viewers, and projectors, from 1940-60
2. Still cameras from 1880s to 1970
3. Novelty, hidden, unusual, and colored cameras
4. Ladies, petite colored cameras
5. Items that look like cameras, but aren't

He asks that you provide a good description, including the camera's color, dimensions, and condition, as well as any serial numbers. A snapshot is helpful.

He pledges to tell you what you have, do appraisals, and make offers if you have properly and completely described the item and included an SASE.

STEREO CAMERAS

Mel Rosenthal, D.C.
507 South Maryland Avenue
Wilmington, Delaware 19804
(302) 994-0874

Dr. Rosenthal is attempting to locate, among a number of other items, stereo cameras and associated equipment.

Unlike most collectors, he is seeking later-model cameras, primarily from the 1940s and 1950s.

If you have one to sell, let him know the manufacturer, the model number, the color, and any serial numbers you can find. If you know whether it works, tell him. Any damage to the case or lens should, of course, be noted.

STEREOVIEW CARDS

Chuck and Trip Reincke
Antique Photography
2141 Sweet Briar Road
Tustin, California 92680
(714) 832-8563

Chuck and Trip Reincke buy photographic stereoview cards for their collection and for resale. They seek more important publishers such as Watkins, Muybridge, Brady, or Houseworth, but will buy most cards in mint condition and better subject matter.

Their favorite cards depict famous people, transportation, expositions and fairs, the Civil War, Indians, lighthouses, California, and mining, although they will purchase other good Americana.

Chuck and Trip believe they "can pay more since we do not depend on the income for a living." Chuck says he will be pleased to advise you about what to do with cards he cannot use. But you must provide a complete description, including publisher, title and title number, and condition. He prefers you to set the price, but has a printed wants list and will make offers.

TINTYPES

George Gilbert
520 West 44 Street
New York, New York 10036
(212) 594-5056

Tintypes are photographic images taken on tin plates, and were a popular form of inexpensive photography for more than three quarters of a century. George Gilbert is interested in tintypes of subjects other than people, especially work scenes, city views, harbors, occupational portraits depicting the tools of the profession, and erotic pictures. Stereoviews on tin are rare and quite desirable.

He also wants pre-1900 catalogs from camera makers Anthony, Scovill, Queen, and others. If you have these catalogs and are unwilling to sell, he will pay a rental fee just to look at them for a week.

Describe your tintype thoroughly. If you are able to photocopy it, do so, since actually seeing the image is important. George warns that he does not answer letters unaccompanied by an SASE nor those requesting offers, so price what you have to sell.

STEREOVIEW CARDS

Steve Jabloner
2131 Greenfield Avenue
Los Angeles, California 90025
(213) 478-8303

Steve Jabloner wants stereoview cards, but only those that are actually photographs, not printed color lithographs. He buys a wide range of subject matter: famous people, aviation, railroad, shipping, sports and games, music, street scenes, mining, the West, photographic equipment, firefighting, circus, military, store interiors, people at work, people at leisure, and general 19th-century way of life. He can supply a one-page wants list, which provides greater detail about these categories and identifies cards that he would especially like to find (such as photographs of Brahms, Verdi, or presidents other than Teddy Roosevelt and McKinley).

He wants to know the subject matter, the title of the photograph (if it has one), and the name of the publisher. Describe the condition, including any stains or creases. He will make an offer for cards he can use.

PHOTOGRAPHS

Janet Lehr
P.O.Box 617 GSS
New York, New York 10028
(212) 288-6234

Janet Lehr is a dealer who seeks to buy fine, old, or rare photographs or photographically illustrated books. She also expresses interest in other photographic ephemera, including reference books, photographers' journals or notebooks, and other unusual items.

She has a wants list, but it is unpriced. You are encouraged to send a photocopy of any photograph you feel might be valuable.

She prefers you to set your own price, but is willing to make offers when you are uncertain. Since occasional photographs sell for more than $1,000, some research is suggested before pricing. Janet is an author and longtime collector, so is well qualified to assist you in reaching a price.

DAGUERREOTYPES AND VINTAGE PHOTOGRAPHS

Marjorie Neikrug
Neikrug Photographica
224 East 68th Street
New York, New York 10021
(212) 288-7741

Marjorie Neikrug operates one of New York's more famous photographic galleries and is always looking for first-class photographic images in mint condition of all types.

She requests that you send a photocopy of the photograph being sold, give an indication of its condition and size, and say whether it is signed.

Appraisals are her business, and a fee is charged. If you have a rare and valuable photograph, she will assist you in pricing it if it is for sale to her.

12
Music,
Radio and Television

SHEET MUSIC

Daniel "Banjo Dan" McCall
50 Grove Street, Apt. 3
New York, New York 10014

"Banjo Dan" McCall wants to buy "all American pictorial popular sheet music, any age or date."

He buys single pieces or large lots. Prices generally run from $1 to $5 for fine-condition pictorial sheets, "I pay more for humorous and ragtime-related illustrations." If selling individual pieces, list the title, writer, publisher, copyright date, and give a description of the design.

"Sellers should note that most sheet music was mass-produced for many years and sold in huge quantities. Therefore it has relatively little value in and of itself. It is unusual titles and interesting pictorial covers that make it of premium interest.

"The condition is most important. List all flaws including soil, frays, and fading. If the seller prices the sheet, the price is subject to my inspection upon receipt of the music." If you have larger quantities to sell, it is suggested that you obtain Dan's wants list, which provides detailed information on how to ship them for inspection and an offer.

"I also want sets of illustrated song slides used to plug popular songs in theaters (1896-1917). They measure approximately three by four inches, are made of glass, and come in sets of about sixteen. I will buy incomplete sets if the subject matter is of interest."

Dan is a professional musician and owner of one of the largest collections of sheet music in the world. He also expresses interest in "anything at all" about the banjo and its players.

SHEET MUSIC

Beverly A. Hamer
Sheet Music Sales
P.O. Box 75
East Derry, New Hampshire 03041
(603) 432-3528

Beverly Hamer is a fifteen-year veteran mail-order dealer in popular American sheet music.

Each month she publishes a large list of sheet music for sale from her own stock, so she constantly needs new items. She will sell sheet music for you on consignment, with a 50-50 split.

The best sheet music is humorous, pictorial, and interesting. She asks for the title, composer, lyricist, and description of the cover. She will do appraisals at no charge and will make offers on unpriced items. She has suggested that items be forwarded for her consideration, but only after contacting her.

SHEET MUSIC

Helen West Cole
H.W. Cole Enterprises
P.O. Box 201
Woodburn, Oregon 97071
(503) 891-7337

Helen Cole buys and sells sheet music of all types, including popular country and western, jazz, folk, movie, stage, or what have you. She'll buy collections or single pieces of music for piano, guitar, organ, or other instruments.

She especially wants (1) large-size popular music with pictures of automobiles, trains, sports, elections, and other Americana; (2) music with colored lithographs on the cover; (3) folios of popular music with words and pictures by or about the artist or composer; (4) music featuring popular performers on the cover; and (5) music with painting by famous illustrators on the cover.

All music must be in excellent condition, no fraying or other tears. To receive her offer, provide the name of the piece, the composer and lyricist, the publisher, the copyright date, and the cover artist. A photocopy would be helpful. "The scarcer the music, the higher the price. Age alone has no bearing on value."

FINE-QUALITY STRINGED INSTRUMENTS

Robert Portukalian
Providence Violin Shop
1279 North Main Street
Providence, Rhode Island 02904

The Providence Violin Shop wants to buy used violins, violas, and cellos "of merit," preferably handmade instruments by known makers.

"I do not want, buy, or sell cheap factory instruments with facsimile labels inside of past famous master makers such as Stradivarius. There are thousands of valuable violins hidden in closets and attics which can be sold for a premium price, yet they rot away unnoticed. There are also several million reproduction violins with famous names but with very little value.

Expert advice is essential, and Robert Portukalian, after thirty years in the business, is one of the experts.

If you have a violin or other fine stringed instrument for sale, he first wants to know who made it, then a complete statement of condition. Are there any cracks or obvious repairs? Describe your instrument well, and he will make offers.

MUSICAL INSTRUMENTS

Sid Glickman
53 Leighton Avenue
Yonkers, New York 10705
(914) 476-7897 (answering machine days)

For more than fifteen years, Sid Glickman has been buying old and new musical instruments, especially odd ones, from any country of origin and in any condition.

"I would also like to obtain anything related to musical instruments, such as catalogs, books, photographs, prints, batons, metronomes, and autographs. I do not concentrate on any particular type of instrument, but rather I am on the lookout for anything that is not in my collection."

He wants the name of the instrument, the maker, and accurate count of the number of keys, valves, and strings, and a statement of its condition. A photograph is desirable, and a serial number should provided if possible. "I like to get the historical background of instruments, and to correspond with other collectors."

Sid is always willing to trade instruments if there is something special you are seeking. He is pleased to make offers if you give him sufficient information.

STRINGED INSTRUMENTS

Steve Senerchia
Music Man
87 Tillinghast Avenue
West Warwick, Rhode Island 02893
(401) 821-2865

For nearly fifteen years, Steve Senerchia has been buying guitars, banjos, mandolins, violins, and basses, and he has developed a reputation for the high quality of his restorations.

Brand names he seeks include Gibson, Martin, B & D, Vega, Paramount, Stromberg, D'Angelico, Orheum, and Tone King. An extensive wants list, which includes descriptions of many other makes and models of instruments, is available.

Describe your instrument by giving the maker's name, the model number or name, the measurements from end to end, and note any alterations or changes you can see. "If possible, send a Polaroid," he asks. He will make offers, but charges a fee for written appraisals.

MISCELLANEOUS MUSIC

Grace Friar
Musical Notes
12 Grafton Street
Greenlawn, New York 11740
(516) 261-2636

Grace Friar is a mail-order auctioneer who specializes in sheet music and piano rolls, so is always willing to obtain new items for sale.

Grace also buys and sells music box disks, cylinder phonograph recordings, and "related items."

If you contact her, she wants to know the type of recording, the brand (label) name, the name of the song, the artist, the length and diameter of the roll, and the condition of both the recording and the container.

Grace does not do appraisals of items that aren't for sale, but she will make offers on items she can purchase for resale.

GLENN MILLER AND BUNNY BERIGAN

John L. Mickolas
172 Liberty Street
Trenton, New Jersey 08611
(609) 599-9672

John Mickolas specializes in "any memorabilia" of two late big band leaders, Glenn Miller and Bunny Berigan.

Included among his wants are photographs, sheet music, autographs, articles, magazine feature stories, newspaper clippings, 78 RPM recordings, 16- inch transcription disks, home recordings, tapes, home movies, newsreels, and what have you. John also buys similar items relating to other popular big band leaders of the 1930s and 1940s.

Simply state what you have and the condition it is in if you want John to make offers.

John is active in many associations having to do with Miller and offers an illustrated and priced wants lists, which you may request.

THE BEATLES AND THE ROLLING STONES

Edy J. Chandler
P.O. Box 20664
Houston, Texas 77225
(713) 668-7864 or (713) 527-8402

Edy Chandler owns most of the common Beatles items, but she is always in the market for the "rare, unique, and unusual."

Among the items that she is actively seeking are:

1. Dinnerware: cups and saucers, mugs, drinking glasses, or plates with Beatle pictures

2. Toy musical instruments: any size, plastic or wooden, including guitars, banjos, drums, and bongos

3. Bobbing head dolls: only the 15½-inch-tall version made by Car Mascots of California and only in complete sets

4. Concert programs: only those from appearances in Europe or Japan

5. Miscellany: including record players, record carrying cases, talc tins, Yellow Submarine banks, and the tin windup Beatles band

She also buys some items from another British rock group, The Rolling Stones. She wants various Rolling Stones magazines, especially those issued in England; Rolling Stones gum cards, and the 7-inch mini-LP records used in jukeboxes (London label only, though).

A brief description, noting condition, is sufficient.

PHONOGRAPHIC MEMORABILIA

Steven I. Ramm
420 Fitzwater Street
Philadelphia, Pennsylvania 19147
(215) 922-7050

Steve Ramm wants a wide range of phonographic items, including (1) cylinder phonographs and records; (2) early phonograph advertising (except magazine ads); (3) phonograph and record catalogs; (4) postcards featuring phonographs; (5) stereoview cards with phonographs or pictures of Edison; (6) phonograph needle tins; (7) recordings of Eubie Blake or Sissle & Blake; (8) Vogue picture records; (9) Vitaphone Discs; and (10) 78 RPM spoken word records.

"I want a few pre-1940 musical 78s, but since there are so many in existence I need a list of what you have to sell. Your list should include the label, the artist, the titles and the condition. I need all this information." He generally does not buy classical records. Send the make and model number of all phonographs. A photograph that shows the condition is helpful.

Steve has agreed to make purchase offers, but he requests an SASE if you want lists or photographs returned.

ANTIQUE PHONOGRAPHS

Larry Donley
Seven Acres Antique Village and Museum
8512 South Union Road
Union, Illinois 60180
(815) 923-2214

The Seven Acres Antique Village and Museum has what its curator describes as "the largest collection of antique phonographs on display in the United States." The museum seeks to buy fine-quality antique phonographs, music boxes, records, and "music-related items."

Larry Donley has been collecting for nearly three decades and is a well-known collector in his field. If you have a musical item to sell, he would enjoy hearing from you. "Just call or write with specifics of the item you have for sale. Your inquiry will be answered and a follow-up will be arranged.

He will make an offer for anything he can use for the museum collection or for resale. He also pays a substantial finder's fee to people who tell him about the location of fine machines that he later purchases.

JUKEBOXES

Ricky Botts
2545 SE 60th Court
Des Moines, Iowa 50317
(515) 265-8324 eves.

Rick wants pre-1955 jukeboxes, especially Wurlitzer, Rock-Ola, and Seeburg. He also wants advertising, brochures, catalogs, service manuals, parts manuals, and other literature about any brand or model of jukebox.

In most instances, you will find a tag on the back of the box that gives the maker and model number. Provide him with that and a general description, noting all defects and cracks, and an offer will be forthcoming. Make a photocopy of advertising, brochures, and other paper ephemera.

Rick is the publisher of the monthly Jukebox Collector Newsletter and author of a book on jukebox restoration.

NONMUSIC AND MECHANICAL MUSIC RECORDINGS

C.L. Batson
5512 Buggywhip Drive
Centreville, VA 22020
(703) 830-0583

C.L. Batson wants to buy a number of unusual recordings:

1. Long-playing records of sound effects, trains, planes, race cars, or any event that is not basically musical or spoken. He particularly wants records on the Riverside label.

2. Long-playing records of mechanical instruments, music boxes, calliope organs, unusual instruments, and electronic music. All labels are wanted except Audio Fidelity and Murry Hill

3. Audiophile orchestral, keyboard, and instrumental records (no jazz or rock), especially the following labels: Sheffield, Direct Disk, Crystal Clear, Varese Sarabande, M & K, Denon, Delos, Telarc, Mobile Fidelity and DBX

4. Long-playing ethnic and specialty recordings of Louisiana Cajun instrumentals, harmonica instrumentals, bluegrass and banjo instrumentals, autoharp instrumentals, Moog synthesizer, and Polynesian music

5. Long-playing records from the London Phase 4 series

6. Any musical or spoken titles on the American Civil War

Don't bother to write unless your record is in excellent to mint condition. In your letter, include the title, the record company and number, and a description of any defects, especially warps or audible scratches. He requests that you state the price wanted, but he has indicated a willingness to make offers for desirable titles.

He is actively seeking other collectors with whom to trade.

ENTERTAINMENT MACHINES

Alvin Heckard
RD 1, Box 88
Lewistown, Pennsylvania 17044
(717) 248-2816

Al Heckard likes a wide variety of entertainment machines. As a result, he is likely to buy: phonographs with outside horns; radios, if they are pre-1930; cathedral-style radios; Atwater Ket and Zenith console radios; pre-1950 TV sets with 7-inch or smaller screens; and any coin-operated amusement machine.

This twenty-five year veteran collector-restorer-dealer also wants to purchase "any parts or literature on the above items."

He asks only that you tell him the "make, model, condition, and price." He does not do appraisals or make offers. Note that a few of these items have values in excess of $1,000, so a certain amount of research is advisable.

MUSIC BOXES AND AUTOMATIC PIANOS

Dave Bowers
P.O. Box 1224
Wolfeboro, New Hampshire 03894
(603) 569-5095

Dave Bowers wants various mechanical musical instruments:

1. Music boxes made by Regina, Polyphon, and others between 1890 and 1910

2. Coin-operated pianos, especially by Wurlitzer and Seeburg

3. Band organs, calliopes, and other automatic musical instruments made for pre-1930 public places

Dave requests "as complete a description as possible, including, whenever you can, a color photograph of what you have to sell."

Dave has written the basic reference work in the field of automatic music, The Encyclopedia of Automatic Musical Instruments, and is available to assist you in pricing.

MECHANICAL MUSIC

William H. Edgerton
Mechanical Music Center, Inc.
Box 88-25, King's Highway North
Darien, Connecticut 06820
(203) 655-9510

"We will buy all types of mechanical musical instruments: cylinder and disk phonographs; cylinder and disk music boxes; organettes; automata; barrel and band organs; nickelodeons; electric player pianos and rolls; and original literature related to any of these items.

"Condition is not important," William Edgerton writes, "although we prefer unrestored instruments. We are interested in any quantity, from one small music box to a garage full of pianos. Mechanical music is our only business." He would like a clear photograph and a good description, including all markings, model numbers, etc.

He does not charge for making offers on items for sales, but does charge a fee for insurance and other appraisals. Edgerton is a senior member of the American Society of Appraisers, among numerous other organizations, and and author of Automatic Musical Instruments Pricing Guide.

PHONOGRAPH RECORDS

L.R. "Les" Docks
Shellac Shack
P.O. Box 32924
San Antonio, Texas 78216
(512) 492-6021

Les Docks buys an enormous range of pre-1965 phonograph records in all sizes and speeds, including radio transcriptions and test pressings.

Just about every record except classical can probably find a market with Les, who lists jazz, dance bands, big bands, swing, jug bands, washboard bands, blues, rhythm and blues, hillbilly, rockabilly, rock 'n' roll, celebrity, and other popular music as the items he seeks.

You can get an extensive wants list of "better" 78 RPM labels from the 1920s through the 1950s by sending him $2. The list contains thousands of records and the price he will pay for each. The $2 is refunded on your first sale to him. It is not necessary to buy the guide, but it is a big help and can avoid a lot of needless correspondence.

Listing of records for sale should include the label and catalog number, the name of the artist, and the title of the song. Les is well qualified, as author of a price guide to records, to make offers for what you have.

MECHANICAL MUSIC

Violet Altman
Vi & Si's Antiques
8970 Main Street
Clarence, New York 14031
(716) 634-4488

The Altmans deal in piano rolls, music box disks, organ rolls, cylinder records, Edison Diamond Disk Phonograph records, and "anything pertaining to mechanical music."

They buy music boxes, organettes, old jukeboxes, and early cylinder and outside horn phonographs. They also buy catalogs and other paper ephemera related to these items.

When describing rolls or records, list the record label, artist, title, and composer. Describe equipment as completely as you can, paying attention to damage and missing pieces. They will make offers on well-described items they can use.

JAZZ LPs

Gary Alderman
G's Jazz, Inc.
P.O. Box 9164.
Madison, Wisconsin 53715
(608) 274-3527

Gary Alderman wants to buy jazz LPs from the 1940s and 1950s. "I am not interested in 78s or 45s," he emphasizes.

He also buys jazz literature and memorabilia from any period, including magazines, year books, record review books, autographed photos, etc.

When selling records, tell him the artist, title, label name and number, and the condition of the record and jacket. When describing literature, pay close attention to condition, as he wants items in very fine condition only. A photocopy is most helpful.

You can state your own price or ask him to make an offer. Please include your telephone number. For twenty-five years Gary has been dealing exlusively in jazz LPs.

PHONOGRAPH RECORDS

Worldwide Collectors
P.O. Box 245
Ormond Beach, Florida 320745

If you have records to sell, Worldwide offers a lengthy (about twenty-page) wants list that shows prices paid for a few thousand different records, 45s, 78s, and LPs. Although a range of performers is included, Worldwide's greatest interest appears to be in the rock 'n' roll and rhythm and blues records of the 1950s.

To sell to Worldwide, you need to have its wants list, which currently costs $5, refundable on your first sale. Purchase of a catalog entitles you to become a member of Worldwide's update service for an aditional $2, thus keeping you posted on wants as they change.

"Everything someone needs to know about selling to us is in the catalog," says the company president.

ROCK & ROLL, R&B, AND
COUNTRY MUSIC RECORDS

Cliff Robnett
7804 NW 27
Bethany, Oklahoma 73008
(405) 787-6703 eves.

Cliff Robnett collects, buys, and sells 45s and LPs from the 1950s and 1960s.

"I prefer rock 'n' roll, rhythm and blues, and country and western music, but can use some pop music of the Doris Day-Eddie Fisher type. I like records with pictures of the artist."

List the label, artist, song or album title, and the condition of the record and the jacket. Note if it is a demonstration copy, radio station copy, etc. He can send a wants list, but prefers you to just list what you have. He has been in business more than twenty years and will make offers.

78 RPM PHONOGRAPH RECORDS

David Alan Reiss
3920 Eve Drive
Seaford, New York 11783
(516) 785-8336

David Reiss specializes in 78 RPM recordings dating before 1940. He buys, sells, and collects popular, classical, jazz, personality, and country and western.

"I buy entire collections and will travel to view collections anywhere in the Northeast or the South."

He also buys books, catalogs, and sheet music relating to music, movies, and the stage of the 1900 to 1930s.

He wants the artist, title, label, and index number of phonograph records. Make certain to include an SASE if you ask for information, an appraisal, or an offer.

Dave is a member of various organizations and is an active speaker on the 1920s and 1930s. He began collecting records forty years ago and has been selling them for the past decade.

1950s ROCK & ROLL AND TV

Dr. Allen B. Radwill
231 West Tabor Road
Philadelphia, Pennsylvania 19120
(215) 927-4624

Dr. Radwill wants pre-1972 items related to television or to rock 'n' roll. Among the things he buys are:

1. Rock 'n' roll records (1952-72)
2. Rock 'n' roll concert posters or programs (all years)
3. Posters from rock 'n' roll movies (1952-72)
4. Rock 'n' roll magazines (1952-72)
5. Sheet music related to movies, television, or rock 'n' roll which pictures the performer on the cover
6. All posters, programs, music, and phonograph recordings that have to do with television shows (any years)

He also buys novelty and Christmas records and recordings of interview shows and public service announcements.

"Condition is important," he notes, and requests that you call him (not collect) or include your telephone number. He will make offers on well-described items.

RECORD COMPANY LITERATURE

Tim Brooks
84-22 264th Street
Floral Park, New York 11001
(212) 664-2078

For fifteen years, Tim Brooks has been buying literature published by phonograph record companies, including catalogs, monthly supplements, and other paper ephemera.

His collection extends from the 1890s to the 1960s and focuses on paper ephemera that both describe and picture phonograph records and covers. He indicates that he will buy company listings of records that are not illustrated, "primarily from, but not limited to, the 78 RPM era."

No appraisals of items not for sale, but offers will be made gladly if you provide sufficient information. A photocopy would be helpful. Tim is president of the Association for Recorded Sound Collections and has written various articles on the recording industry and other entertainment media.

OLD BROADCAST AND SHORTWAVE RADIOS

J.E. Howell
P.O. Box 73
Folly Beach, South Carolina 29439

J.E. Howell is interested in "old broadcast and shortwave radios, preferably unmodified."

He has been a collector-dealer in early radios for thirty-five years, but does not publish a wants list, does not make appraisals, and will not make purchase offers on equipment.

What he does do is publish the Electronics Trader, a biweekly swap sheet for persons to advertise radios or electronic equipment for sale. Ads generally cost between $3 and $10 and may help you find just the right buyer. Inquire for current advertising and subscription rates.

Collectors want to know the make, model, year, condition, and whether there are modifications. The latter will be difficult for most amateurs to tell, but do the best you can. It is customary for the seller to advertise the price wanted, but you may also ask readers to "inquire if interested."

ATWATER KENT AND McMURDO SILVER RADIOS

Arthur Axelman
19652 Weeburn Lane
Tarzana, California 91356

Art Axelman is a fairly new, but expert, collector of Atwater Kent radios and their less well known line of automotive items. In addition to the radios themselves, Art buys wood, tin, cardboard, or paper display signs intended as in-store advertising.

He also buys McMurdo Silver radio receivers, advertising, catalogs, "and anything else that bears the name McMurdo Silver."

Art would like to obtain personal correspondence from Atwater Kent or McMurdo Silver, the men for whom these two brands of radio were named, as well as photographs of the men or their factories, news accounts involving the men or their companies and products, and all other related material.

He wants a photograph or photocopy, which he will return. He requires you to set the price desired in the first letter. Provide all model names or numbers and a "candid and accurate" description of the item's condition. These radios often have values in excess of $100, and a little research is suggested.

EARLY RADIOS

Charles J. Hinkle
Route 11, Box 3
Fredericksburg, Virginia 22405
(703) 373-6546

Charles Hinkle wants battery radios, "cat's whisker" crystal sets, horn speakers, old tubes, and radio parts made before 1926. He is particularly interested in "wireless era" items of World War I vintage or before, including military radio receivers and transmitters.

"I also want radio and wireless magazines and catalogs issued before 1926, telegraph items, and stock market tickers. I am interested in pre-World War II ham equipment. I am not interested in electric radios that run on house current unless they are unusual, such as grandfather clock radios or radios with chrome-plated chassis like the Scott or McMurdo Silver."

He continues, "When inquiring, list the brand name and/or manufacturer and model number of other identification informations. Describe interior and exterior condition, including whether parts appear to be broken or missing. If you cannot find the manufacturer's name or model numbers, send a sketch or photograph." Purchase offers or appraisals will be forthcoming if your radio is of interest.

PRE-1946 TELEVISION SETS

Arnold L. Chase
9 Rushleigh Road
West Hartford, Connecticut 06117
(203) 521-5280

Arnold Chase collects pre-1946 television sets, including the "mechanical" spinning disk sets of the 1920s and the electronic sets of the late 1930s.

Upon request he will send you a fairly lengthy wants list, which includes "all known models from the 1938-40 period, each of which is worth upwards of $1,000 in reasonable condition and physically complete." A favorite specialty of his is the "mirror-in-the-lid" type of sets. These feature a mirror on the underside of a lift lid, which reflects the image an of upward-pointing picture tube. A good way to identify pre-1946 sets is to look at the channel selector, he says, since "no pre-1946 set could tune above channel 6."

He is also interested in catalogs, literature, advertisements, owner's manuals, and other ephemera dealing with pre-1946 television sets. "A substantial finder's fee is paid for successful leads which result in the purchase of any of these sets," he adds, so even if you don't own one, but know where one is that could be purchased, it may be worthwhile to contact him.

If you have one of these early sets, he wants to know the brand name, the model number, and the general physical condition. Warning: If the set has not been turned on for a long time, do not plug it in. You could cause a great deal of damage.

Arnold is a television broadcast professional who is gradually restoring all the sets he buys to working order. The ultimate goal is for them to be housed in a museum of early television in Hartford.

OLD RADIOS AND TVs

Mel Rosenthal, D.C.
507 South Maryland Avenue
Wilmington, Delaware 19804
(302) 994-0874

Dr. Rosenthal wants to buy pre-1930 radios, both battery and AC (wall plug) operated. He is particularly interested in unusual portables, radios covered with mirrors, and ornate radios of all types. Among the most interesting makes are Kennedy, Federal, Atwater Kent, and DeForrest. He also buys any pre-World War II television sets.

Indicate the manufacturer, the model number, and the condition of the radio or TV. Mel is a veteran collector attempting to build a display of radios and TVs for a local museum, so good-condition items only, please. Mel will make offer on well-described sets he can use.

RADIO HORN SPEAKERS

Floyd A. Paul
1545 Raymond
Glendale, California 92101
(213) 242-8961

For nearly ten years, Floyd Paul has been collecting unusual radio speakers from the 1920s.

"Some horns have bells, goose necks, and bases," he writes, "while others are curled like early air auto horns. Some horns are in cabinets. Some are shaped into table lamps, and so on. They are known to have been made of sea shells, porcelain, aluminum, copper, papier-mache, pressed wood, solid wood, amethyst, and other materials. More than 315 manufacturers and over 600 models of radio horns have been identified, and more than 5 million horns were made, so there are still a lot of them around."

Your description should include the manufacturer, the model number or name, the color, the type of finish, and the condition. If you send a photograph along with your description and an SASE, he will quote a price on all horns offered.

Floyd has written a book on radio horn speakers and is an officer in the Southern California Antique Radio Society.

RADIO TRANSCRIPTION DISKS

Larry F. Kiner
P.O. Box 724
Redmond, Washington 98052-0724

Larry Kiner wants transcription disks from "the network days" of radio, roughly 1930 to 1960. "Any transcription disks, any size, any speed, may be of interest," he writes, "including AFRS World War II era re-pressings of network and AFRS programming. I will consider tape copies of items in lieu of actual disks but would prefer to make my own copies."

Particular favorites include Bing Crosby, Al Jolson, Fats Waller, Art Tatum, Artie Shaw, and the other bands and musicians of the period. Also of special interest are dramatic, adventure, and comedy programs such as Lux Radio Theater, "The Thin Man," "Terry and the Pirates," "Fibber McGee and Molly," and the like.

He is also interested in radio magazines from the 1930s and 1940s, and scripts of early radio programs.

Include as much information about the item as you can. Please state the price you would like for what you have. He will sometime make offers on unpriced items.

PRE-1927 BATTERY RADIOS

David Shanks
115 Baldwin Street
Bloomfield, New Jersey 07003
(201) 748-8820

For more than ten years, David Shanks has been a collector of pre-1927 battery radios, crystal sets, and wireless equipment.

He provides a long list of radios he is seeking, almost all of which are worth at least $50. At the top of the list, bringing in excess of $100, are radios by Atwater Kent, De Forrest, Kennedy, and Federal.

Dave also buys tubes, parts, magazines, books, and related items pertaining to early radio. Indicate the make, model number, and condition. "A photo is often useful in determining information about your radio," he says. He will make offers on unpriced items for amateur sellers.

PRE-1935 RADIOS

Gary Schneider
6848 Commonwealth Boulevard
Cleveland, Ohio 44130
(216) 582-3094

This fifteen-year veteran collector wants to purchase radio items dating between 1905 and 1935.

"My interests are (1) wireless receivers and transmitters; (2) crystal sets; (3) battery-operated radios of the 1914-28 period; (4) small electric table model radios made between 1928 and 1935; and (5) catalogs, magazines, service manuals, advertising, dealer literature, and promotional items related to pre-1935 radios." He does not want the large console model radios of the 1930s unless they are highly unusual or have chrome-plated interiors.

Also wanted are radio speakers, tubes, and parts for all radios dating before 1935. Early television and telegraph items are also of interest.

Gary Schneider strongly urges people to send a good, clear photograph of the radio or other items they have to sell. Photocopies or sketches are helpful. We will make offers on items he can use.

13
Books, Catalogs, Magazines, Newspapers and Autographs

ALICE IN WONDERLAND AND ILLUSTRATED BOOKS

Joel Birenbaum
7917 Chelsea Court
Woodridge, Illinois 60517
(312) 985-8560 eves.

"I am looking for editions of Alice In Wonderland and Through the Looking Glass by Lewis Carroll that are illustrated by other than John Tenniel. I am basically interested in obtaining first editions of these illustrated versions. I also collect other Lewis Carroll-related material, as well as Alice parodies. I am currently expanding the scope of my collection to include other Alice material such as figures, games, toys, posters, and ephemera.

"I also deal in out-of-print illustrated children's books. I will consider purchasing first editions of books illustrated by such artists as Jessie Wilcox Smith, Charles Robinson, Willy Pogany, Alice Woodward, Charles Folkart, Arthur Rackham, and Maurice Sendak. I am also anxious to hear about any unusual books or books with moving parts. I will buy single volumes or large quantities of books."

For all books, Joel Birenbaum wants to know the title, author, illustrator, publisher, place of publication, and date of publication and copyright. A full description should also include the color and type of binding, the number of illustrations and whether they are in color and/or black and white, and the number of pages. Note all chips, bumps, tears, loose pages, missing pages, marks, writing, soiling, discoloration (fading), shelf wear, etc.

Joel will make offers on items he can use for his collection or for resale.

TUNEBOOKS AND HYMNBOOKS

Carl N. Shull
436 North Mt. Joy Street
Elizabethtown, Pennsylvania 17022
(717) 367-5346

Carl Shull is primarily interested in oblong tunebooks (singing school books) published in the 18th and 19th centuries. These were compiled by Tansur, Billings, Walker, Wyeth, Mason, Hastings, Bradbury, and others.

He also wants German and American hymnbooks, English psalters, and bound collections of 19th-century sheet music.

This twenty-five-year veteran collector-dealer wants to know the author or compiler, the title of the book, the date of publication or copyright, the condition of the contents, and the condition of the cover and spine. For bound sheet music, he want to know the number of pieces, selected copyright dates, and general condition.

In all instances, he prefers you to set a price, but he will make offers for works he can use for his collection or for resale.

RARE BOOKS

David and Anne Bromer
Bromer Booksellers, Inc.
607 Boylston Street
Boston, Massachusetts 02116
(617) 247-2818

The Bromers are in their third decade as dealers in rare books. For their stock, they seek the following: fine and rare first editions; fine and rare first editions; private press books; pre-1900 books containing paper dolls; pre-1900 trick or mechanical books; English or American children's books before 1850; and books less than three inches tall in any language (except Bibles or dictionaries dating after 1900).

When offering books, include the author, title, publisher, place and date of publication, description of the binding, and a statement of condition covering both the text and the binding.

Describe your items well, and the Bromers will make you an offer if they are genuinely for sale.

BIBLES

Miles Eisele
Hunters Woods Fellowship House
2231 Colts Neck Road
Reston, Virginia 22091
(703) 620-4450

Miles Eisele, manager of this Lutheran Fellowship house, writes, "I will buy English-language Bibles and New Testaments (no foreign languages) which were published in England or the United States between 1550 and 1850. No Bibles after 1850, as millions have been published."

Owners of pre-1850 Bibles are encouraged to ship them for his offer or return. He pays approximately $30 for Bibles from the early 1800s. A Bible from the 1700s will generally bring $50 to $150, depending on age, printer, text, style, etc.

If you decide not to ship but would like to sell, tell him the date the Bible or New Testament was published and the name and address of the publisher, as well as the depth, height, and width of the book. Are the covers attached? Are all pages, including title pages, intact? Are there tears or water stains? "It doesn't have to be a professional description of the Bible, just a general, commonsense idea of its overall condition and appearance."

SCIENCE FICTION AND MYSTERY PAPERBACKS

Leonard D. Dick
P.O. Box 3711
Bartlesville, Oklahoma 74006
(918) 335-2179 eves., weekends

Leonard Dick wants science fiction and mystery detective paperback books, magazines, digests, and pulps.

He buys for his own collection and for resale, wants only good-condition goods, and will buy small or large lots. You may request his wants list.

He asks for the title, author, publisher's name, book or issue number, printing date, and condition. He will make offers if he can use what you have.

ELBERT HUBBARD AND THE ROYCROFTERS

Thomas and Rosaline Knopke
The House of Roycroft
1430 East Brookdale Place
Fullerton, California 92631

The Knopkes want to buy "everything of, by, about, or related to Elbert Hubbard, the Roycrofters, the Larkin Soap Company, and the Buffalo Pottery Company."

They prefer to buy larger lots, but will gladly buy single items or small quantities. Tom notes, "While we do not purchase every piece, we appreciate having the opportunity to bid. We are not interested in Wise & Co. publications but do try us for anything else." Roycroft items are marked with an "R" in a circle with a two-armed cross atop.

Include a brief description and an indication of how you came to own the item. They ask that you also indicate how you heard of their interests, since they advertise and exhibit widely. Don't forget an SASE if you inquire.

LONGFELLOW BOOKS AND MEMORABILIA

Laraine Lange
4157 North 79th Street
Milwaukee, Wisconsin 53222
(414) 462-3664

Laraine Lange wants a wide range of items related to American author Henry W. Longfellow, including busts, photographs, pictures, and souvenirs of Longfellow and his family. "I would also love to find items such as statuary relating to his poems or characters within them, especially Evangeline, Hiawatha, and Minnehaha."

As for books by Longfellow, she wants only first editions, complete sets, and foreign editions of his work. She will also buy biographies of Longfellow.

Tell her the publisher, publication date, and size of all books. A photograph is requested for statuary. "Describe everything as much as possible, especially condition." She will make offers on items she can use.

MATH, SCIENCE, AND SCIENCE FICTION

Merlin D. Schwegman
Merlin's Bookshop
6543 Pardall Road
Isla Vista, California 93117
(805) 968-7946

Merlin's Bookshop wants an interesting assortment of books:

1. Any books on recreational mathematics
2. Pre-1930 books on higher mathematics in any language
3. Anything by or about the Wright Brothers, Thomas Paine, James Clerk Maxwell, Nikola Tesla, Copernicus, Galileo, Archimedes, Scipio Africanus, Isaac Newton
4. Fantasy and science fiction first editions
5. Books on book binding

This fifteen-year veteran collector-dealer would like you to provide him with the author, title, edition or date of printing, and condition. You must set the price wanted, as he does not make offers.

MYSTERY AND DETECTIVE BOOKS

Martha W. Rhodes
1220 Third Avenue
Picayune, Mississippi 39466
(601) 798-3482

Martha Rhodes, a retired librarian, is a mystery fan seeking to complete her collection of Unicorn Mystery Club 4-in-1 books and Detective Book Club 3-in-1 books.

Martha collects these because she enjoys reading them and sharing them with friends, not because they are worth much money. She generally pays from $1 to $3 per volume for those needed. "I don't have much spare cash," she writes, "but love to read, trade books, and correspond with other mystery fans."

If you have any of these multivolumes to part with, she'd like you to list the title and author of the first story in the book. She can supply a list of books she needs and books she has extra copies of for trade or sale.

DIME NOVELS

Edward T. LeBlanc
87 School Street
Fall River, Massachusetts 02720
(617) 672-2082

Ed LeBlanc is the nation's expert on dime novels, the turn-of-the-century popular escape fiction. He is always eager to obtain more of them for his own collection or, primarily, for resale.

This forty-year veteran collector-dealer also buys boys' and girls' series books, such as the Rover Boys, Tom Swift, and others.

He requests that you provide the title, author, publisher, date of publication, series number when appropriate, as well as a description of the illustrations (if any), and a statement of condition of the paper—does it crack, tear, or crumble when bent? He will make offers for books he can use.

ASSORTED BOOKS

Ben Hamilton
Hampton Books
Route 1, Box 202
Newberry, South Carolina 29108
(803) 276-6870

Ben Hamilton is a veteran book dealer with a number of active specialties. He buys books, magazines, photographs, and "all memorabilia of good quality" on aviation history, from its beginning to space travel; movie, radio, and TV history; history of photography, including original photographs; general southern Americana, with an emphasis on South Carolina.

Tell Ben the author, title, publisher, date and place of publication, condition of the text and bindings, number of pages, and number and type of illustrations. Photocopying a page or two from items other than books is recommended. He prefers you to price what you have, but will make offers in some cases.

GERMAN-AMERICAN BOOKS AND DOCUMENTS

Donald R. Hinks
Obsolescence
24 Chambersburg Street
Gettysburg, Pennsylvania 17325
(717) 334-8634

Don Hinks buys all German-American books and other paper ephemera printed, written, or drawn in American before 1830. Wants include books, pamphlets, newspapers, birth certificates, baptismal certificates, posters, fraktur, and handwritten documents. Anything published by or about early German printers and publishers, especially the Brethren Church, the Dunkards, or the German Baptists, is also of interest, including copies of their various magazines.

In addition, Don seeks books and other printed ephemera about the Civil War or the history of Pennsylvania and surrounding states.

When describing books, include the author, title, publisher, place and date of publication, number of pages, approximate size, type of binding, and language in which it is published. Condition of both the text and binding should be clearly spelled out.

ENGINE MAGAZINES AND CATALOGS

Alan C. King
4790 River Road
Radnor, Ohio 43066

For nearly thirty years, Alan King has been buying a wide variety of magazines dealing with gasoline engines, tractors, aviation, and other topics. Among his extensive wants are:

1. Gasoline engine manuals, catalogs, parts books, and repair guides of all types before 1940

2. Tractor manuals, catalogs, parts books, and repair guides of all types before 1940

3. Camera manuals, catalogs, and sales brochures before 1940

4. Radio manuals, catalogs, amd sales brochures before 1940

5. Flying magazines: Popular Aviation, Flying, Flying Aces, and Aero Digest, all pre-1945

6. Tractor and gasoline engine magazines: Gas Power, Gas Review, and Tractor & Gas Review, all pre-1925

He does not want books on these topics, only magazines. He asks that you tell him the issue(s) available, the dates, the condition, and the approximate price you would like. In exchange for an SASE, he will make you an offer.

MAGAZINES

The Old Book Store
2040 Lafayette Street
Portsmouth, New Hampshire 03801
(603) 436-7250

For more than two decades, The Old Book Store has been buying bound and unbound runs of magazines, particularly early and less common publications.

They want to know the name of the magazine(s), the dates covered, the total number of issues involved, and whether the run is complete. Describe the condition, noting loose covers, cut-out pages, and other damage. It is not necessary to give long lists of individual dates.

They charge for appraisals and prefer not to make purchase offers on magazines.

In addition to magazines, the store also buys large quantities of new or old erotica, including books, girlie magazines, photos, films, and other items.

GIRLIE MAGAZINES

Warren Nussbaum
A.A.A.
29-10 137th Street
Flushing, New York 11354
(212) 886-0558

Warren Nussbaum is a dealer in secondhand girlie magazines.

He buys, for resale, excellent-condition only girlie magazines of any vintage, particularly 1920 to 1970. Among the more familiar titles he seeks are Taboo, Cavalier, Fling, Gent, Frolic, Playboy, Rapture, Night and Day, and many more.

You might try him as well with old copies of scandal sheet magazines, movie magazines, sports guides, and detective and action pulps. He will make offers on large or small lots of magazines with resale potential. He wants to know the date of publication, who is on the cover (if known), and any unusual or celebrity features the issue contains.

TEACHERS' AND CHILDREN'S MAGAZINES

Shirley Jane Hedge
Route 2, Box 52
Princeton, Indiana 47670
(812) 385-4080

Shirley Hedge is a twenty-year veteran collector of dolls, toys, and similar items who is listed elsewhere in this book. There are a number of magazine-related items she seeks, including:

1. Children's magazines printed between 1900 and 1960, such as Little Folks, Jack & Jill, Children's Playmate, The Friend, Wee Wisdom, Children's Activities, and Child Life

2. Teachers' magazines printed between 1920 and 1950

3. Magazine advertisements or covers printed in color between 1900 and 1950 that feature Santa Claus

4. Magazine advertisements printed in color between 1900 and 1950 depicting animals dressed as humans

5. Magazine or newspaper advertising that features paper dolls

When selling magazines, give the title, date, and an indication of whether any pages or items are missing. When offering advertisements, indicate the name and date of the publication from which they were removed; state condition. Note that Shirley will respond to requests for appraisals or offers, but only if you include an SASE.

KITCHEN AND HOUSEWARES CATALOGS

Linda Campbell Franklin
P.O. Box 383, Murray Hill
New York, New York 10016
(212) 679-6038 until 9 p.m. EST

Linda Franklin wants pre-1930 catalogs and brochures that feature advertising, particularly pictorial, for kitchen or household tools and gadgets. Catalogs dating before 1890 are particularly important, and she indicates, "I badly want an F.A. Walker catalog from the 1870's and will pay well for it."

Condition is important, as are the number of pages, the rarity of the items pictured, the number of pictures, and the amount of information contained. It is suggested that you send her a photocopy of the front (title) page and a sample of the contents.

Linda is an important name in the world of kitchen collectibles, author of From Hearth to Cookstove and other books, and the editor of Kitchen Collectibles News.

TV GUIDE

Jeffrey M. Kadet
P.O. Box 90
Rockville, Maryland 20850
(301) 654-1876

Jeff Kalet is a collector-dealer of TV Guide magazines and similar regional publications from the 1940s and early 1950s such as Chicago's TV Forecast, Philadelphia's TV Digest, and the like.

Provide Jeff with the year and date of the magazine, and a statement of condition that notes all tears, creases, and the like. If you send him an SASE he will make an offer by return mail.

OUTDOOR BOOKS AND MAGAZINES

George Bryant
Bryant's Book Shop
P.O. Drawer T
Hanson, Kentucky 42413

Bryant's Book Shop wants to buy:

1. Outdoor magazines having to do with hunting, fishing, trapping, or camping, including Field & Stream, Outdoor Life, Sports Afield, American Woodsman, Fur-Fish-Game, Outing, and many others
2. Gun magazines, Shooters Bible, and Gun Digest
3. Catalogs for fishing tackle, guns, or furs
4. Older farm magazines
5. Trapping methods books
6. Books on hunting, fishing, and the outdoors
7. Books about the fur trade or early settlements, especially those that describe the outdoor life of early mountain men

George Bryant wants to know the title and dates for magazines, author and publisher for books. He will buy some early magazines without covers, but notes that they are worth much less. He is willing to make "reasonable offers" is asked to do so.

EARLY NEWSPAPERS

Richard W. Spellman
Olde and Rare Newspapers
610 Monticello Drive
Brick Town, New Jersey 08723

Richard Spellman is a dealer in old newspapers and will buy English or American newspapers in bound or unbound runs, dating between 1600 and 1900.

He wants the name of the newspaper, the dates of the run, and the condition. Note all defects such as tears, stains, yellowing, brittleness, and serious creases. Any news that is either historically important or unusual should be pointed out.

Spellman is a noted authority in the field of journalism history and the evolution of the newspaper. He issues ten catalogs each year of newspapers for sale, so he is always in the market for more. He will make offers if you provide a good description.

NEWSPAPERS AND OTHER PAPER

Gordon Totty
576 Massachusetts Avenue
Lunenburg, Massachusetts 01462
(617) 582-7844

Gordon Totty is a veteran dealer who specializes in a variety of paper items:

1. Pre-1800 newspapers of all types
2. Pre-1875 newspapers with coverage of any war
3. Pre-1875 illustrated newspapers such as Harper's Weekly
4. Pre-1875 maps and atlases
5. Civil War paper items, including letters, documents, and photographs
6. Stereoview cards, especially Civil War views, early American city and town views, nautical views, and depictions of the military or Indians
7. Stereoviewers of all types
8. Pre-1875 books on the Civil War, Revolutionary War, or the military.
9. Early leatherbound books
10. Early books with color illustrations
11. Pre-1875 books on the sea, California, gold mining, travel, and discoveries
12. Saturday Evening Post and other magazines with covers by Norman Rockwell

Gordon says he'd like you to tell him the date, size, contents, condition, and price of what you have to sell. He does not make offers.

POTTERY CATALOGS

Jo Cunningham
Haf-a-Shoppe
P.O. Box 4929 GS
Springfield, Missouri 65808
(417) 865-3722

Jo Cunningham buys old books and catalogs that depict American pottery and dinnerware. Catalogs may be issued either by the manufacturer or by the retail industry.

Jo is a sophisticated collector and a well-known author on the topic of American dinnerware, so she is seeking good early items that will provide historical information.

Please price what you have, as Jo does not care to make offers. You may request appraisals for a small fee.

TECHNICAL CATALOGS AND MAGAZINES

C. L. Batson
5512 Buggywhip Drive
Centreville, VA 22020
(703) 830-0583

This longtime collector seeks to buy catalogs and magazines that pertain to the following types of equipment and apparatus: electric, electronic, radio, laboratory, scientific, medical, and dental.

C. L. Batson wants catalogs dating before 1950. He also wants World War II military surplus catalogs and advertisements dating between 1945 and 1955.

If you have catalogs to sell, state the title, copyright date, number of pages, condition, and price wanted in your first letter.

AUTOGRAPHS

Charles and Pat Searle
Searle's Autographs
P.O. Box 630
St. Mary's, Georgia 31558
(912) 882-5036

The Searle's are mail-order dealers in autographs who issue a catalog almost every month.

To keep up their stock, they need to buy letters, signed photographs, documents, manuscripts, signatures, and autographed books from all areas of autograph collecting, especially presidents, statesmen, authors, poets, artists, sports figures, movie stars, and explorers. They encourage you to write regarding any autograph.

Please describe the type of document you have, its size, its condition, and who signed it. They want to know the condition of both the paper and the signature. It is advisable to provide some details about the content of the document or letter. A photocopy is always helpful. The Searles will make an offer for anything they can use.

AUTOGRAPHS OF THE FAMOUS

Herman M. Darvick
Herman M. Darvick Autographs
P.O. Box 467
Rockville Centre, New York 11571
(516) 766-0093

For nearly three decades, Herman Darvick has been buying signatures, letters, documents, signed photographs, autographed books, manuscripts, Civil War diaries, and the like written by or about famous people in all walks of life, "from Queen Elizabeth I to Elizabeth Taylor to Zachary Taylor, or from Tom Edison to Tom Seaver."

The ideal inquiry, he says, would include four things: a photocopy of the entire item, your telephone number, a self-addressed stamped envelope, and the price you would like.

The latter is not absolutely necessary, Herman points out, as he is willing to make offers for documents or other salable items.

He is currently president of the world's largest autograph collector's club, editor of its newsletter, and author of a book on autograph collecting.

244   WHERE TO SELL ANYTHING AND EVERYTHING

AUTOGRAPHS AND DOCUMENTS

Charles Hamilton
Charles Hamilton Galleries, Inc.
200 West 57th Street
New York, New York 10019
(212) 245-7313

Perhaps the country's best-known dealer in autographs, Charles Hamilton wants to obtain autographs, letters, and documents of famous persons, or any handwritten material "that is intrinsically interesting" such as diaries, traveler's journals, or firsthand reports of experiences or famous events.

In addition, Hamilton Galleries buys signed photographs of movie stars, sports hereos, statesmen, authors, and composers as well as autographed books by established authors. Sketches and drawings by well-known artists will also be purchased.

Hamilton points out that it is extremely difficult to accurately judge the value of an autographed document without actually seeing the item. He urges you to write for his free pamphlet, "How to Sell Your Autographs," that describes exactly what steps must be taken if you are to receive top dollar. Ultimately, you will be required to ship what you have for inspection and a free appraisal. For more than thirty years Hamilton Galleries has been evaluating documents, making appraisals, and buying and selling. If you are not pleased with an offer, it will carefully pack and return what you have sent for examination.

Two important warnings come from Hamilton: Do not attempt to make any repairs to any document and do not destroy any old handwritten materials without consulting a reliable dealer or expert. "You may inadvertently throw out or give away the most valuable material."

Hamilton is the author of eight books and more than two hundred articles about autographs.

LETTERS AND AUTOGRAPHS OF THE FAMOUS

Leon H. Becker
Memorabilia, Ltd.
7624 El Camino Real
Carlsbad, California 92008
(714) 436-2321

Leon Becker specializes in letters written and signed by famous people, although he buys other autographs as well.

He wants you to describe the contents of the letter and the physical condition of the paper, of the letter itself, and of the signature. In addition, he wants to know when and where you obtained the item, and why you believe it to be a genuine signature rather than a mechanically reproduced one. Whenever possible, please include a photocopy with your inquiry.

If you have a specific price in mind, Leon would prefer that you price the item. He will, however, make offers for suitable items. His shop frames autographed documents and photographs into attractive ensembles for resale.

HANDWRITTEN DOCUMENTS

Terry Alford
Manuscript Company of Springfield
P.O. Box 1151
Springfield, Virginia 22151
(703) 256-6748

"I am interested in hearing from people who have old handwritten letters, journals, documents, ledgers, and similar things which they wish to sell.

"My interests are twofold. I always want to purchase things written by famous people, but I am equally anxious to buy things written by 'nobodies' who were at an interesting place or who lived during an important period and had something of historical interest to say. Diaries and collections of letters are particularly good in this period.

"Regardless of the subject matter or period of time involved, if you have material that is old and handwritten, do let me hear from you." A photocopy is suggested for single items or smaller lots. An overall description (including content, condition, dates, and authors) is necessary for larger collections.

Terry Alford is a professor of history at a local college and operates his manuscript business as a sideline. "The prices I pay are competitive with anyone's" he writes, as he expresses a willingness to help amateur sellers by making appraisals and offers.

PICTURES OF CHILDREN

Marguerite Cantine and Elizabeth Kilpatrick
P.O. Box 798
Huntington, New York 11743
(516) 271-8990

These two ladies are most famous for their outstanding collection of teddy bears, but they have other serious collecting interests:

1. Children's books from 19th-century Germany, England or the U.S. that contain color or black-and-white illustrations of children

2. Advertising signs and pieces that depict children

3. Calendars picturing children

"We prefer pictures of girls or girls with animals, but we also buy pictures of groups of children," writes Marguerite. She asks that you describe what you have and "suggest a price." Don't forget to include your name, address, telephone number, and an SASE. Marguerite and Elizabeth will send you a wants list and other information about their needs.

14

Paper Goods
of All Sorts; Coins

OLD POSTCARDS

John H. McClintock
P.O. Box 1765
Manassas, Virginia 22110
(703) 368-2757

For more than twenty years, John McClintock has been in the business of buying and selling pre-1930 postcards.

Among his favorites are expositions and fairs, small town events, transportation, aircraft, snowmen, Santa Claus, Main Street scenes, and cards showing coins and stamps. But there are many others he will buy.

"Old postcards must be seen to put a fair market value on them," according to John, so he encourages you to pack your cards and send them for an appraisal. Do make certain to take out any damaged cards and all cards after 1930. He does not want them, and you are just wasting postage to include them.

He pledges to have an appraisal and a check in the mail within three days of receipt of your cards. If you do not accept his offer, he will return your cards and reimburse your postage. He claims to pay more than other mail dealers, and will send you a most informative one-page dissertation entitled "Four Ways to Dispose of Antique Postcards" in exchange for a long SASE.

John is the founder of the Postcard Club Federation and the International Federation of Postcard Dealers. He is also the editor and publisher of Postcard Dealer Collector magazine, now in its sixth year.

PRE-1920 POSTCARDS

Thomas J. Boyd
140 Andover Lane
Williamsville, New York 14221
(716) 626-0089

Tom Boyd is a specialist in pre-1920 postcards, especially those published by PFB or Winsch. Although "all pre-1920 cards will be considered," Tom prefers those picturing Halloween, Santa Claus, fire stations, and railroad depots. He also buys:
  1. Advertising trade cards
  2. World's fair and exposition postcards and other memorabilia, especially from the Buffalo Pan American Exposition
  3. Pin-back buttons, both political and advertising
  4. U.S. stamps and envelopes from before 1930
Describe what you have, including a photocopy of the more important items. Include your telephone number and asking price. Tom will travel to inspect large or important collections. He does not appraise collections, but will make offers for items he can use.

POSTCARDS

Bryan Lizotte
The Post Card Exchange
P.O. Box 842
Shelton, Connecticut 06484
(203) 736-9532

Bryan Lizotte buys postcards. He prefers pre-1925 views of Connecticut cities and towns, but buys a wide range of other cards.
  It is suggested that you write for his wants list, which shows the specific subject matter and publishers he will buy.
  If you write him concerning cards, indicate the type of cards, their age, and the number of them you have. A sample of some of the cards is suggested if you find it inconvenient to make a few photocopies as examples. Make certain to describe the average condition of your card collection.

POSTERS AND OTHER PAPER, WINE, TOBACCO

George Theofiles
Miscellaneous Man
P.O. Box 1776
New Freedom. Pennsylvania 17349
(717) 235-4766

The Miscellaneous Man is a well-known eastern dealer in posters and all sorts of other paper memorabilia, largely items purchased through the mail. Among George Theofiles' principal wants are:

1. Posters of all types, all subjects, pre-1950
2. Movie memorabilia, including movie magazines, posters, souvenir books, and "anything having to do with film"
3. Transporation memorabilia, especially steamship and airline calendars, travel posters, and other promotional literature
4. Wine cooling buckets, unusual corkscrews, and other wine items
5. Pro- or anti-smoking material, advertising, catalogues, books
6. Menus, wine lists, ashtrays, napkins, and other memorabilia from restaurants, especially European bistros from before 1960
7. Cocktail shakers in unusual shapes or with advertising on them

Since his wants are so varied, it is best to telephone or write him and ask for instructions on describing what you have. George has a wants list, but does not make offers on unpriced items. He promises fast responses and "quick checks," but you set the price.

POSTCARDS

Chester Ashby
The Ashbys
2232 East Maple
Enid, Oklahoma 73701
(405) 233-5532

For more than a decade, Chester Ashby has been specializing in buying and selling postcards. His extensive wants include cards depicting railroad depots, trains, ships, and Oklahoma and Kansas street scenes.

He also buys cards featuring Santa Claus, New Year's, leap year, Labor Day, St. Patrick's Day, cute children, Sunbonnet girls, possums, bears, pigs, and outlandish exaggeration. He does not want greeting cards or postcards containing scenes of parks, trees, rivers, or bridges.

He would like an accurate description, a statement of condition, and the age of the cards offered. He prefers you to price your cards but will make purchase offers.

POSTCARDS OF COURTHOUSES

Volney J. Seaver
1408 Escalada Avenue
Rowland Heights, California 91748
(213) 964-5597

Volney Seaver buys postcards, but his wants are quite specific.

Postcards of U.S. and Canadian courthouses are his fancy, and he will buy them used or unused, from the days of the undivided backs down to modern chromes. He is particularly eager to hear from you if you know any of the history behind the courthouse. As a matter of fact, Volney would like to hear from you if you have interesting information about any U.S. or Canadian courthouse, even if you don't have a picture of it.

He requests that you tell him the type of postcard, the date it was cancelled, and its condition. He warns not to send cards on approval, as he buys only from lists.

POSTCARDS

Edy J. Chandler
P.O. Box 20664
Houston, Texas 77225
(713) 668-7864 or (713) 527-8402

Edy Chandler has a long list of postcards she will buy.

Her wants include cards illustrated by more than fifty artists, generally from the 20th century. She also wants postcards that are advertisments for automobile, motorcycle, airplane, airline or chewing gum companies.

She buys mechnical and hold-to-light postcards as well as cards depicting all sorts of other things. If you have postcards for sale, you will undoubtedly find it worthwhile to send a self-addressed stamped envelope for a long, specific wants list.

VALENTINES

Evalene Pulati
Valentine Collectors Association
P.O. Box 1404
Santa Ana, California 92702
(714) 547-1355

Evalene Pulati buys fancy pre-1900 valentines for her collection or for resale at club auctions. She will on occasion buy later valentines, but only very elaborate or unusual ones.

As she describes it, "I need large, showy lacey types and large foldouts or pull-downs in the shape of ships, carriages or other items. I will consider anything nice and unusual, and will accept fine-condition early valentines on approval."

If you don't send them on approval, a photocopy is almost essential to accurately describe the large, elaborate valentines Evalene buys. When photocopying or describing a valentine, the maker's name and marks on the back of the card are important. Your price is requested, but she will also make offers.

STAMPLESS LETTERS

Dale Ferber
Orion Philatelics
P.O. Box 1007
Brandon, Mississippi 39042
(601) 981-0113 or 992-2550

Dale Ferber specializes in "stampless letters," mail sent before standard postage stamps were issued by the government in 1847. These stampless letters will usually have the postage hand-stamped or written on the envelope or folded letter itself. Dale wants all stampless mail from before 1855 and all Civil War stampless mail, both Union and Confederate. Letters with interesting contents are especially desirable.

Dale also buys stamped envelopes or folded letters that predate 1870. "Never remove stamps from a stamped letter or early envelope," he warns, "since that reduces the value greatly."

"I would prefer a good photocopy showing all postmarks. If the contents are interesting, I would like a photocopy of the entire letter. Do not send any material unless instructed to do so by me. I will reimburse postage. I will make an appraisal and an offer based on your photocopies. If I don't want it but know someone else who does, I will refer the writer to the proper person."

STAMPS & COINS
STAMP COLLECTION

Herman Herst, Jr.
P.O. Box 1583
Boca Raton, Florida 33429
(305) 391-3223 or 391-8869

Herman Herst, Jr. is among the nation's best-known stamp dealers and author of more than a dozen books and thousands of magazine and newspaper columns on stamp collecting.

If you're curious about your old stamps, a great way to begin is to send fifty cents and a self-addressed stamped envelope to Mr. Herst for a copy of his most informative "Stamp Seller's Guide." This twenty-page booklet begins with a note saying, "We believe you will find that most, if not all, of your questions are answered in the following pages." You probably will. It is clear and informative for the amateur seller.

Herst buys stamp collections, stamped envelopes from before 1920, and autographs and manuscripts of important people (not movie stars or other entertainers). If you have items for sale, follow the directions in his pamphlet.

DOCUMENTS WITH REVENUE STAMPS

Michael Mahler
1725 The Promenade 204
Santa Monica, California 90401
(213) 393-1394

Michael Mahler is a collector of 18th- and 19th-century documents, especially those bearing U.S. or state revenue stamps. His special interests include documents with Civil war-era revenue stamps; western, southern or territorial stamped documents; and engraved or ornate documents with or without stamps.

He wants to know the type of document, the year it was executed, the place of execution, the type and denomination of stamp affixed, and any additional details you think significant. Mike does not require that you price what you have, as he is willing to make purchase offers on good-quality items he would like to add to his collection.

PAPER MONEY

Harry B. Wigington
P.O. Box 1538
Erie, Pennsylvania 16507
(814) 864-3371

Harry Wigington buys a number of items related to money:

1. Foreign paper money dating between 1700 and 1950, with particular interest in the Notgeld (inflation money) of Germany, 1914 to 1924

2. Obsolete U.S. and state paper money from before 1900

3. Depression scrip (paper money) issued by U.S. or Canadian towns or companies

4. Checks, bank drafts, stocks, bonds, and other paper related to banking and financial affairs.

Harry writes that he always prefers you to send photocopies, but if they are not practical, provide the denomination and the name of the bank, the city, the country, or the firm that issued the money. The date of issue and a description of any pictures (vignettes) on the money are also important. Condition of money is vital when establishing value, so be careful to note its appearance and general condition, including wear, tears, or other damage.

COINS

Ronald G. Aldridge
617 Lakeway Drive
El Paso, Texas 79932
(915) 584-4775

For more than two decades, Ron Aldridge has been buying and selling U.S. and foreign coins through the mail.

He will buy collections or single pieces, and is particularly interested in obtaining older coins in better condition. He considers gold and other high-grade coins from the U.S. and Canada his specialty.

A complete description of coins should include the country of origin, the denomination, the mint mark, the condition, and the owner's estimated selling price. "I will pay above that price if the coins warrant it," he promises. "A fair offer will be made after examination. The only cost to the owner is the postage and registration both ways." Write him for further instructions if you have coins to sell. El Paso National Bank West, P.O. Box 12826, El Paso, Texas 79912 has been provided as a reference.

ANCIENT COINS AND ARTIFACTS

David Hendin
Amphora
P.O. Box 661
Bardonia, New York 10954

David Hendin has been a collector and dealer in ancient coins, art, and artifacts for more than twenty years.

He seeks items from Greece, Rome, Egypt, and Israel in particular, but should be contacted for any ancient items from the Mideast.

Hendin requests that you send a photograph of art or artifacts, a rubbing or close-up photograph of coins. There is a fee for appraisals, but he will make offers on items genuinely for sale. Hendin is listed in Who's Who in America and can provide numerous references.

REBUS PUZZLES

Linda Campbell Franklin
P.O. Box 383, Murray Hill
New York, New York 10016
(212) 679-6038 until 9 p.m. EST

Linda Franklin wants to buy hand-drawn rebus puzzles from before 1900.

Rebus puzzles are sentences (or even entire letters) wherein pictures are used to represent words or parts of words. For example, a drawing of an eye usually stands for "I" and a drawing of a deer for "dear," and so on. "I would especially like to find long messages, such as the 1880s letter I have with more than forty pictures."

A photocopy is recommended, as these puzzles are difficult to describe. Linda will make offers if she can use what you have.

── 15 ──
Americana

VIKINGS

W.R. Anderson
Lief Ericson Society
P. O. Box 301
Chicago, Illinois 60690
(312) 761-1888

W. R. Anderson wants figures of Vikings less than sixteen inches tall and rare books on the Vikings in pre-Columbian America.

He is the founder of the Lief Erickson Society and author of Viking Explorers and the Columbus Fraud. Any item related to his interests would be appreciated. Send a complete description and photograph of what you have.

You may set the price or request an offer.

1907 JAMESTOWN EXPOSITION MEMORABILIA

W.T. Atkinson, Jr.
P.O. Box 4112
Hampstead, North Carolina 28443
(919) 686-0921

W. T. Atkinson is a collector-dealer who buys all the items he can find from the Jamestown Exposition (the 1907 world's fair), which was held in Virginia to commemorate the three hundredth anniversary of the founding of England's first successful colony on these shores.

If you have memorabilia from that fair, write to him giving a complete description and a statement of condition. This ten-year veteran has indicated a willingness to make offers on unpriced items.

ALASKA-YUKON-PACIFIC EXPO OF 1909

W.E. Nickell
432½ South Franklin Street
Juneau, Alaska 99801
(907) 586-1733

"I wish to purchase postcards, trade tokens, watch fobs, encased cents, and other memorabilia of the Alaska-Yukon-Pacific Exposition held in Seattle in 1909. I also wish to buy Alaskan "good for" trade tokens and old picture postcards.

"All such items must be sent on approval," W. E. Nickell notes, but he indicates that a photocopy "may suffice." He will make offers on items he needs for his extensive collection.

He promises to respond to all letters promptly and expresses willingness to answer questions about Alaskan memorabilia. Upon request, he will send an illustrated descriptive brochure on the topic.

THE OLD WEST

Joe Gish
P.O. Box 1587
McAllen, Texas 78501
(512) 686-3476

Joe Gish, an artist of western subjects, began collecting artifacts to help him keep his illustrations authentic.

After thirty years, he still wants to buy any "old-time" items used by cowboys, including cowboy hats, chaps, vests, scarfs, cartridge belts, holsters, leather cuffs, boots, spur straps, saddle bags, quirts, and the like.

Joe also wants pre-1925 saddle catalogues, old photos of cowboys and lawmen, guns used by westerners from the time of the Civil War to the early 1900s, and any western law enforcement items such as badges, handcuffs, and leg irons.

"A photo of some kind is most helpful," Joe writes, but don't forget a complete description. Joe will make offers, but prefers that sellers telll him what they would like to receive for their memorabilia. He will send a simple illustrated wants list upon request. Joe is building a western museum in Fredericksburg, Texas, which he plans to open to the public when he retires.

INDIAN ARTIFACTS

Ben W. Thompson
1757 West Adams
St. Louis, Missouri 63122

Ben Thompson has been buying and selling Indian artifacts for more than forty years, and now that he is retired it has become his full-time business.

He wants arrowheads, stone relics, pottery, beadwork, baskets, rugs, carvings, jewelry, Kachinas, and any other "Indian items."

When you contact him, include the size, coloring, weight, and price of what you have for sale. "A Polaroid picture is desirable, but, if not available, at least send a tracing of smaller items. Ben is reluctant to make purchase offers, preferring the seller to set the price.

Ben's knowledge and experience in the field are impressive. He has been associated with various archaelogical societies for fifteen years and is the editor-publisher of a series of books on collectors of Indian relics.

NEW YORK CITY NEWSBOYS

Peter J. Eckel
1335 Grant Avenue
South Plainfield, New Jersey 07080
(201) 757-0748

Peter Eckel wants to buy any item relating to the more than 40,000 homeless children who wandered the streets of New York City during the 19th century, surviving by selling newspapers.

He will buy photographs, paintings, prints, magazine articles, passes, badges, and other items relating to these children, the giants of Printing House Square and Newspaper Row who employed them, and the man who made their physical and spiritual salvation his life's mission, Father John C. Drumgoole of Mount Loretto on Staten Island.

"All pertinent information, including a description or photocopy, is requested, including the date, the dimensions, and a statement of condition." If it is something he can use, Peter Eckel will make you an offer.

SPACE AGE MEMORABILIA

Barry Burros
160 East 48th Street
New York, New York 10017

Barry Burros has been seeking "small, good condition, easy to display items" commemorating specific space missions, American or foreign, for fifteen years.

Items he will purchase include plates, cups, mugs, glasses, bottles, jars, decanters, paperweights, ashtrays, plaques, coin banks, books, buttons, magazines, bookmarks, nonmechanical toys, canisters, tiles, key chains, medallions, cards, jewelry, lunch boxes, jigsaw puzzles, fabrics, tapestries, placemats, pennants, and much more.

Barry does not make offers and wants all items to be described fully and to be priced by the seller. When pricing, be certain to include cost of postage in your quote. Barry is a member of various clubs and associations for space memorabilia collectors.

APOLLO 11 LUNAR LANDING

Bernard Passion
3517½ Kinney Street
Los Angeles, California 90065
(213) 256-8291

Ever since the first lunar landing took place, in the summer of 1969, Bernard Passion has been collecting glasses, cups, plates, toys, jewelry, playing cards, ashtrays, and every other souvenir you can think of connected with that famous landing.

He would like you to give a complete description, noting any defects or damage. A sketch, photograph, or photocopy should accompany your description whenever possible.

Bernard prefers that you set the price you would like, but he will make offers on especially good items he can use.

CAMP FIRE GIRLS MEMORABILIA

Alice O'Rear
Wo-He-Lo Museum
113 North 19th Avenue
Cornelius, Oregon 97113

Although Alice O'Rear has been collecting for forty years, there are still many items she wants for her museum. She requests you contact her with "anything made by or for the Camp Fire Girls which pre-dates 1950 and is marked with the Camp Fire Girls insignia."

Among things she seeks are Wo-He-Lo magazine (1913-20), Every Girl magazine (1920-38), Guardian magazine (1920-46), the 1912 Camp Fire Manual, membership cards (1910-40), calendars (1910-50), all catalogs, pocket knives, hat pins, honors, certificates, stationery and forms. Upon request, she will return your SASE with a substantial list of early girls' series books she will buy relating to camping and the Camp Fire Girls.

For thirty-five years, Alice has been a Camp Fire leader, camp director, and volunteer for nearly everything associated with the girls' outdoor movement. She will be pleased to make an offer for items she can use.

BOY SCOUT MEMORABILIA

Doug Bearce
P.O. Box 7081
Salem, Oregon 97303
(503) 363-1715 mornings

After twenty-five years in scouting, and fifteen as a scouting collector, Doug Bearce is particularly interested in older items having to do with the Order of the Arrow, jamborees, and other national or world scouting events.

His lengthy wants list include magazine from before 1950, books from before 1945, older postcards, photographs of clearly identified subjects, uniforms (adult pre-1940; Cub pre-1945), everything about the Philmont Scout Ranch, everything by or about Dan Beard, all scouting medals, patches (pre-1950), pins (pre-190), Lone Scout (everything), as well as toys, banks, posters, movies, recordings, sheet music, and similar items that have scouting as a theme.

You are encouraged to send an SASE for his simple but helpful wants list, which includes greater detail about the types of scouting items likely to find a home with him. His wants list is not priced, but he will make appraisals and offers.

Doug lists condition as a most important consideration. If your items are in good shape, describe them completely, making certain to give any dates. Make a photocopy or take a picture of patches and other things you find difficult to describe.

HOMOSEXUAL MEMORABILIA

L. Page Maccubbin
1724 20th Street, NW
Washington, D.C. 20009
(202) 387-6688

Page Maccubbin buys pre-1950 books, magazine articles, prints, pamphlets, photographs, and artwork that is related to the homosexual community or lifestyle.

He is especially seeking items from before 1920, including ads that use the word "gay," such as "have a gay breakfast." Items connected with famous homosexuals are also wanted, such as correspondence from Oscar Wilde, photos of Gertrude Stein, and the like. "Nudes are okay," he writes, "but no hardcore porn."

Send a complete description, including a statement of condition and your asking price. Since they are for resale, please offer fine-condition items only. He will make offers if an SASE is enclosed, and points out that photocopies are extremely helpful if you are asking him to price things.

RECREATIONAL DRUGS

L. Page Maccubin
1724 20th Street, NW
Washington, D.C. 20009
(202) 387-6688

Page Maccubbin's interests include the historical use of recreational drugs, specifically opium, marijuana (cannabis), and cocaine (coca).

Items sought include patent medicines containing these drugs, advertising and information about the drugs and their use, antique opium pipes and tools, and books relevant to the subject. All items associated with Vin Mariani, Metcalf's Wine of Coca, and French or Pemberton Coca Wines are especially sought.

Page is a dealer of antique memorabilia as well as a collector, so condition is critical. "I want quality more than quantity," he notes.

A complete description is requested, along with a statement of condition. Photographs or sketches are helpful, depending on the item you have to sell. Page will make offers.

HALLOWEEN PARAPHERNALIA

Scott J. Anderson
1500 LaSalle, Apt. 322
Minneapolis, Minnesota 55403
(612) 871-6288 eves.

Scott Anderson would like to hear from you if you have any Halloween candy containers, Halloween figures and other decorations, or Halloween toys for sale. These can be made of papier-mache, composition, celluloid, wood, glass, bisque, or tin. Scott most likes pre-1940 German-made items featuring witches, cats, jack-o'-lanterns, pumpkin-headed people, or other traditional Halloween creatures.

"Please note," he says, "that I do not buy postcards, costumes, tin noisemakers, or anything made of plastic, crepe paper, or wax."

He requests that you give the size and material of what you have to sell, and provide an accurate description, noting any chips, missing parts, dents, rust, etc. "I will answer all inquiries which include an SASE," he promises, "but if no SASE is included I will answer only if the material offered is of interest to me."

Scott prefers that sellers set the price they want, but will make offers when requested.

WORLD'S FAIR MEMORABILIA

Michael R. Pender
148 Poplar Street
Garden City, New York 11530
(516) 741-4884

Michael Pender is president and cofounder of the World's Fair Collector's Society, and described himself by saying, "I collect items from all world's fairs, past, present and future."

After forty-five years of collecting he still wants books, maps, pamphlets, china, medals, tokens, spoons, stamps, photographs, first day covers, tickets, matchbook covers, flags, postcards, elongated cents, pavilion models, buttons, badges, ashtrays, mugs, glasses, manuals, clippings, slides, programs, silverware, tablecloths, towels, plates, and virtually everything else marked with the name of one of the fairs.

He requests a complete description of what you have for sale, including the type of material, the size, the condition, and the name of the fair associated with the item. Appraisals and offers may be solicited, but he cautions, "Each request must be submitted with a self-addressed stamped envelope if they want a reply."

EARLY WORLD'S FAIR MEMORABILIA

Douglas D. Woollard, Jr.
11614 Old St. Charles Road
Bridgeton, Missouri 63044
(314) 739-4662 eves. or weekends

Books, souvenirs and miscellaneous memorabilia from early world's fairs have been Doug Woollard's hobby for nearly fifteen years.

Doug prefers relics from Missouri's own 1904 St. Louis World's Fair, also known as the Louisiana Purchase Exposition. But most items from earlier American fairs and expositions are also of interest, as are most things from the 1933 Chicago and 1939-40 New York fairs.

He writes, "I will also buy selected items from other fairs and expositions, including foreign. But I have no interest in items dating after 1940." Among those he seeks are fair or exposition stock certificates, hold-to-light postcards, souvenir watches, clocks, lamps, toys, steins that have lithopane bottoms, larger china items (such as pitchers, mugs, and bowls), attractive decorative plates, ribbons (particularly silk woven ribbons), and unusual or attractive celluloid mirrors or pin-back buttons.

He goes on, "Items should be described fully, with the condition carefully noted. I'd prefer the owner to state the price wanted, but I will make offers on any material that it is of interest to me. If the owner does not wish to sell but is interested in knowing the value of an article, I will estimate value if an SASE is furnished. I will also do written appraisals for a nominal fee."

WORLD'S FAIR

Ron Mahoney
Department of Special Collections
California State University Library
Fresno, California 93740
(209) 487-2595

As head of the Department of Special Collections, Ron Mahoney would like to obtain items related to various world's fairs.

He notes, "Our collection is very large, so we need only unusual items, including rare books, pamphlets, maps, plans for buildings or exhibits, photographs, postcards, sheet music, and manuscripts. They can be from any fair or exposition from 1851 to 1940, but they must be scarce and in fine condition. We do not collect items from state or regional fairs."

When writing, follow standard form, listing the title, author, publisher, date and place of publication, number of pages, and type and number of illustrations. Ron is willing to appraise what you have and make an offer, but calls attention to the fact that as a member of a government agency, he is not allowed to prepay orders.

WORLD'S FAIRS BEFORE 1905

Andy and Irene Kaufman
4th Dimension Collectibles
P.O. Box 383
Manchester, New Hampshire 03105
(603) 622-7404

The Kaufmans write, "Our interest in world's fairs is concentrated on the 1851 Crystal Palace, the 1853 New York Crystal Palace, the 1893 Columbian Exposition, the 1901 Pan American Exposition at Buffalo, and the 1904 St. Louis World's Fair, but we will buy other early world's fair items. We particularly like toys from or relating to any pre-World War I world's fair."

They want to know what the item is, the material from which it is made, and its size and color(s). Accurately describe condition. Photocopies are always helpful when you want to sell complicated artwork or text.

Andy and Irene will make offers, but they caution you not to send anything to them without prior authorization.

MARDI GRAS MEMORABILIA

Arthur Hardy
P.O. Box 8058
New Orleans, Louisiana 70182
(504) 282-2326

Virtually anything related to the New Orleans Mardi Gras is likely to be purchased by Art Hardy, especially items from the 1800s.

Among the most desirable memorabilia are invitations to the various carnival balls and elaborate chromoliths called "Carnival Bulletins," which were published in newspapers and picture the various floats. Since Art and his wife publish the annual New Orleans Mardi Gras Guide, they can use most postcards, photographs, magazine and newspaper articles, periodicals, railroad brochures, and other illustrated ephemera from before World War II.

In exchange for an SASE, the Hardys will send you a wants list that although not illustrated, indicates the range of prices Mardi Gras items will bring. Art is available to do appraisals and will make an offer on items that you feel insecure about pricing. When inquiring about an item for sale, describe it carefully, including its date and condition. A photocopy would be extremely helpful.

Art owns one of the largest private collections of Mardi Gras memorabilia, and is well known for his frequent radio and television appearances in the South and his willingness to lend items for museum displays.

ICE CREAM MEMORABILIA

Allan "Mr. Ice Cream" Mellis
1115 West Montana
Chicago, Illinois 60614

Allan Mellis buys a wide range of ephemera associated with ice cream and the ice cream industry, including
  1. Unusual advertising items featuring ice cream, such as pocket mirrors, bill hooks, matchsafes, etc.
  2. Trade cards from ice cream stores and ice cream freezer companies
  3. Photographic postcards depicting interiors of old soda fountains or ice cream factories
  4. Humorous cards of all types involving ice cream
  5. Soda fountain supply catalogues and menus
  6. Serving and tip trays picturing women or children eating ice cream
  7. Trade magazines from the ice cream industry before 1930
  8. Patent models of ice cream scoops or freezers
  9. Glass lantern slides depicting people eating ice cream
  10. Stereoviews, match covers, sheet music, valentines, letterheads, an most other paper ephemera
Allan can send you a lengthy, unpriced wants list in exchange for your SASE. If you write him, include an accurate statement of condition. Allan will make offers on occasion, but prefers the seller to set the price. When offering more valuable items, include a clear photograph or photocopy.

This eleven-year enthusiast was a founding member of The Ice Screamers, a national association of soda fountain collectors.

DUELING

Lt. Col. William R. Orbelo
912 Garraty
San Antonio, Texas 78209
(512) 828-1873

William Orbelo buys anything associated with dueling in America, including American-made dueling pistols, original handwritten correspondence regarding duels or dueling, court documents having to do with duels, duel challenges issued from one person to another, pamphlets, letters, postings, and early books having to do with duels, dueling, or duelists.

He requests that you provide "as accurate a description as possible, preferably including photocopies of paper items and photographs of guns or other objects." If you know any of the history of the item(s) you are offering, make certain to note it. Orbelo will make offers for items he can use for his extensive collection and traveling exhibit.

McDONALD'S MEMORABILIA

Jane H. Bramberg
44 Connecticut Avenue
Natick, Massachusetts 01760
(617) 653-7039

Jane Bramberg was one of the first people in the country to recognize the collectibility of memorabilia from the various fast-food chains. A McDonald's specialist, she is most interested in items from the earliest days of the company in the 1950s, but buys all sorts of things, including giveaways, jewelry, advertising, toys, equipment, furniture, etc., from this country and around the world.

Jane points out that there seems to be an almost endless supply of McDonald's memorabilia, since there are not only national and regional items but also things created for a single franchise.

If you have things she may be able to use, send a description that includes size, color, material, condition, and age of the item. She also would appreciate learning how you obtained it. You may price your item(s) or ask her to make an offer.

PRISON MEMORABILIA

Jerry and Carol Zara
J & C Collectibles
P.O. Box 248
Brick Town, New Jersey 08723

The Zaras buy a wide range of items associated with prisons, jails, and reformatories, especially tokens or paper scrip, which is used instead of money.

The Zaras seek medals, homemade items, weapons, badges, uniforms, buttons, shields, ID cards, handcuffs, leg irons, and the like. They also want postcards or photographs that picture prisons or depict prison life.

If selling a token, please indicate the size, metal it is made of, information inscribed thereon, and condition. Send a sketch or photocopy of paper scrip. Whatever items you offer, indicate the prison from which they came. Don't forget your SASE and Jerry will respond promptly with an offer.

NEW JERSEY

Jerry and Carol Zara
J & C Collectibles
P.O. Box 248
Brick Town, New Jersey 08723

Carol and Jerry Zara are avid collectors of items from their home state of New Jersey, seeking such things as:

1. Tokens of all sorts, including transportation, parking, and "good for" in trade
2. Wooden money, scrip, trade checks, paper money, elongated coins, encased coins, countersigned coins, flipping coins
3. Advertising items, spinners, mirrors, and signs related to New Jersey and its business and trade activities
4. Similar coins and ephemera from other states that can be used for trading with other collectors

The Zaras want you to send a drawing, description, or photocopy "sufficient to determine value." It is helpful, Jerry says, if you include the price you want since it saves a great deal of time. Jerry buys, sells, and makes offers.

NEVADA AND WESTERN RELICS

Ron Bommarito
Genoa Museum
P.O. Box 114
Genoa, Nevada 89411
(702) 782-3893

Ron Bommarito is a collector, an antique dealer, and the curator of a museum in Genoa, Nevada. In all three capacities, he is always in the market for a wide range of items related to the state of Nevada, including: tokens, stocks, bonds, letterheads, bottles, maps, law badges, lodge badges, railroad items, fire department memorabilia, store signs, hunting licenses, advertising, military items, mining notary stamps, Tahoe beer cans, photographs of towns, cowboys, Indians, or ranches, and just about anything else marked as being from Nevada.

You should describe your item carefully, making certain to note all damage, no matter how minor. Whenever possible, send a photocopy of what is for sale. List the maker and any other information or dates marked or printed on the item. Ron will make an offer on anything that he can use for his collection, the museum, or resale.

NEW JERSEY

Randall Gabrielan
71 Fish Hawk Drive
Middletown, New Jersey 07748
(201) 671-2645

Randall Gabrielan buys books, photographs, maps, postcards, and various other paper memorabilia having to do with New Jersey.

Describe books in the standard manner - author, title, publisher, date and place of publication, number of pages, etc. Note all damage, soil, foxing, etc. Photocopies of other paper items are helpful if he is to make the best possible offer.

NEVADA

Douglas B. McDonald
P.O. Box 348
Silver Springs, Nevada 89429

"I am interested in just about anything from or pertaining to the state of Nevada, particularly things of a financial nature such as tokens, stock certificates, checks, certificates of deposit, and anything else from Nevada banks, including photographs of the banks themselves. I want photographs of street scenes, business interiors and exteriors, town panoramas, mines, ranches, and disasters. I also need items pertaining to prostitution, both in Nevada and elsewhere, and am particularly eager to locate items that actually came from Nevada brothels."

When describing three-dimensional items, give the size, exact wording or lettering, the type of material, and its condition. For flat items, a photocopy is highly advised and generally brings the best selling price. Douglas McDonald wants you to state the price wanted, and he will make counteroffers. If you price your item too low, he will tell you, just as he will if you price too high.

NEVADA AND DEATH VALLEY

Gil Schmidtmann
Route 1, Box 371
Mentone, California 92359
(714) 794-1211

Gil Schmidtmann buys "almost anything old" from or about Nevada and Death Valley.

His wants include books, newspapers, magazines, diaries, letters, postcards, maps, promotional brochures, photographs, medals, stock certificates, checks, merchant tokens, stereoviews, souvenirs, and just about anything else printed or written on a piece of paper.

All he requests from the seller is a good description of the item(s) offered for sale and a fair asking price. Gil will make offers on unpriced items he'd like to purchase, however.

FRESNO AND THE SAN JOAQUIN VALLEY

Ronald J. Mahoney
Department of Special Collections
California State University Library
Fresno, California 93740
(209) 487-2595

The Department of Special Collections would like to obtain books, pamphlets, maps, photographs, postcards, and manuscripts relating to Fresno and the San Joaquin Valley. "Our collection is large," Ron Mahoney notes, "and only the rarer books are needed."

If you are offering books for sale, provide the title, author, publisher, place and date of publication, number of pages, number and type of illustrations, and a description of the binding. Pay very close attention to condition when describing paper goods.

Ron indicates that he will appraise what you have and make an offer, but warns, "Because we are a state institution, we are not allowed to prepay orders. Several weeks must be allowed to clear invoices."

FALL RIVER, MASSACHUSETTS

John J. Gleason
Fall River Antiques
272 Ray Street
Fall River, Massachusetts 02720
(617) 672-4259

John Gleason wants virtually anything from Fall River, Massachusetts, and/or the Fall River Line, a passenger steamer that made runs to New York City.

There are thousands of Fall River collectibles, including books, postcards, photographs, stereoviews, souvenir plates, and advertising memorabilia from breweries and mills.

Identify what you have, describe its condition, and set a price. Jack will make counteroffers or assist you if you find pricing difficult.

EUREKA SPRINGS, ARKANSAS

John Cross, President
Bank of Eureka Springs
Eureka Springs, Arkansas 72632
(501) 253-8241

"We are searching for art, furniture, coins, pictures, books, articles, buttons, pins, certificates, or anything else which relates to the past of our quaint town. We are deeply involved in our local history and restoration projects which revive our past. Any items which have their origin in Eureka Springs are of interest to us."

Describe the item(s) you have, including an explanation of how it is connected with Eureka Springs, one of the South's more popular resort communities. Make certain to note any damage.

"We ask that items be priced," John Cross says, but admits, "it is not absolutely necessary since we will make offers on appealing unpriced items."

NORTHERN AND WESTERN CANADA

Tom Williams
Box 4126, Station C
Calgary, Alberta
Canada T2T 5M9
(403) 264-0184

"If it's old and Canadian," says Tom Williams, "I want you to contact me."

Tom seeks books, pamphlets, maps, photos, and any other printed material relating to Canada, especially the west, northwest, and far north. Early explorations and travels are particularly wanted, but "anything interesting" might find a buyer. Wants include old view books, political tracts, and items having to do with immigration, settlement, railroads, politics, ranching, business, Indians, Eskimos, the Klondike, or the Arctic.

When describing books, include the author, title, place and date of publication, type of illustrations and binding, and detailed and specific information about condition. A photocopy is recommended for items other than books. Setting the price is your responsibility.

CUBA

Manuel Alvarez
Alvarez Stamps and Coins
1735 SW 8th Street
Miami, Florida 33135
(305) 649-1176

If it's pre-Castro and from Cuba, Manuel Alvarez may well want to buy it.

Although silver Cuban souvenir spoons are his specialty, he also buys stamps, coins, postcards, documents, labels, cigar bands, and other collectibles from Cuba.

A complete description is necessary, as is a statement of condition. A photograph or, better yet, a photocopy of things for sale would be appreciated. He will make purchase offers on unpriced items.

PANAMA AND THE CANAL ZONE

Brad Wilde
Star Route 2, Box 480
Susanville, California 96130

"I am interested in purchasing anything concerning the country of Panama or the Panama Canal. This includes books, photographs, postcards, medals, tokens, magazines, stamps, stereoviews, covers, autographs, correspondence, and miscellaneous memorabilia. About the only thing not wanted is Panamanian coins."

Brad Wilde offers $3 for any pre-1925 postcard bearing Canal Zone stamps. No SASE is required, and he promises a finder's fee of 10 percent for purchases over $50.

He asks for "a reasonably detailed description of the item, plus the price they are requesting." He will, however, make offers on unpriced merchandise if it appeals to him.

16
Miscellany

TWINS

"Miss Helen" Kirk
Supertwin Statistician
P.O Box 254
Galveston, Texas 77553-0254
(409) 762-4792

If it has anything to do with twins, famed twin-expert "Miss Helen" Kirk (formerly Lauve) wants to know about it. This retired medical practitioner plans to open a museum of twins, and can use just about everything related to multiple births that might have research or historical value, including:

1. Books of all types, from chidren's to scientific and medical
2. Magazine, newspaper and other printed articles
3. Personal correspondence about being a twin or having twins
4. Souvenirs of the Dionne Quints or other multiple births
5. Photographs of twins or multiples
6. Clothing worn by twins or multiples
7. Toys and paper dolls featuring twins

Miss Helen buys on a limited budget, makes offers, and gratefully accepts donation of materials on twins or other multiple births. Remember the purpose for which she is buying, so describe fully, noting all dates. Photocopies are helpful.

FREAKS, ODDITIES, AND CURIOSITIES

Harvey Lee Boswell
Palace of Wonders
P.O. Box 446
Elm City, North Carolina 27822
(919) 291-6308

If it's unusual, one of a kind, bizarre, strange, weird, dwarfed, freaky, two-headed, shrunken, or in any way out of the ordinary, there is a good chance Harvey Boswell will buy it.

Handcuffs, leg irons, tombstones, coffins, jungle relics, circus and carnival banners, Indian relics, fossils, skeletons, torture instruments, mounted animals, mounted snakes, mummies, shrunken heads, freak animals (alive or stuffed), and so on, are of interest. He especially wants photographs of freak humans and animals.

Describe it well, including size, age, and condition. A color photo is a must. This fascinating wheelchair-bound showman, with more than thirty years of experience, requests your "lowest price."

RATIONING AND VITICULTURE

Ron Mahoney
Department of Special Collections
California State University Library
Fresno, California 93740
(209) 487-2595

As head of the Department of Special Collections of this western university, Ron Mahoney would like to obtain materials suitable for the library's research collection in these areas:

Rationing: Fine-condition ration forms, books, coupons, and posters relating to rationing of food or commodities anywhere in the world during any period of history. The library does not need any more red tokens, blue tokens or ration books from the United States during World War II.

Grape Growing-Winemaking: "All pre-1920 books, pamphlets, photographs, manuscripts, and sheet music related to viticulture (grape growing) and oenology (winemaking) from any country, in any language."

It is recommended that you make photocopies of paper goods you would like to sell. Describe all books by author, title, date and place of publication, publisher, number of pages, number and type of illustrations, type of binding, and condition. Inspect condition carefully and describe accurately. Ron is willing to make offers, but reminds that, as a state agency, the library is not permitted to prepay orders.

DEATH, BURIAL, HEAVEN AND HELL

Michael E. Justings
210 West 78th Street Suite 1-B
New York, New York 10024

Mike Justings buys, sells, and collects small objects relating to death, burial, heaven, and hell.

Objects can be in almost any form, including metal, wood, bones, paintings, prints, drawings, photographs, and what have you. He wants real human skulls and any representation of them. Mike requires only that all objects be at least fifty years old and pass his personal test for authenticity.

Mike suggests that a photograph acompany a good clear description of what you have. Please include a statement guaranteeing him the right to return an item for any reason. You must set the price you'd like. He may make a counteroffer, since "I'm willing to pay what the item is worth to me, which may be more or less than its retail value."

HANDCUFFS AND RESTRAINTS

Stan Willis
6211 Stewart Road
Cincinnati, Ohio 45227
(513) 271-0454

Stan Willis is a longtime collector of handcuffs, leg irons, nippers, thumbcuffs, twisters, Oregon boots, and other restraints. He also saves police equipment and badges.

He has an extensive research library on these topics, and is always eager to obtain more catalogs and other informative literature. Send for his illustrated wants list.

If you want to sell, or just ask about what you have, Stan expresses a willingness to assist others to identify items they own. He needs a photo or sketch showing all markings. Note whether keys are present and whether the item works. Describe its condition. "Please price it," he says, but he will make offers when necessary.

HANDCUFFS AND OTHER RESTRAINT DEVICES

Joseph and Pamela Tanner
Wheeler-Tanner Escapes
P.O. Box 349
Great Falls, Montana 59408
(406) 453-4961

The Tanners specialize in the buying and selling of restraint and escape devices used by jails, prisons, asylums, or magicians.

They deal in handcuffs, leg irons, balls and chains, prison convict uniforms, old law badges, padlocks, strait jackets, and any type of locking or restraining device. In addition to the devices themselves, they buy books and posters related to magic, magicians, and escape artists.

A brief description is sufficient, as long as it includes a photograph, photocopy, or sketch. A statement of condition should note whether the item has its original keys and whether it works. "Of course, people should tell us the price they want, but if they have no idea, we will make a reasonable offer."

PLASTER CARNIVAL PRIZES

Thomas G. Morris
Unique Junque
49 Monterey Drive
Medford, Oregon 97504
(503) 779-3164

Tom Morris has a longtime interest in the plaster (chalk) figures given as carnival prizes between 1900 and 1950.

He buys all types of figures, especially those containing lamps. Both the early hand-painted figures as well as the later air-brushed versions are collectible, but figurines of dogs, cats, horses, pigs, and birds are of no interest unless they are cartoon animals. Movie stars, circus characters, fictional folk such as the Lone Ranger and Tonto, and larger, more elaborate pieces are all desirable.

Make a sketch, including dimensions, of your plaster pieces. Be sure that you note any chips or other damage when you describe your statue. Items worth more than $40 require a good clear photograph before judgment will be made about value. Tom prefers to buy assortments or large collections, but will also buy good single pieces.

AMUSEMENT PARKS AND ROLLER COASTERS

Tom Keefe
161 Forest Street
New Lenox, Illinois 60451
(815) 485-4653

If it's amusement park memorabilia you have, especially from roller coasters, Tom Keefe wants to hear from you.

Old photographs, blueprints, posters, catalogs, and memorabilia of any sort are wanted if they pertain to amusement parks and rides, but especially interesting are "materials, no matter how small or unusual, even remotely related to roller coasters.

"Send me the best description possible, including the size, shape, date, and condition. I will appraise and make offers on any items well described." All inquiries are welcome regarding the national collectors organization. A bibliography on roller coasters and amusement parks may be requested.

AN ASSORTMENT OF ITEMS

Clay Tontz
4043 Nora
Covina, California 91722
(213) 338-9976

Clay Tontz's specialty is woodworking tools, but he also collects a large number of other items, including:

1. Old kitchen utensils, both mechanical and static, including egg beaters, can openers, and tinware
2. Unusual safety razors, especially those made by Collins. No common hoe-shaped razors, please
3. Figural razor blade banks
4. Mouse and rat traps that are both old and unusual
5. Duck, goose, and snipe decoys that pre-date 1940
6. Tiny cameras, such as those made by Expo Watch Camera, Kombi, Expo Detective Camera, and Pupile

Describe what you have fully, noting all brand names, maker's marks, and serial numbers. Make careful note of condition, and say whether items actually work as they should. A sketch or photograph is helpful.

He is willing to make offers, but requests that if you have a price that you would like, please state it. An SASE is essential if you want an answer.

BRICKS, TINS, AND MOVIE STILLS

Ken D. Jones
100 Manor Drive
Columbia, Missouri 65201

Ken Jones buys three decidedly different items:
1. Casting directories, Academy player directories, and 8-by-10 inch glossy movie stills from the 1930-55 era
2. Building bricks marked with the name of the manufacturer, city, state or combination thereof; no firebricks
3. Pocket tobacco tins, early tobacco packages, and tin signs related to the smoking tobacco industry

Ken requests a complete description of the item(s) for sale, making certain that you accurately describe condition, pointing out all flaws or damage. Please set the price you want, as Ken feels pricing is the seller's responsibility and prefers not to make offers. Since a number of tobacco tins are valued at more than $1,000, some research is advisable.

THE FOWLERS AND PHRENOLOGY

Marion Sauerbier
RD 2
Cohocton, New York 14826

Marion Sauerbier collects books, pamphlets, and other paper ephemera related to Orson, Lorenzo, or Charlotte Fowler and their theories on phrenology, water cures, octagonal houses, child rearing, love and marriage.

"I am building my collection around the family rather than one type of item," she writes, "But I am especially interested in the Phrenology Journal published by Fowler and Wells."

If you have anything by or about the Fowlers or their theories, she would like to know the age, condition, and price. Describe published matter by author, title, date and place of publication, publisher, and the number of pages. She will make offers for items she can use.

ALL SORTS OF INTERESTING THINGS

Betty and Harold Yingling
Yingling's Collectibles
15 Chapel Road
Gettysburg, Pennsylvania 17325

Betty and "Reds" Yingling run a large shop devoted exclusively to all sorts of interesting collectibles. As a result, they buy a wide range of items:

1. Glass and tin candy containers
2. Figural bulbs and other pre-1930 Christmas items
3. Calendars and posters that predate 1940
4. Advertising signs, posters, and trays
5. Figural cast iron lawn sprinklers
6. Cast iron doorstops
7. Pendulum clocks by Lux, Keebler, Columbia
8. Planters peanut items
9. Advertising from Victor and other phonograph companies
10. Comic character collectibles
11. Toys and "soaky plastic figural bottles"
12. Pennsylvania car, dog, hunting, and other licenses
13. Oyster and other seafood tin cans and signs
14. String holders

There are many more items, so send for their wants list.

They would like to know what it is, its size, and its approximate age. Condition is important, as is the percentage of remaining paint. The Yinglings encourage you to set your price, and promise "no haggling." They promise to answer all mail, make offers, and pay finder's fees if you tip them off to a collection or a few important items which they purchase.

CAVE HISTORY

Jack H. Speece
711 East Atlantic Avenue
Altoona, Pennsylvania 16602
(814) 946-3155

Jack Speece seeks "any cave-related items, foreign or domestic, including books, articles, maps, photographs, advertisements, postcards, and other paper ephemera."

He'd like to hear from you if you have anything related to caves. Tell him what cave your item is from or about, the age of the item, its condition, and give a brief general description.

He prefers you to set the price, but he will make offers.

ALL SORTS OF THINGS

Ron Bommarito
Genoa Museum
P.O. Box 114
Genoa, Nevada 89411
(702) 782-3893

Ron Bommarito is a collector, a dealer, and the operator of the Genoa museum. As a result, there is an enormous range of items included on his wants list:

Good guns, old rusty guns, spurs, photographs of western scenes, lamps, posters, handcuffs, leg irons, safes, strong boxes, music boxes, barber items, Wells Fargo items, stuffed animals, Indian baskets, clocks, old car parts, telegraph keys, mining items, gambling equipment, cheating devices, playing cards, political buttons, telephones, doctor and dentist tools and memorabilia, back bar bottles, cowboy hats, bowie knives and daggers, fishing plugs and lures, horse bits, dolls, Victorian walnut furniture, scales, iron toys, and paper, tin, and porcelain signs.

Decribe what you have carefully, especially noting any defects. Make photocopies or take photographs whenever possible. Give dimensions and all marks, dates, and numbers you can find. Ron will make offers for what he wants.

ASSORTED COLLECTIBLES

Paul Hartunian
65 Christopher Street
Montclair, New Jersey 07042
(201) 746-9132

Paul Hartunian runs a mail-order auction house and buys a variety of items for resale, including:

1. Autographs of anyone famous or infamous

2. Items owned or used by any president of the United States or made for use in the White House

3. Anything made by NASA or a NASA contractor for the space program, including medallions, parts of the spacecraft, patches, and space suit material

4. Artifacts associated with any famous building or event

Send a good photocopy of paper items you wish to sell, and a clear, thorough description of everything else. If you are requesting an offer, an SASE is greatly appreciated. "Please do not send items until I request them," he notes.

FRENCH CULTURAL LIFE

Patricia Scoales
6726 Wandermere Road
Malibu, California 90265

Pat Scoales is a historian of French life. She seeks a wide range of items that can be described as "exemplifying the culture of France between 1600 and 1900."

She will purchase selected maps, atlases, books, art catalogs, exhibition catalogs, pamphlets, magazines, tax bills, administrative documents, medals and medallions, and general artifacts that reflect French culture during those three centuries. Observations in the foreign (especially British) press about the French are also welcome.

Include information about size, color, age, and condition of any item you describe. If it is a book, include the name of the publisher, the number of pictures, and the number of pages. Send a photocopy of other items, if at all possible. She prefers that you price what you have, but she is willing to make offers on items she can use.

FIRECRACKER LABELS

Hal Kantrud
Route 7
Jamestown, North Dakota 58401
(701) 252-5639

Hal Kantrud has spent nearly forty years collecting and writing about the colorful labels from packs of Chinese firecrackers. He also buys catalogs of fireworks.

If you have something you think he might like, tell him about the brand name, the dimensions, and any writing. Indicate whether it is just a label or a full package of fireworks. A photocopy is always preferred.

You may request his wants list. Hal will make offers for what he does not have.

Index